Comic Theory in
the Sixteenth
Century

From *Terentius cum Quinque Commentis*, Venice, 1504

Comic Theory in the Sixteenth Century

PN 1926
H 56 C

67048

Marvin T. Herrick

University of Illinois Press, Urbana, 1964

Originally published as Vol. 34, Nos. 1-2, in the Illinois
Studies in Language and Literature.

Copyright 1950 by the Board of Trustees of the University
of Illinois. Manufactured in the United States of America.
Library of Congress Catalog Card No. 50-9785.

Preface

IT IS IMPOSSIBLE now to recall the many aids that members of the staff of the University Library have given me during the preparation of this monograph. I wish, however, to mention in particular the unfailing kindness of Miss Isabelle Grant, Librarian of the Rare Book Room, and of Miss Georgia Coffin, her assistant. Dr. Marguerite Little, Graduate Research Assistant, not only helped me with books but also read the typescript. Dr. Edwin W. Robbins, now at Ohio State University, who used to share a table with me in the Rare Book Room, also used to share his researches among the Terentian commentators. To Professor Kenneth M. Abbott of Ohio State University I owe a special debt. In fact, without Professor Abbott's expert advice, I probably would not have tried to translate the long, involved periods of Robortellus' Latin essay on comedy, here included in an appendix. Professor Harris Fletcher, my colleague and an editor of this series, suggested several changes for the better in the original typescript. Neither Professor Fletcher nor Professor Abbott, however, can be held responsible for any errors remaining in my interpretations of critical matter or in my numerous English translations from the Latin. Any one who has struggled with Renaissance Latin well knows the difficulty of finding suitable English words for the original. In many instances, literal translation is impossible; we can merely hope to preserve what we hope is the sense. For well known ancient rhetoricians and critics, such as Cicero, Horace, Quintilian, and Aristotle, there are excellent English translations, and I have made extensive use of the invaluable Loeb Classical Library. There are no adequate English translations, however, for many lesser known ancients and for most of the Renaissance rhetoricians, critics, and commentators; with these I have had to do the best I could. Proper identification of the passages translated will, I trust, enable scholars to check what I have done. Most of the material in Chapter II, and some of that in Chapter III, has already appeared in the *Quarterly Journal of Speech*.

Urbana, 1949   MARVIN T. HERRICK

Contents

Chapter I: Introduction

TERENCE and the Terentian commentators furnished the principal matter for the discussion of comedy in the sixteenth century. The study of Terentian comedy in the first half of the century laid the main foundations of Renaissance theories of comedy.

For some time, twentieth-century students of the drama have been dissatisfied with conventional explanations of the origin and development of Renaissance theories of comedy. For the most part we have accepted, without much challenge, Spingarn's statement on page 101 of the *History of Literary Criticism in the Renaissance:* "The treatment of comedy in the literary criticism of this period is entirely confined to a discussion and elaboration of the little that Aristotle says on the subject of comedy in the *Poetics.*" But every serious student of the drama knows that comedy was flourishing in western Europe long before the Greek text of the *Poetics* was rediscovered and translated into Latin.

It is a historical commonplace, for example, that the plays of Terence were read and imitated in the so-called Dark and Middle Ages. It is well known that Renaissance comedy was modeled principally upon the plays of Terence, as its tragedy was modeled upon the plays of Seneca. Educated men did not become generally aware of Aristotle's theory of poetry until some time after Paccius' Greek-Latin edition of the *Poetics* appeared in 1536; they did not become familiar with Aristotle's dramatic criticism until after the great commentaries on the *Poetics* by Robortellus and Madius appeared in 1548 and 1550. We know that scholars, playwrights, and critics of the Renaissance were discussing comedy long before the middle of the sixteenth century. There were other ancient authorities, well known in the fifteenth century, who had something to say about comedy; chief among these were Cicero, Quintilian, Diomedes, and above all Donatus, the fourth-century grammarian, rhetorician, and commentator on Terence.

Professor J. W. H. Atkins, in his recent book on English literary criticism in the Renaissance, has presented a much more satisfactory account of comedy than Spingarn's. Professor Atkins points to one of the right sources when he says, "For the earliest contributions, which were concerned with inculcating the value of dramatic literature in general, we must look primarily to the Humanists, who accepted all ancient classics as a priceless legacy, though on educational grounds."[1] He is certainly right in pointing to the humanists of the early Renaissance. These humanists, besides providing important matter on the value of dramatic literature, lead us to a more important source of comic theory, namely to Terence and to the great commentaries on the plays of Terence. Erasmus was one of these humanists who had something to say about comedy. Melanchthon was another. Erasmus apparently took little or no interest in the *Poetics* of Aristotle beyond including the treatise in the Basle edition of Aristotle in 1531, and Melanchthon left only perfunctory references to it.

Both Erasmus and Melanchthon, however, together with many other humanists, were well acquainted with Cicero, Quintilian, and Donatus. Further, both Erasmus and Melanchthon wrote annotations on the comedies of Terence. Erasmus' annotations are preoccupied with metrical problems and throw little light on the criticism of comedy in general. Scattered throughout other works of this great humanist, however, are various important observations on comedy, on Terentian comedy in particular. Melanchthon's "arguments" of Terence's plays have been valuable. Even had they not proved valuable, they had to be considered, for Melanchthon's great reputation in the sixteenth century assured any work of his a respectful hearing from other scholars. Actually, I suppose, I have learned more from the rhetorical writings of Melanchthon than from his remarks on Terence.

In this study, therefore, I propose to examine the leading commentaries on Terence from the fourth-century work of Donatus to the annotations by Willichius, first published in 1550. In these commentaries there is a wealth of critical matter, greatly varying in quality, to be sure, on comedy in general and on Terence in particular. I hope to show before I am through that by the middle of the sixteenth century there was a large amount of comic theory well established in western Europe, and incidentally that comic practice more often than not went hand in hand with comic theory during most of the sixteenth and seventeenth centuries. In fact, I hope at least to indicate that our present theories of comedy are largely indebted to the detailed analyses and observations worked out by Donatus and his sixteenth-century followers. Since the comments of Donatus and his disciples are sporadic and repetitious, I shall try to reduce them to a few systematic general principles of dramatic criticism. After preliminary chapters on the relationship between rhetoric and poetics

---

[1] *English Literary Criticism: The Renascence* (London, 1947), p. 218.

and on the traditional conceptions of comedy and tragedy, including the theory of the laughable, I shall try to analyze the comic theory of the sixteenth century in terms of Plot, Character, Sentiment, and Diction.

But Plot, Character, Sentiment, and Diction are borrowed from Aristotle's critical procedure on tragedy in the *Poetics*. It looks as though I were merely doing what, according to Spingarn, every critic of comedy in the Renaissance did. It is true that I am doing what ultimately most critics of the late Renaissance did, that is, transfer Aristotle's critical method from tragedy to comedy. I have no wish to minimize the influence of Aristotle on modern dramatic criticism; in fact, I have included in this book my translation of Robortellus' essay *On Comedy* (1548) to show how the Aristotelian approach to tragedy was made to serve as an approach to the criticism of comedy.

There is no questioning, it seems to me, the superior system of Aristotle's dramatic criticism, and I propose to use this superior system to bring order to the scattered remarks of ancient and Renaissance authorities on comedy. This method is precisely what Robortellus, Antonius Riccobonus, and others adopted. My point, however, is that Aristotle's contribution to the discussion of comedy in the Renaissance was mainly a critical method plus a few critical terms; the details of specific anyalsis of comic function, comic plot, characterization, intellectual content, and style came not from Aristotle's *Poetics*, but from the commentators on Terence, who drew upon the rhetoricians, ancient and modern. Aristotle's *Rhetoric*, in fact, provided more matter for the discussions of comedy in the first half of the sixteenth century than did his *Poetics*. In other words, the groundwork of comic theory was already laid before the *Poetics* became a major influence in dramatic criticism.

A few words about the early Renaissance commentators on Terence may help the reader of the following pages. The names of these commentators, once well known and even celebrated, are now almost forgotten. These learned and able scholars were mostly Italian, French, and German by birth, cosmopolitan in education and scholarship. I shall list here only those commentators that have proved most useful in this study. I have made some use of others who will be mentioned from time to time. Needless to say, perhaps, all these scholars wrote in Latin, and I shall refer to them by their Latin names.

The dean of modern commentators on Terence was Joannes Calphurnius (d. 1503), who supplied the first commentary on the *Self-Tormentor*, the one play of Terence that Donatus omitted from his ancient commentary. Guido Juvenalis (d. 1507) was apparently the first man to write commentaries on all six plays of Terence. Therefore his work is of historical importance, although its value as criticism was largely displaced by the work of a greater scholar, Iodocus Badius Ascensius (*ca.* 1462-1535). Badius, who became famous as a printer in Paris, issued several notable scholarly works, including commentaries on Horace and Terence. The *Prenotamenta* to his annotations on Terence constitute one of the important critical documents of the Renaissance; his discussion of poetry and poet, of tragedy and comedy, anticipate many of the critical commonplaces that Minturno, Julius Caesar Scaliger, and other critics made famous in the second half of the century.

Petrus Marsus (1442?-1512) was a commentator whose notes on Terence were reprinted many times during the century. Marsus is particularly useful for studying the didactic elements in the discussion of comedy. Joannes Rivius (d. 1553) was another whose criticism of Terence emphasized the didactic and philosophical elements; his castigations were reprinted several times. Bartholomaeus Latomus (1485-1566) was specially interested in dramatic structure, i.e., the structure of comedy. Latomus' remarks on Terence are very useful in the study of comic plot. Adrianus Barlandus (1488-1542) left unusually full annotations, and while, like most of the early sixteenth century commentators, he often repeated the observations of Donatus, his criticism has been among the most valuable I have encountered.

Many German scholars in the sixteenth century were active in Terentian scholarship. The earliest of this group was Ambrosius Berndt (d. 1542), who was professor of rhetoric at Wittenberg. Berndt left several *prolegomena* on Terentian comedy which were published in Stephanus Riccius' edition of Terence. Another German commentator was Joannes Stigelius (1515-62), poet and scholar, who held professorships at both Wittenberg and Jena. Stigelius' criticisms of Terence were also published by Riccius. The castigations on Terence by Georgius Fabricius (1516-71), noted German poet and scholar, were first published in 1548. Fabricius was probably the first sixteenth-century commentator on Terence to make any significant use of Aristotle's *Poetics*. Iodocus Willichius (1501-52), whose elaborate edition of Terence first appeared in 1550, has proved, next to Donatus, the most valuable of all the Terentian commentators; he is specially useful for the rhetorical analysis of comedy. Nathan Chytraeus (1543-98), another German poet and scholar, published an annotated edition of the *Brothers* in 1576. Included in this edition were the editor's "propositions" on comedy, which furnish one of the most convenient summaries of comic theory I have ever seen.

Why did Terentian comedy monopolize the sixteenth-century discussion of comic theory? Aristophanes is certanly a greater poet than Terence, and Plautus is certanly a much livelier comedian. Both Aristophanes and Plautus were read, admired, and imitated in the Renaissance. J. C. Scaliger and Ben Jonson, to mention two prominent arbiters of literature, preferred Aristophanes and Plautus to Terence.

The commentators whose pronouncements on comedy I shall try to analyze in the following pages often referred to other comic poets than Terence. Nevertheless, so far as I can discover, the sixteenth-century critics may have liked Aristophanes and Plautus, but they distrusted them. The Athenian Aristophanes was too vulgar, too indelicate; the Roman Plautus was sometimes too vulgar and often too "irregular." The later Roman poet, Terence, offered safer and more familiar ground upon which schoolmasters and critics could expatiate on art, on manners, and on morals. Furthermore, and here is the real reason, I suspect, for the dominant role of Terence, there was already at hand the great Terentian commentary of Donatus, the famous Roman grammarian and rhetorician, the tutor of St. Jerome.

In Donatus' justly celebrated commentary, Renaissance scholars found not only detailed analyses of five out of the six plays of Terence, but also two excellent prefatory essays on the origin and development of both comedy and tragedy. Donatus had already worked out the main outlines of comic theory. The sixteenth century had only to elaborate his observations. Renaissance scholars added new details, and they compared the theory of Donatus with authoritative pronouncements in other ancient rhetoricians, such as Cicero, the author of the *Ad Herennium*, Quintilian, Hermogenes, Aphthonius, and, when they came to know him, Aristotle.

Although the following chapters will be mainly devoted to a study of comic theory in the sixteenth century, and specially to the development of comic theory in the first half of the century, I shall occasionally refer to writers of later periods. Often a remark of Dryden or of his disciple John Dennis, for example, will demonstrate how firmly established in dramatic criticism this comic theory of the sixteenth century had become. Likewise, the comic practice recommended by sixteenth-century critics will sometimes be most conveniently illustrated for the modern reader by playwrights of a later time.

English playwrights of the Restoration, for example, usually followed the dramatic "rules" more faithfully than did their Elizabethan predecessors. These dramatic "rules" were established during the sixteenth century, and for comedy they were largely derived from the practice of Terence. I have made no attempt, however, to present any systematic account of comic theory after 1600. Such an account would require another book.

Chapter II: The Place of Rhetoric in Poetics

THE SUB-TITLE of an important edition of Terence, published at Zurich in 1550, contains the following:

The commentaries of Iodocus Willichius Resellianus on the same, in which is presented an account of invention, disposition, and style in each of the scenes, with an explanation of some obscure passages.

Willichius, who prepared the edition for use in schools, proceeded to do just what the title promised; he rhetorically analyzed every scene in the six plays of Terence, pointing out how Terence invented his arguments, how he put them together, and how he clothed them in the proper sentiments and figures. He tried to classify each scene as deliberative, judicial, or demonstrative, finding some scenes, to be sure, mixtures of two or even three types of oratory.

Willichius thought of each scene in a play as an oration; the short scene was often a little oration, an *oratiuncula*. When he could, he analyzed the quantitative structure of the scenes according to the conventional rhetorical scheme of exordium, statement of facts (*narratio*), proof (*confirmatio*), disproof (*refutatio*), and peroration. He did not neglect the traditional dramatic analysis (itself rhetorical in origin) of *prologue*, *protasis*, *epitasis*, *catastrophe*, but showed how the rhetorical form and expression of individual scenes supported the dramatic pattern of the play.

Willichius' analysis of the *catastrophe* of the *Eunuch* (5.9.1031 ff.) furnishes a good illustration of his method, which, in turn, is similar to methods employed by other commentators in the sixteenth century. This scene contains the final resolution wherein all errors and misunderstandings are cleared up. Chaerea wins Pamphila for his bride; Phaedria wins Thais for his mistress; the old people are satisfied; Gnatho, the parasite, wins a new patron; Thraso, the braggart soldier, wins an amnesty and is allowed to provide the purse for Phaedria and Thais. According to Willichius, the scene is built up as follows:

EXORDIUM: Chaerea opens the scene with an outburst expressing his overflowing happiness. As is proper in an exordium, this speech secures good will and attention.

NARRATIO: The *narratio* tells why Chaerea is happy. Pamphila, the slave girl, has turned out to be an Athenian citizen and therefore

6

eligible to become his bride. Furthermore, his brother Phaedria has now disposed of all rivals and has sole possession of the beautiful Thais.

PROOF: The happiness of Phaedria and Chaerea is confirmed by the generous action of their father, who has consented to become the patron and protector of Thais.

DISPROOF: There is also some use of disproof in this scene. Gnatho, the clever parasite, tries to persuade Phaedria and Chaerea, for their own interests, to make up with Thraso, whose purse, Gnatho argues, will be very useful. Gnatho removes the objections that the young men have to such an alliance by pointing out that "there is no man who entertains better or more liberally."

PERORATION: Any attention to peroration in this scene was unnecessary since it is the last scene in the play and ends with the conventional "Farewell and clap your hands!"

Such an analysis may strike a twentieth-century student of comedy as a strange exercise and one better calculated for oratory than for drama. It did not strike the sixteenth-century student as strange; it was the usual procedure, a procedure that had been followed by interpreters of Terentian comedy since the time of Donatus in the fourth century. Willichius was more systematic, perhaps, than Donatus and others in his application of classical rhetoric to Terence, but he was following an established practice. And his chief authorities were the conventional authorities on rhetoric and poetry in the sixteenth century: Cicero, Quintilian, Hermogenes, Aristotle, Plato, Horace, and Donatus. This strictly rhetorical analysis was not the only approach to the study of Terence in the century. Some scholars, in fact, seemed to disapprove of Willichius' method. Matthias Bergius objected to studying a Terentian comedy as a whole play or as an oration. "Much more ridiculous," he asserted, "is the labor of those who seek sedulously and even at great length what they call arguments, not only of whole comedies, which might appear bearable, but also of every scene."[1] Bergius favored a grammatical and metrical study of Terence. Christopher Johnson, who became headmaster of Winchester in 1560, found fault with the use of plays at school: "For what else is comedy than a laborious nothing? Invention difficult, disposition laborious, the description of parts [characterization] difficult."[2] These complaints, however, suggest that the rhetorical analysis of drama was standard practice. So it was.

---

[1] *P. Terentii Afri comoediae sex*, edited by Matthias Bergius (Leipzig, 1574), p. 401.

[2] Quoted by T. W. Baldwin, *William Shakspere's Small Latine and Lesse Greeke* (Urbana, 1944) 1.329.

The twentieth-century student of literary criticism has to keep in mind that the medieval trivium of logic, grammar, and rhetoric was still in force during the sixteenth century, though considerably modified. For centuries the study of literature, of poetry, had been by way of logic, grammar, and rhetoric; and the sixteenth-century student still studied literature by way of logic, grammar, and rhetoric. In recent years the position of rhetoric and poetry has been radically changed.

Today the student of literary criticism generally dismisses the older rhetoric as something that went out of fashion with William Jennings Bryan and Chautauqua declamations and gives his whole attention to poetics, to what he likes to think is a purely aesthetic approach to literature. But our modern poetics, including our modern theories of dramatic art, are outgrowths of this older rhetoric. Modern poetics, including the theory of comedy, were built up largely by schoolmasters and commentators whose training and outlook were rhetorical. Some students of these schoolmasters learned their lessons well.

As Professor T. W. Baldwin has brilliantly demonstrated,[3] the literary training of our greatest English playwright, Shakespeare, was rhetorical. Much of our difficulty and misunderstanding today would be removed if we could remember that poetry and rhetoric are not oil and water that refuse to mix. We must combat the depreciation of rhetoric and oratory that romantic critics have foisted upon us.

John Stuart Mill's statement that eloquence is *heard* and poetry *over*heard is clever and partly true, but it is very misleading if we conclude from it that all eloquence is unpoetic. If we decry rhetorical eloquence, then we must condemn as unpoetic the major compositions of our greatest poets, Milton and Shakespeare.

The ancients and their Renaissance disciples did not make such a mistake; they rightly regarded oratory and poetry as cognate arts, nourished by the same disciplines of logic, grammar, and rhetoric. Plato treated poetry and rhetoric together in the *Phaedrus*. Aristotle repeatedly referred the reader of his *Poetics* to the *Rhetoric*, and vice versa. Cicero time and again drew upon poetry, including the plays of Terence, for illustrations of rhetorical principles. Probably the best known, most often quoted, comparison of poet with orator came from Cicero's *De Oratore* (1.16.70): "The poet, indeed, is closely allied to the orator, being somewhat more restricted in numbers, but freer in the choice of words, yet in many kinds of ornament his ally and almost his equal." Quintilian, who exerted a profound influence upon the schools of the Renaissance, often illustrated gen-

---

[3] *Ibid.*

eral observations on rhetoric from the poets. His remarks in the *Institutio Oratoria* (10.1.69) on Menander, the chief model for Terence, may be cited as typical of the ancient, and Renaissance, attitude towards poetry and oratory:

The careful study of Menander alone would, in my opinion, be sufficient to develop all those qualities with the production of which my present work is concerned; so perfect is his representation of actual life, so rich is his power of invention and his gift of style, so perfectly does he adapt himself to every kind of circumstance, character, and emotion.

Quintilian also joined in praise of Homer's eloquence; some of the speeches in the *Iliad*, he maintained, "display all the rules of art to be followed in forensic or deliberative oratory." Hermogenes, who was well known to scholars in the sixteenth century, offered an even greater eulogy of Homer, "the best of all poets, orators, and writers."[4]

Aphthonius, the fourth-century rhetorician whose *Progymnasmata Rhetorica* was a popular schoolbook in western Europe throughout the sixteenth century, emphasized, in his first sentence, the common ground between poetry and rhetoric: "In the beginning the fable belonged to the poets. Afterwards, because it was suitable for instructing boys, it was adopted by the rhetoricians."

An early Italian humanist, Gasparino Barzizza (d. 1431), remarked that orator, grammarian, and poet were necessarily allies and interdependent. "What," he asked, "would Cicero profit me without Priscian and Terence and other poets; what, Priscian, without Cicero and Terence; finally, what, Terence, without Cicero and Priscian? Nothing certainly."[5]

Landinus, whose celebrated commentary on Horace first appeared in 1482, called special attention to the common precepts guiding orator and poet, both of whom had to consider invention, disposition, and style. He took for granted that Horace, in his *Art of Poetry*, was concerned with invention, disposition, and style. Landinus was one of the first to transfer to the poet, Cicero's praise of the ideal orator as the supremely learned man. According to Landinus, the poet especially should try to adorn his poetry with all the arts and sciences.[6]

Parrhasius, whose commentary on Horace was first printed in

---

[4]*De Formis Orationum* 2.10.375.

[5]See Karl Vossler, *Poetische Theorien in der Italienischen Fruhrenaissance* (Berlin, 1900), p. 69.

[6]See his comment on *Ars Poetica* 309.

1531, remarked: "If the oratorical power and art of speaking are lacking, the poet will forthwith be dumb."[7]

Daniello, author of an early Renaissance poetics (*La Poetica*, 1536), was primarily interested in poetry, especially in Petrarch, yet his approach was naturally rhetorical. For him, the three principal parts of poetry in general were invention, disposition, and style. Daniello said (*La Poetica*, 47-49) that the poet must master the three kinds of oratory—panegyric, deliberative, and forensic— and that his procedure should be by way of exordium, arguments, and conclusion. As was fashionable at the time, Daniello devoted most space to style, which he analyzed in the traditional Ciceronian pattern of grand, middle, and humble. He was fond of illustrating his rhetorical generalizations from the *canzoni* of Petrarch.

Bartholomaeus Lombardus, who together with Madius published an important commentary on the *Poetics* of Aristotle in 1550, expressed the current attitude that poet and orator make use of the same faculty and devices. Lombardus echoed the suggestion of Landinus that poetry, while a counterpart of rhetoric, is more learned than common speaking.[8]

This elevation of poetry over oratory is not classical, but belongs to the Renaissance and anticipates the modern separation of poetry and rhetoric. The ancients could discriminate between poetry and rhetoric without separating the two arts; they regarded Homer as a great rhetorician as well as a great poet.

Julius Caesar Scaliger presented one of the clearest illustrations of this change of emphasis from the ideal orator to the ideal poet. Minturno before him, however, was quite as enthusiastic in his praise of Virgil as the omniscient artist, and he was even more specific in his rhetorical demands on the poet. "Now, indeed" wrote Minturno in 1559, "what kind of poet and how great a poet will he be who ignores the precepts of the rhetoricians and does not excel in the power of speaking which these rhetoricians challenge?"[9] The great poet, like Virgil, must be a master of persuasion, of praise, and of debate.

Scaliger, who was not an original critic but followed traditional paths, neatly expressed the evolution of oratory and poetry as an exchange of functions. The early orators sought only to persuade and move; the early poets sought only to please. "In due time, however,

[7]*Ecphrasis in Horatii Flacci artem poeticam* (Naples, 1531), p. 3r.

[8]*In Aristotelis librum de poetica communes explanationes* (Venice, 1550), p. 2.

[9]*De Poeta*, p. 95.

orator and poet secured from each other that which they lacked respectively."[10] The orators acquired grace and the poets became more thoughtful and didactic until both orators and poets achieved what Horace in his *Art of Poetry* prescribed, the mingling of profit and delight. In the first chapter of his *Poetices*, Scaliger asked and answered this question: "Now is there not one end, and one only, in philosophical exposition, in oratory, and in the drama? Assuredly such is the case. All have one and the same end—persuasion." The orator in the forum, according to Scaliger, debates on life, on vice and virtue; philosopher, poet, and historian treat of the same matter in the same spirit; but only poetry is all-inclusive, "excelling those other arts in this, that while they, as we have said above, represent things just as they are, in some sense like a speaking picture, the poet depicts quite another sort of nature, and a variety of fortunes; in fact, by so doing, he transforms himself almost into a second deity."

By 1561, when Scaliger's *Poetices* first appeared, there was obviously some critical separation of orator from poet, and poetry was becoming more carefully discriminated from oratory. Rhetoric, however, was still fundamental in the theory and practice of both oratory and poetry, for poetry was still regarded as rhetorical, and the tools for examining poetry were still primarily rhetorical. Nevertheless, the rhetorical terminology of literary criticism was already becoming somewhat modified. This modification, which ultimately produced modern literary criticism, grew out of an increasing knowledge of the *Poetics* of Aristotle, first made readily available to the sixteenth-century student in 1536, when the Latin version of Alexander Paccius was first printed. The chief pioneer in the formulation of our modern poetics was Franciscus Robortellus, the first (1548) and one of the greatest commentators on the *Poetics* of Aristotle.

Robortellus was thoroughly familiar with the ancient arts of rhetoric; he read and used Plato, Aristotle, Cicero, Quintilian, Hermogenes, Dionysius of Halicarnassus, and virtually all the other classical writers on rhetoric. He had no thought of exalting poetry over oratory, for he believed, as did his contemporaries, that oratory and poetry are sister arts. Nevertheless, Robortellus learned from Aristotle and Horace that there is an art of poetry, specifically an art of dramatic poetry, that can be discriminated from the art of rhetoric in general. This art of poetry is itself rhetorical in large part, but there are peculiar qualitative and quantitative elements that distinguish it, *per se*, that form tragedies, comedies, and epic poems.

---

[10] *Poetices* 3.25.

RHETORIC IN TERENCE

Before trying to demonstrate how Robortellus and his followers succeeded in squaring the classical theory of rhetoric with the Aristotelian analysis of poetry, it is necessary to examine this rhetorical theory in more detail and to determine the role of Terence as rhetorician and poet. Terence and Cicero were the "foundation-stones" for the study of both prose and poetry in the sixteenth century."[11] Terence shared with Cicero the principal authority in rhetoric and Terence himself was the first model in poetry. For comedy, Terence was preferred to the livelier Plautus. Scaliger, for one, attributed this preference to the rhetorical superiority of Terence: "Why then do we make more of him than of Plautus? For the reason that today we are most intent on the art of good speaking (*bene loquendi*)."[12]

Cicero[13] more than once praised Terence as a model for the orator. Even if any prompting from Cicero had been wanting, and even if the schoolmasters had not been using Terence as a model, the commentators would have found rhetoric enough in Terence. In the prologue to the *Self-Tormentor*, for example, the speaker professes to be a pleader (*orator*) delivering an appeal to the audience, defending the practice of the author and refuting the attacks of his enemies. Willichius called this prologue a mixed form with a large part of it belonging to the judicial, or forensic, type. Similar is the Prologue to the *Mother-in-law*, which Donatus admired: "This prologue has been written with great art and beyond measure oratorically."[14] Paulus Malleolus added that it is "most observant of the rhetorical rules."

All the commentators admired good rhetorical passages, and they found many in Terence, not only in the prologues but throughout the plays. Donatus, for example, called special attention to an illustration of sound oratorical method in the *Mother-in-law* 4.2.589 ff. Here, Pamphilus, the young man who has refused to live with his wife, Philumena, replies to his mother's offer to step aside and retire to the country:

Shall her [Philumena's] folly drive you from town to country? It shall not be; nor will I allow the censure that the cause was my obstinacy and not your good nature. I am unwilling that, for my sake, you give up friends, relations, and festivities.

Donatus observed: "See how oratorically he has gathered everything together, from persons, causes, places, and actions." Pamphilus was

---

[11]Baldwin, *op. cit.*, 1.448.   [12]*Poetices* 3.97.
[13]*De Inventione* 1.23; *De Oratore* 2.80.326-28.
[14]Donatus on *Mother-in-law* 9.

speaking in the manner approved by Cicero and Quintilian (5.10.23), both of whom stated that all arguments are drawn from persons or from things, which include causes, places, and actions.

Another example is the *Self-Tormentor* 2.2.233. Here Clinia, just returned from military service abroad, is worried about his mistress whom he had left behind; he thinks of many reasons why she may have been unfaithful: opportunity, place, her age, and her unscrupulous, avaricious mother. Calphurnius, who supplied the leading commentary on the *Self-Tormentor*—Donatus did not leave one for this play—saw that Clinia, by means of "rhetorical art," is here drawing up confirmatory agruments, all of which come from persons or from things. Barlandus supplied the proper reference to Cicero's *De Inventione* 1.24.

It is hardly necessary to argue whether or not the speeches in Terence follow the prescriptions of rhetoricians or that Cicero learned rhetoric from Terence; the point is that Donatus and his Renaissance followers took for granted that a good comedy is constructed upon sound rhetorical principles, and that the practice of Terence naturally harmonizes with the theory of Cicero and Quintilian. While the commentators took good rhetoric in Terence for granted, they rightly called attention to the more brilliant illustrations of fine rhetoric.

Hegendorphinus was particularly struck by the masterly exposition, or *narratio*, of the *Mother-in-law* 1.2. Here Parmeno, in a lively dialogue with Philotis, presents the background of the main argument of the play. "Notice," wrote Hegendorphinus, "the matchless art of the poet in this scene, how excellently he has observed oratorical topics (*loci*) and the decorum of character." In fact, the Renaissance commentators on Terence apparently looked first for rhetoric and then considered the qualities that might particularly distinguish the poetic or dramatic manner.

The comment of Calphurnius on the use of the word *morari* in *Self-Tormentor* 1.1.172 will illustrate. Chremes excuses himself with the remark, "I am keeping my guests waiting (*egomet convivas moror*)." Calphurnius remarked that the use of *morari* here instead of *expectare* is "poetic rather than oratorical"; in other words, one would normally expect *expectare* in comedy. The commentators, in their minute interpretations of the Terentian comedies, overlooked virtually no canon of classical rhetoric. They carefully distinguished the three kinds of oratory to be found in the plays. They kept always in mind the qualitative parts of a discouse (invention, disposition, style).

They analyzed individual scenes in terms of the quantitative parts (exordium, *narratio*, proof, disproof, and conclusion).

The comedies of Terence abound in examples of deliberative, forensic, and demonstrative oratory. Far from being confused by the variety displayed by Terentian characters, the commentators welcomed these rhetorical riches. Willichius, on the *Andrian* 4.2, neatly summed up this phenomenon: "Therefore, many very short forms of oratory are mingled and sometimes interrupted, in which Terence is a notable master." Many a scene, consequently, had to be labeled "mixed discourse" (*oratio mista*). Sometimes a commentator might venture to classify a whole comedy as belonging to one type of oratory. Thus Melanchthon called the *Andrian* deliberative: "The whole play is like the persausive type of oration, for old men, youths, and servants deliberate (*consultant*) on the whole matter in various ways."[15] Willichius, possibly following Melanchthon, summarized the argument of the play in similar terms: "It belongs to the deliberative kind. . . . Here are both persuasions and dissuasions of youths, old men, and servants."

Deliberative Rhetoric

By common consent of classical authorities, deliberative oratory is the highest type, and its function is persuasion and dissuasion. Trapezuntius, a follower of Hermogenes and a translator of Aristotle's *Rhetoric*, who was very influential himself in the sixteenth century, held that deliberative oratory should persuade and dissuade and that its main end is honor or dignity (*honestas*), which may be divided into "prudence, justice, manliness, and moderation."[16] Scenes involving these virtues would normally be deliberative. In the *Mother-in-law* 3.2(336 ff.), for example, Parmeno dissuades Sostrata from interfering in the domestic crisis of her daughter-in-law Philumena. Parmeno urges prudence and moderation on the part of the mother-in-law, who should wait until the son is reconciled to his wife. Quite naturally, then, the commentators from Donatus to Willichius labeled this scene deliberative, containing, as it does, persuasions and dissuasions.

An important element in the comedies of Terence is *consilium* (counsel). According to Melanchthon,[17] "Comedy is nothing unless it is the image of human counsels and events." *Consilia* have to do with doubtful matters, involving consulations about what is right and wrong, what is expedient, and thus naturally belong to deliberative

---

[15]*Terentii Comoediae* (Paris, 1552), p. 3a.
[16]*Rhetoric* (Basle, 1522), p. 94v.   [17]*Op. cit.*, p. 3a.

discourse. "Deliberation," said Quintilian (3.8.25), is "always about what is doubtful," and the Terentian commentators echoed him. These *consilia* appear most frequently in the quieter plays like the *Self-Tormentor* and the *Mother-in-law*, but they are prominent throughout all the comedies.

A good example of *consilium*, for instance, appears early in the *Eunuch* (1.1), the liveliest of all the plays of Terence. In this scene, Parmeno gives his young master Phaedria realistic advice on how he should extricate himself from the love affair with Thais. Hegendorphinus called the scene deliberative. Melanchthon found the whole play mostly deliberative: "In the foregoing play there are many consultations, and as a whole it is generally of the deliberative kind."[18] Donatus, upon at least one occasion, used the term "comic deliberation"; he applied it to the *Andrian* 1.3.206 ff., wherein Davus debates with himself on the most expedient course of action, i.e., whether he should throw in his lot with young master Pamphilus or obey old master Simo. The deliberation is comic, to be sure, because Davus is a humble slave.

Another element in oratory that may have influenced the classification of comic scenes as deliberative is impersonation (*prosopopoeia*), which Quintilian discussed under deliberative oratory. An important accomplishment of good orators, according to Quintilian (3.8.51-52), is the ability to impersonate various characters:

As a rule, they impersonate sons, parents, rich men, old men, gentle or harsh of temper, misers, superstitious persons, cowards and mockers, so that hardly even comic actors have to assume more numerous roles in their performances on the stage than these in their declamations. All these roles may be regarded as forming part of impersonation, which I have included under deliberative themes.

Quintilian's list of roles that the orator must be able to assume certainly looks like a cast of characters in almost any domestic comedy from Terence through Ben Jonson and Molière.

I do not wish to emphasize *prosopopoeia*, however, as a major factor in comic deliberation since another classical authority of influence in the sixteenth century offered a different classification. Aphthonius' scheme of rhetoric as interpreted by Rodolphus Agricola, put *imitatio*, which was virtually synonymous with *prosopopoeia* and *ethopoeia* in the Renaissance, under demonstrative discourse.[19] In addition, although Quintilian discussed *prosopopoeia* under deliberative themes (2.10.12-13), he did call attention to the similarity between the

---

[18]*Ibid.*, p. 4a.   [19]*Progymnasmata rhetorica* (Salamanca, 1550), p. 1v.

heightened delivery of comic actors and the air of elegance in epideictic, or demonstrative, oratory.

FORENSIC RHETORIC

Forensic oratory was perhaps not so often connected with comedy as were the deliberative and demonstrative types. The principal quantitative scheme for analyzing comic scenes, however, was borrowed from forensic oratory exordium, *narratio,* proof, peroration and later on I shall discuss the use of proofs in comedy. Willichius, for one, classified many scenes in Terence as primarily forensic. Such a scene is the *Andrian* 4.1. Here Charinus accuses his friend Pamphilus of treachery; he believes that Pamphilus is going to marry Philumena although his own lady love is Glycerium. Pamphilus, who is still in love with Glycerium, answers the charge by disclaiming any personal desire for the match and shifts the blame to his scheming servant Davus. The servant, in turn, defends his past failure by promises of better advice and better action in the future.

A more obvious example of the forensic manner is *Phormio* 2.1. In this scene, Demipho returns to Athens from abroad to find that his son Antipho has married during his absence. The old gentleman, highly incensed at this unfilial conduct, accuses Antipho and Geta, his slave, of shameful behavior. Antipho lacks the courage to face his father, but his cousin Phaedria defends him by means of an argument fabricated and rehearsed beforehand by Geta. Phaedria argues that the inexperienced Antipho was helplessly caught in legal toils and forced into marriage. There was a law which required that orphans be married to the next of kin, and Geta had suggested that the girl was kin to Antipho. Geta defended himself by reminding Demipho that a slave had no right to appear in court and therefore he (Geta) was unable to help his young master. As Willichius observed, this scene is a "legal issue (*status*) in which the inquiry concerns an established law."

DEMONSTRATIVE RHETORIC

Demonstrative oratory deals primarily with praise and blame. It is calculated to delight rather than to persaude, and thus may be closer to the spirit of poetry than are the other types of oratory. In the minds of some classical and medieval authorities, the art of praise and blame was closely connected with poetry. The rhetorical scheme in sixteenth-century editions of Aphthonius listed *praise, blame, imitation,* and *comparison* under the demonstrative discourse. As I have suggested previously, comedy, which naturally made large use of *mimesis* or *imitatio* (or *prosopopoeia* or *ethopoeia*), may have been specifically connected with demonstrative oratory. Averroes certainly supports such a conjecture. According to a sixteenth-century Latin version of Averroes' paraphrase of Aristotle's *Poetics*, "All poetry and every poetic fable is classified as either praise or blame."[20]

Poetic fables are "imitative discourses" (*sermones imitatorii*). The best art of praising is tragedy, which praises distinguished actions. Comedy, on the other hand, deals mainly with blame; it blames bad actions, but only those bad actions that are ridiculous and not painful.[21] That Averroes, or his Latin translator, was not using terms loosely is indicated by another passage in the paraphrase, where Averroes was trying to follow Aristotle's discussion of the quantitative parts of a tragedy. Even Arabic poems, it seems, were divided into parts that correspond to the divisions of a rhetorical speech, namely, exordium, praise or episode (*laudatio vel episodium*), and conclusion.[22]

At all events, demonstrative speeches and scenes are prominent in both tragedy and comedy. Speeches of praise and blame abound in Terence. Such speeches are specially prominent in the *Brothers,* for example, since this play is a representation of what constitutes proper behavior in the guardian-parent and in the son. There is much to praise in the behavior of the city-bred brother, Micio, and something to blame. There is much to blame in the intolerant behavior of the rustic brother, Demea, and something to praise. Willichius found that a good part of the *Brothers* 3.4.(364 ff.) belongs to the demonstrative kind. Certainly a good part of the scene deals with praise and blame. Syrus, with his tongue in his cheek, praises Ctesipho, the country-bred son of Demea; flatters Demea; and blames the other son (Aeschinus) and the city-bred brother (Micio) for all the family troubles. Donatus called attention to the *laudantis oratio* in the *Brothers* 4.5.(707 ff.). Here Aeschinus delivers an ecstatic eulogy of his generous uncle Micio. Any highly emotional speech in comedy was likely to be classified as demonstrative.

It is hardly necessary, I believe, to cite further examples of deliberative, forensic, and demonstrative discourse in Terence. As Quintilian (2.21.23) remarked, the Aristotelian tripartite division brings virtually everything that may arise within the province of the orator. A more important task now is to examine the relationship that the

---

[20]"Omnis Poesis omnisque fabula poetica in vituperandi vel laudandi genere consistit." *Averrois paraphrasis in librum poeticae Aristotelis,* edited by Fridericus Heidenhain, in *Jahrbucher fur classische Philologie, Supplementband* 17 (1890), 354.

[21]*Ibid.,* pp. 358-59, 368.   [22]*Ibid.,* p. 367.

sixteenth century established between the qualitative and quantitative elements of rhetoric and the qualitative and quantitative elements of poetry. After some necessary discussion of these rhetorical elements I shall try to show how the sixteenth century squared invention, disposition, and style with Aristotle's plot, character, thought, and diction; and how it squared exordium, *narratio*, proof, and peroration with the Aristotelian prologue, episodes, choral odes, and exode.[23]

THE QUALITATIVE PARTS OF RHETORIC

The chief classical authority on rhetoric in the sixteenth century was Cicero, closely followed by Quintilian, and the favorite classical text was apparently Cicero's *Partitiones Oratoriae*, which briefly and clearly discusses the functions of the orator and the structure of a speech. From Cicero came the accepted definition of the aim or purpose of oratory: "to teach, to delight, and to move."[24] The functions of the orator are intimately related, of course, with this threefold purpose of oratory. Johann Sturm, probably the best known interpreter of the *Partitiones Oratoriae* in the sixteenth century, stated this relationship clearly:

First is invention, next disposition, third style, then delivery, all four of which are preserved by the memory. All these are related to the three [aims], that he should teach, delight, persuade, that is, that he should prevail with what is necessary to victory.[25]

In other words, the successful exercise of invention, disposition, style, etc., will teach, delight, and persuade.

Of these five functions of the orator, or the qualitative parts of oratory, disposition (*dispositio* or *collocatio*) will be discussed in some detail in a later chapter on plot in comedy. Style (*elocutio*) will be discussed in a later chapter on thought and diction. Delivery and memory, important functions of the orator in action, belong rather to the actor or the declaimer than to the poet. Therefore I shall now examine invention, the first qualitative element in rhetoric, and long considered a fundamental element in all art.

---

[23]Two other quantitative parts of rhetoric, partition and disproof, were often added. See the *Ad Herennium* 1.3.

[24]See *Brutus* 49.185. Cf. *Orator* 21.69.

[25]*Ioannis Sturmii in partitiones oratorias Ciceroni, dialogi duo* (Strassburg, 1539), p. 18.

Invention and Imitation

The sixteenth century regarded both invention and disposition, i.e., the finding of arguments and their artistic arrangement, as common to both logic and rhetoric. Aristotle had recognized the kinship between the two arts; the first sentence of his *Rhetoric* reads:

Rhetoric is a counterpart of Dialectic; for both have to do with matters that are in a manner within the cognizance of all men and not confined to any special science.

Some sixteenth-century scholars found it difficult to separate rhetorical invention from logical invention; others objected to any such separation.

Melanchthon and Ramus may be taken as typical authorities, both of whom found that the characteristic distinction between logic and rhetoric lay in style. According to Melanchthon, dialectic discovers and organizes arguments but does it briefly and dryly; rhetoric dresses up these arguments in an ornamental, pleasing style.[26] Ramus went further; he insisted that invention and disposition were logical elements which were borrowed by the rhetoricians.[27]

Leonard Cox, an Englishman of the sixteenth century who followed Melanchthon, summed up the difference as follows:

For this is the difference that is between these two sciences, that the logician in disputing observeth certain rules for the setting of his words, being solicitous that there be spoken no more nor no less than the thing requireth and that it be even as plainly spoken as it is thought. But the rhetorician seeketh about and borroweth when he can as much as he may for to make the simple and plain logical arguments gay and delectable to the ear. So then the sure judgment of arguments or reasons must be learned of the logician, but the craft to set them out with pleasant figures and to dilate the matter longeth to the rhetorician.[28]

Alexander Richardson, a seventeenth-century English schoolmaster, followed Ramus and was therefore more biased in favor of logic:

Now indeed the rhetoricians have taken invention to be a part of rhetoric, and so judgment, but when they come to explain them, they teach logic: and their *dissertus* is not only rhetorician but the grammarian and logician, their orator is *omnium horarum homo*, a man for every turn, so that he

---

[26]"Verum hoc interesse dicunt, quod Dialectica res nudas proponit; Rhetorica uero addit eloquutionem quasi uestitum." (*Elementorum rhetorices libri duo* (Strassburg, 1533), p. 12.)

[27]See *Scholae in liberales artes* (Basle, 1569), pp. 253 ff.; Talaeus, *Rhetorica et P. Rami praelectionibus observata* (Frankfort, 1584), p. 29.

[28]*The Arte or Crafte of Rhethoryke*, edited by F. I. Carpenter (Chicago, 1899), p. 48.

is a man in whom there is a confusion of all arts: neither is orator belonging to rhetoric, but he is a general man, that hath all the arts, and chiefly he is a logician.[29]

I have already indicated how the conception of the ideal orator, the "man for every turn," advanced by Cicero and Quintilian was being transferred during the sixteenth century to the ideal poet, specifically to Virgil or Homer.

The most important modification of this logical-rhetorical *inventio*, when applied to the poet, came about with the modification of the traditional notions of imitation; it began to appear when Plato and Aristotle became better known to those who were interested in poetry, when Plato's and Aristotle's explanations of imitation were added to the familiar remarks in Horace, Cicero, Quintilian, and Donatus. Apparently every educated man in the Renaissance was familiar with the Ciceronian definition of comedy known only through Donatus: "the imitation of life, the mirror of custom, the image of truth." Donatus himself drew mainly upon Cicero and Quintilian, although he may have been familiar with an earlier conception of imitation that goes back to Plato.

Socrates, in the *Republic* (392-94), restricted the imitative style to the drama. According to Socrates, there are three styles in poetry: (1) simple narration, as in the dithyramb; (2) imitation, as in tragedy and comedy; (3) mixed narration and imitation, as in the Homeric epic poem. Aristotle, in the *Poetics* (3), thought of imitation in a wider sense:

Given both the same means and the same kind of object for imitation, one may either (1) speak at one moment in narrative and at another in an assumed character, as Homer does; or (2) one may remain the same throughout, without any change; or (3) the imitators may represent the whole story dramatically, as though they were actually doing the things described.

The narrower Platonic view was that imitation is the assimilation of the speaker to another character. When Donatus used the term *mimesis*, and he often did, he usually meant mimicking. He was familiar with the notion of a mixed style, though precisely how he distinguished between the two is not altogether clear. For example, on the *Andrian* 4.5.773, where Davus describes to Mysis what thoughts must be going on in the mind of Glycerium, Donatus observed: "It is μίμησις. He passes from a mixed style to an imitative." Now Davus

---

[29]*The Logicians School-Master* (London, 1657), p. 55. Cf. Abraham Fraunce, *The Lawiers Logike* (London, 1588), p. 115r.

passes here from a simple relating of events to a mimicking of Gly-cerium's own words and actions. Evidently Donatus thought of narrative passages in comedy as not pure narrative, but as mixed; they were narrative and yet partly imitative because the author was after all putting words into the mouth of a character all the while. Upon at least one occasion Donatus came close to a conception of imitation as a dramatic representation of life created by the author, which is not quite the same thing as an aping of character by another character. In commenting on the somewhat garrulous exchange of courtesies between old Laches and the courtesan Bacchis in the *Mother-in-law* 5.1.741, Donatus remarked: "Here is imitated a senile and womanish tediousness of speech." Here Terence is the imitator, not one of his characters. I am not quite sure just what Donatus did believe, but it seems fairly certain that his notion of imitation was closer to the Platonic interpretation than to Aristotle's wider mean-ing. *Mimesis* or *imitatio* usually meant the assimilation of the speaker to another character.

The Terentian commentators did not have to go to Plato's *Republic* for this narrow meaning of imitation; they found it in the rhetorical discussions of *mimesis*, *prosopopoeia*, *prosographia*, *ethopoeia*, and *dialogismus*. All these terms were used more or less synonymously.[30] Quintilian (9.2.58) said: "The imitation of other persons' characteris-tics, which is styled *ethopoeia* or, as some prefer, *mimesis*, may be counted among the devices which serve to excite the gentler emotions; for it consists mainly in banter, though it may be concerned either with words or deeds." And Quintilian illustrated from the *Eunuch* (1.2.155-57) of Terence, where Phaedria mimics his mistress Thais. Barlandus, for one, quoted Quintilian on the passage, and doubtless all the commentators were familiar with the illustration. Although all the terms for imitation mentioned above were interchangeable, some rhetoricians tried to discriminate. Aphthonius[31] called *prosopopoeia* a kind of *ethopoeia*, specifically a portrait of manners such as Menan-der fashioned. Menander, of course, pointed straight to Terence.

According to Professor Baldwin,[32] English schoolboys were taught that in *prosopopoeia* the speaker feigns talking by himself, in *dialog-ismus* he feigns carrying on a dialogue by means of question and answer. The commentator Barlandus would support such a distinc-tion; he called Phaedria's debating with himself in the *Eunuch* 1.1.46 a *dialogismus* and cited a Virgilian parallel in the *Aeneid* (4.534 ff.),

---

[30]See Donatus, Latomus, and Willichius on the *Mother-in-law* 5.3.803; on the *Andrian* 1.5.286.
[31]*Op. cit.*, p. 16v.   [32]*Op. cit.* 2.233.

where Dido debates with herself. These rhetorical terms persisted for some time, long after Aristotle's broader conception of imitation became well known. Sir Philip Sidney, praising the poetry of David's Psalms, wrote, "His notable *prosopopoeias*, when he maketh you, as it were, see God coming in his majesty.[33] Sir John Harington took care to point out a "*pretty prosopopoeia*" in the *Jerusalem Delivered* of Tasso.[34]

In addition to the technical conception of imitation as a rhetorical device particularly appropriate to comedy, there was the conception of imitation as the copying or emulation of models, best illustrated for the sixteenth century by Virgil's imitation of Homer, by Cicero's imitation of Demosthenes, and by Terence's imitation of Menander. Vida, in his *Art of Poetry* (1527), made famous this Virgilian kind of imitation that appropriates and refines upon the work of another author. Ben Jonson defined and practiced it as faithfully as any one: "The third requisite in our poet or maker is *imitation*, to be able to convert the substance or riches of another poet to his own use.[35] Cicero and Quintilian had strongly advocated the imitation of good authors as a necessary part of sound training in rhetoric. Horace had recommended the emulation of Greek authors. This notion of imitation, like *prosopopoeia*, persisted long after the Aristotelian imitation was well established.

By the middle of the sixteenth century, scholars were quoting Aristotle's statement in the *Physics* (2.2.194ª22), that "art imitates nature." After 1536, when the Latin version of the *Poetics* by Paccius appeared, there was an increasing acquaintance with Aristotle's more specific explanation of imitation. Imitation, according to Aristotle and the Aristotelian commentators, is the characteristic quality of the poet, who imitates by fabricating idealized representations of human beings in action. The sixteenth-century commentators and critics, by combining this Aristotelian imitation with theories found in Plato, Cicero, Horace, and Quintilian, arrived at a concept of imitation that closely corresponded to the traditional invention of logic and rhetoric. In fact, by the middle of the century, *imitatio, inventio, fictio,* and *fabula* were corollary terms, often used as synonyms.[36] Thus Lionardi, in 1554, could use imitation and invention interchangeably, and could

---

[33]*Defense of Poesie* (1595), in Gregory Smith, *Elizabethan Critical Essays* 1.155.

[34]*Briefe Apologie of Poetrie* (1591), *ibid.* 2.199.

[35]*Discoveries* (Bodley Head Quartos, London, 1923), p. 93.

[36]See my discussion of poetic imitation in the *Fusion of Horatian and Aristotelian Literary Criticism* (Urbana, 1946), pp. 28-38.

say that invention is the "soul of all poetic imitation."[37] Long after the middle of the century *imitatio* and *inventio* continued to appear together in critical writings too numerous to mention. Examples from two of the most illustrious critics will suffice. Ronsard, in his *Brief on the Art of French Poetry* (1565), maintained that the "main point in poetry is invention, which comes as much from the right nature as from the lesson of good and ancient authors.[38] The aim of invention, said Ronsard, is to "represent, to describe, to imitate."[39] Sidney, in his *Defense of Poesie* (1595), raised a common question of the day, namely, whether or not a philosophical or historical poet, such as Lucretius or Lucan, is a "right poet" since he "takes not the free course of his own invention." Poetry, for Sidney, was an "art of imitation, for so Aristotle termeth it in his word *mimesis*, that is to say, a representing, counterfeiting, or figuring forth."[40]

In 1548, Robortellus brought imitation and invention together in a way that satisfactorily harmonized Aristotle's theory with the "learned imitator" (*imitator doctus*) of Horace and with the ideal orator of the rhetoricians. The ignorant man and the learned man, argued Robortellus, do not learn in the same way, although all men, as Aristotle said, delight in learning something and delight in viewing works of imitation. The common man who views a work of imitation, such as a picture or a carving, perceives only particulars, the particulars he has already experienced. The philosopher, however, applies universals to these particulars, for he is able to reason. The common man exercises reminiscence; the philosopher is also provided with *invention*.[41]

Castelvetro, approaching the problem from the poet's point of view rather than from the spectator's, offered a similar interpretation. Although Castelvetro was opposed to imitation in the sense of copying ancient authors, he did approve of the right kind of imitation, which evidently was the same thing as poetic invention. In commenting on *Poetics* 9, wherein Aristotle asserted that the proper distinction between Homer the poet and Herodotus the historian is not that the

---

[37]Alessandro Lionardi, *Dialogi della inventione poetica* (Venice, 1554), p. 14.

[38]*Oeuvres* (Paris, 1914-19) 7.45.

[39]*Ibid.* 7.50. Cf. Robortellus, who said the same thing in *In librum Aristotelis de arte poetica explicationes* (Florence, 1548), p. 2.

[40]Smith, *Elizabethan Critical Essays* 1.158.

[41]"Differt autem cognitio philosophi a cognitione illa vulgari, quoniam philosophus applicat vniuersale ad singularia, et sic colligit, ac recognoscit res ipsas; differt etiam, quoniam in philosopho inest vtraque cognitio, et quae per reminiscentiam, et ea simul, quae per inuentionem paratur; in vulgari autem homine est tantum reminiscentia." (*Op. cit.*, p. 31.)

one wrote in verse and the other in prose but rather that Homer
exercised a creative faculty while Herodotus reported facts, Castelvetro said that the essence of poetry "consists in invention, and without invention there is no poet."[42] Versified history, said Castelvetro,
is not poetry, for the mere versifier "endures no labor in invention;
invention is the most difficult thing that the poet has to do, and it
appears in that part from which he takes his name, that is, ποιητής."[43]

Castelvetro's statements on invention offer striking parallels to
statements on imitation by other sixteenth-century scholars who were
also following Aristotle. In *Poetics* 1, Aristotle argued that a poet is a
poet by reason of his imitation, not by reason of his meter, that Empedocles, though a versifier, was a physicist rather than a poet. Robortellus (14) summed up the argument thus: "Homer imitates; therefore he is a poet. Empedocles does not imitate; . . . therefore he is
not a poet." The sixteenth century could substitute "invents" for
"imitates" and the meaning would remain the same; Lucretius, Lucan,
Virgil (of the *Georgics*) could be substituted for Empedocles.[44]

The sixteenth-century interpretation of Aristotelian imitation
brought out an important distinction between oratorical invention and
poetic invention. Robortellus (p. 2), in comparing the ends of rhetoric and poetry, decided that it is imitation that specially distinguishes
poetry, persuasion that specially distinguishes rhetoric:

What other end, indeed, do we say the poetic faculty serves than to delight by means of representation, description, and imitation of all human
actions, of all motions, of all matter both animate and inanimate? And
since imitation or representation is done by means of speech, we say that
the end of poetry is imitative discourse, as the end of rhetoric is persuasive discourse.

Then Robortellus proceeded to back this statement by quoting the
Ciceronian definition of comedy—"the imitation of life, the mirror
of custom, the image of truth"—which, he maintained, could be applied to all poetry.

This distinction, most clearly set forth by Robortellus, was not new
at the time. Even before the revival of good Greek texts, with compe-
tent Latin translations, Averroes had pointed out the same difference.
Robortellus, by the way, knew a Latin version of Averroes' paraphrase of Aristotle's *Poetics*, and often referred to it. Averroes argued
that rhetoric exercised its office "by means of persuasive speech,

---

[42]*Poetica d'Aristotele* (Basle, 1576), p. 216.
[43]*Ibid.*, p. 78.
[44]See Herrick, *op. cit.*, pp. 34-38.

poetry rather by means of imitative speech."[45] He emphatically insisted that persuasive speech is not becoming in poetic art, which should use speech that is "feigned and imitative"; in fact, he went so far as to assert that poetic art, especially tragedy, is not devised for argumentation and disputation.[46]

Most sixteenth-century schoolmasters, I suspect, would not have agreed with Averroes. Certainly Willichius, who found virtually every kind of argumentation and disputation in Terence, and who wanted schoolboys to find them, would have agreed with him. Nor would Scaliger, who maintained that philosopher, orator, and poet, "all have one and the same end—persuasion." This attitude, that poet and orator exercise essentially the same function of persuasion,[47] that the poet differs from the orator only in his being more restricted in his "numbers," that verse is merely an appendage of poetry,[48] persisted long after the time of Scaliger.

There was little or no disagreement in the sixteenth century, however, on the importance of imitation in poetry, especially in dramatic poetry. There was little disagreement, moreover, that this poetic imitation was largely a making of fiction. In the eyes of most scholars and critics of the time, this imitation, this making of fiction, was what chiefly characterized the poet.[49] I have already shown that Averroes promoted this theory. Robortellus (p. 2), restated it as well as any:

[45]*Op cit.*, p. 361.

[46]*Ibid.*, p. 362.

[47]For example, Fenelon (1651-1715), in his dialogues on eloquence, said:
"C. But if true Orators be Poets, I should think that Poets are Orators, too; for Poetry is very proper to persuade.
A. Yes; they have the very same end."
Then Speaker A reminded his companions of Cicero's comparison of the Orator with the Poet. (*Dialogues Concerning Eloquence*, translated by Wm. Stevenson (London, 1722), p. 80.)

[48]Late in the eighteenth century, George Campbell could say that "poetry indeed is properly no other than a particular mode or form of certain branches of oratory." (*The Philosophy of Rhetoric* (London, 1776), 1.14.) Verse, Campbell believed, is merely an appendage, not a constituent of poetry. In 1800, it will be recalled, Wordsworth could say that the language of poetry differs in no essential way from the language of prose. Was Coleridge, who tried to set Wordsworth straight, the first critic who emphasized the innate formal character of verse, which is essential to poetic form?

[49]Scaliger, though he believed in imitation, did object to the grading of poets according to the imitative powers. He maintained, contrary to the majority of leading critics, that a poet is a poet because he writes verses. See *Poetices* 1.2.

Since, therefore, poetry must use feigned speech for its matter, it is plain that poetry should fitly contrive fable and false tale; in no other art is the mingling of false tales more characteristic than in this one. According to Aristotle,[50] Homer, from whom all poetry has been derived, first taught how a lie should be fitly expressed.

During the Renaissance, and long afterward, invention remained the first quality necessary to the good orator and the good poet. The orator exercised his invention by discovering arguments, proofs, testimony. The poet exercised his invention, which was peculiarly imitative, by imitating nature in general and human actions in particular; he feigned and counterfeited, he made fictions. Both orator and poet aimed to teach, delight, and move. The orator put the main emphasis upon persuading his audience. The poet put the main emphasis upon delighting his. The poet, as Sidney said, "cometh unto you with a tale which holdeth children from play, and old men from the chimney-corner."

THE QUANTITATIVE PARTS OF RHETORIC

As I have remarked at the beginning of this chapter, the conventional quantitative analysis of any formal speech or writing was borrowed from forensic rhetoric: exordium, *narratio*, proof, conclusion. Sometimes partition and disproof were added to the list of parts. There were some attempts in the sixteenth century to make a whole comedy, from prologue through protasis and epitasis to catastrophe, fit this rhetorical plan. Generally, however, the commentators were happier in analyzing individual scenes. Thus Willichius seldom discussed the exordium of a whole play; rather he would discuss the numerous exordia that appeared in the scenes. Again Aristotle pointed the way to a consideration of the composition as an organic whole, and once his *Rhetoric* and *Poetics* became better known more attention was given to the pattern of the whole comedy.

Exordium

Aristotle, in the *Rhetoric* (3.14.1-6), remarked that the "exordium is the beginning of a speech, as the prologue in poetry and the prelude in flute-playing." The exordia of forensic speeches ought to produce the same effect as do dramatic prologues and epic exordia; their special function is to make clear what is the end or purpose of the composition. Long before the modern publication of the *Rhetoric*, Averroes, in his paraphrase, had called attention to the similarity between

---

[50]See *Poetics* 24.60a19.

the exordia of orators and poets: "Not only orators use this, but also poets, both those who make use of praise and other kinds of poets."[51]

This view of the exordium was commonly held in ancient times. Donatus, who probably had no direct acquaintance with either the *Rhetoric* or *Poetics* of Aristotle, argued that the author of a comedy should use the opening of his play to inform the audience about the origin and the end of his plot:

This order and compass of poetic art or power, not only the tragic and comic authors have followed, but also Homer and Virgil have held to.[52]

Donatus thought that the main function of the prologue was to narrate the argument. He recognized that the Terentian prologue is not an integral part of the main action. At all events, he praised Terence for the lively opening, i.e., Act 1, Scene 1, of the *Andrian:*

This scene, in which the grounds of the story (*fabula*) are set forth, is offered in place of a narration of the argument, so that by virtue of the poet and without the service of prologue or "gods out of the machine" people may obtain a summary of the comedy and the matter may be seen acted rather than narrated.[53]

Certainly the typical Roman prologue in comedy did not fulfill Aristotelian requirements, as Robortellus pointed out. Robortellus showed that the Roman prologue, which was usually a mere appendage, "something short and trifling," is different from the Aristotelian ideal of prologue as an integral part of the play.[54] The principles that traditionally governed the making of an exordium were therefore applied to the opening scenes of the play proper rather than to the Terentian prologue. Commentators like Willichius, to be sure, managed to find exordia of some sort or other in almost every scene.

Mainly for introduction, the exordium should not be too emotional; the best place for strong emotional appeal is in the conclusion. According to Quintilian (4.1.5), the author best prepares for receptive listening by making his audience well disposed, attentive, and ready to learn. Donatus, as I have shown above, found a good illustration in the opening scene of the *Andrian*. Later commentators found another admirable illustration in the opening scene of the *Self-Tormen-*

---

[51]"Non agunt hoc solum oratores, sed etiam ipsi poetae, et qui utuntur laudatione, et qui sunt aliarum specierum poetarum." (*Aristotelis . . . opera . . . Averrois Cordubensis in ea opera omnes qui ad nos pervenere commentarii . . .* (Venice, 1550-52) 2.63v.)

[52]Preface to his commentary on the *Andrian.*

[53]On the *Andrian* 1.1.28.

[54]See p. 229.

tor, where Chremes tries, and successfully, to win the confidence of his crotchety neighbor Menedemus so that he may help him overcome his domestic troubles.

The exordium of Roman comedy, then, does not correspond to the Roman prologue; it appears in the opening scene, or scenes, of the play. The exordium of comedy, in fact, overlaps with the next quantitative part, the *narratio;* often it is impossible to determine just what is exordium and what *narratio.*

NARRATIO

The commentators on Terence used the term *narratio* in two ways: first they applied it to the necessary statement of the main argument or to any statement of facts in any scene; secondly they applied it to any narrative passage which might occur anywhere in the five acts. Generally speaking, *narratio*, when applied to comedy, meant either the statement of facts in a particular scene or merely a narrative passage as opposed to the give-and-take of rapid dialogue. Exposition (*expositio*), which nowadays means the necessary explanation of the background of action and character, was apparently used in the sixteenth century, as indeed it was used by the author of the *Ad Herennium* and by Quintilian,[55] interchangeably with *narratio.* Perhaps one commentator, Latomus, did mean to distinguish between *narratio* and *expositio.* Latomus, on the argument of the *Eunuch* 3.5.(549 ff.) called Chaerea's account of his amorous adventure in the house of Thais the "exposition of the protasis of the other part of the play"— i.e., the exposition of the protasis of the sub-plot. But he called Dorias' account of the quarrel between Thais and Thraso, in the *Eunuch* 4.1(615 ff.), the *narratio* of the occasion of the epitasis in the main action. Did Latomus apply *expositio* only to the *protasis*, namely the first act of a play, and thus anticipate our present-day use of the term exposition? I cannot be sure. Unfortunately Willichius does not help much.

Willichius did remark that in the *Phormio* 1.2.(57 ff.) the poet has come to the "exposition of the argument," and this is the protasis of the play. On the other hand, Willichius referred to the whole scene as *narratio:* "Here is the *narratio*, in which the argument of the play is set forth (*exponitur*)." Although it is tempting to argue that *expositio*, in the sixteenth century, was coming to mean the statement of facts in the protasis, thus directly pointing to our present-

---

[55]See Quintilian 3.9.7; 4.2.2. *Ad Herennium* 1.3.4 reads as follows: "Narratio est rerum gestarum aut proinde ut gestarum expositio." Cf. Cicero *De Inventione* 1.19.

day "exposition" in drama, I do not now have sufficient evidence to support such a claim, likely as it appears. Certainly *narratio* was a much commoner term in the century than *expositio*, whether applied to the "exposition" of the whole action, to the "exposition" of individual scenes, or merely to narrative passages.

The classical rhetorical rules for constructing a *narratio*, which the commentators found exemplified in the comedies of Terence, are better discussed in a later chapter on plot. I shall mention here only one important observation that Donatus contributed. Donatus, who had a keen appreciation of the dramatic, called attention to the skillful way in which Terence diversifies his *narratio* in the *Mother-in-law* 1.2.104, 131 by means of many pleasing by-plays of character and by shifting from narrative to *mimesis*. This observation, which had sound Ciceronian authority,[56] is consistent with the best oratorical and dramatic practice. Convenient illustrations may be observed in the early comedies of Shakespeare. The *narratio* in the *Comedy of Errors*, for example, consists of long narrative speeches by old Aegeon, only rarely broken by remarks from the Duke. The *narratio* in the opening scene of the more mature *Midsummer Night's Dream*, however, is diversified by lively by-plays of character and rapid dialogue.

PROOF

The third quantitative element, proof (*confirmatio*), played an important part in many commentators' analyses of Terence. Willichius was the most indefatigable; seldom did he fail to find examples of proof or disproof in a scene. Furthermore, from the rhetorician's point of view, the use of proof in any discourse, oratorical or poetic, furnished the critics with an important basis for artistic evaluation. Aristotle and Quintilian classified proofs as "inartificial" and "artificial"; the artificial proofs were superior since they represented the author's own invention.[57] Donatus and his followers applied this division into artificial and inartificial proofs to the Terentian comedies and judged the artistic merit of some scenes on this basis. There are numerous illustrations; perhaps the best are Donatus on the *Brothers* 3.4.478, and Willichius on the *Andrian* 2.2.359. Nevertheless, while it was easy to find many examples of proof and disproof in Terence, it was difficult to square this third quantitative part of a forensic oration with the third part of a comedy. In other words, proof or dis-

---

[56]"A *narratio* is delightful moreover which has surprises, suspense, and unexpected issues, mingled with human emotions, dialogues between persons, grief, rage, fear, joy, and desire." (*Partitiones Oratoriae* 9.32.)

[57]See Aristotle *Rhetoric* 1.2.2; Quintilian 5.1.1, 5.8-9.

proof as a quantitative element did not fit the pattern of comedy very well; the epitasis is not one long proof or even a consistent series of proofs or disproofs. Averroes had pointed out a real difficulty when he said that poetry is not devised primarily for argumentation and disputation. Aristotle, however, in *Poetics* 19, had mentioned proof as a legitimate part of the intellectual element (διάνοια) in tragedy, and suggested that it properly belongs to the art of rhetoric. Therefore, in time, this phenomenon of proof and disproof in the drama, tragedy or comedy, along with the whole process of reasoning and arguing, was shifted in dramatic criticism from the quantitative scheme of oratory to the Aristotelian qualitative scheme of dramatic poetry where it fitted the third qualitative element of Thought or Sentiment. Consequently I shall reserve my detailed discussion of the use of proofs, of syllogisms and enthymemes, in Terentian comedy for a later chapter on sentiment and diction.

CONCLUSION

Any detailed discussion of the conclusion, the peroration, the epilogue, will be in the chapter on plot. A few general observations on conclusion will have to suffice at this point.

The peroration of a speech, according to Quintilian (6.1.1-2), may deal with either facts (*res*) or emotions. The speaker may repeat his facts in order to refresh the memory of the judge, and he may make his final emotional appeal. Cicero[58] divided the peroration into three parts: (1) the reckoning up, (2) the arousing of indignation, (3) the arousing of pity. When applied to poetry, Cicero's division obviously fits tragedy and the epic poem better than it does comedy. Nevertheless, the adjustment to comedy was not difficult; comedy also has its reckoning up or recapitulation in the catastrophe; it substitutes good humor for indignation, and laughter for pity.

Actually, the commentators on Terence paid little attention to perorations in the plays, doubtless because the pattern of New Comedy was firmly set and all conclusions were similar; they were happy settlements of domestic troubles and happy reunitings of quarreling families and neighbors. Willichius, to be sure, occasionally pointed out a good illustration of peroration in a particular speech or at the end of a particular scene.[59] But the usual conclusion of a scene in Terence is a transition or preparation (παρασκευή) for the next scene. Only one traditional principle for making a good conclu-

---

[58]*De Inventione* 1.52-55. Cf. Trapezuntius, *op. cit.*, pp. 87 ff.
[59]See Willichius on the *Brothers* 1.2.123; *ibid.* 4.3.608.

sion calls for special comment here. Quintilian had insisted that the conclusion be as brief as possible.[60] This rhetorical rule, which must have been hammered into the heads of many schoolboys in the Renaissance, helps to explain a rather common phenomenon in the comic drama of the sixteenth and seventeenth centuries, namely the hurried conclusion. Every student of the drama must have observed it, often in notable plays.

THE REUNION OF RHETORICAL AND POETIC THEORY

The traditional schemes, then, of analyzing literature, whether oratorical or poetic, were two: the qualitative (invention, disposition, style, memory, delivery) and the quantitative (exordium, *narratio*, proof, conclusion). With the rediscovery of Aristotle's *Poetics* in the sixteenth century it was inevitable that sooner or later the traditional rhetorical analysis and Aristotle's poetic analysis would come together, that the two methods, the rhetorical and the poetic, would either be fused or one be raised in importance over the other. So far as I can make out, both these results obtained; the rhetorical and the poetic methods of analyzing literature were fused and in time the Aristotelian analysis by means of plot, character, thought, and diction emerged triumphant in the study of dramatic and epic poetry, in the study of novel and short story.

Robortellus, in 1548, was the first to place these analyses side by side. He paralleled Aristotle's qualitative analysis of tragedy, which also applied to epic poetry and to comedy, with the rhetorical qualitative analysis, enumerating the parts in the reverse of their intrinsic importance:

And there are Spectacle, Music, next Diction, Thought, Character, Plot. Just so in rhetoric, if you proceed in the same order, there will be the constituent parts: Delivery, Memory, Style, Disposition, Invention.[61]

Robortellus found that not only were the qualitative parts parallel, but that the Aristotelian quantitative parts of dramatic poetry corresponded to the quantitative parts of rhetoric:

In the rhetorical faculty the same kind of parts have been called by the rhetoricians Invention, Disposition, Style, Memory, Delivery. So in the poetic faculty, Plot (to which are joined Discovery, Peripety, Perturbation), Character, Thought, and the rest. It should be understood that

---

[60] 6.1.2. Cf. Aristotle *Rhetoric* 3.13.3; 3.19.4.

[61] "Sunt autem Apparatus, Melodia. Dienceps vero Dictio, Sententia, Mores, Fabula. Sicuti etiam in Rhetorice, si eodem ordine progrediaris. Sic erunt partes constituendae, Pronunciatio, Memoria, Elocutio, Dispositio, Inventio." (Commentary, p. 56.)

these are the parts that belong to the form, that are exercised in the very mind of the artist. There are other parts, moreover, within the work itself, that are ascribed to the quantity. Such in rhetoric, to be sure, are Exordium, Narratio, Partition, Proof, Disproof, Conclusion. Likewise, such in poetry are Prologue, Episode, Exode, Chorus.[62]

Aristotle's quantitative division of a play into prologue, episodes, choral interludes, and exode was squared, in the sixteenth century, with Donatus' scheme of prologue, protasis, epitasis, and catastrophe, and with the five-act formula worked out by Terentian commentators.[63]

Robortellus very wisely did not push this parallel between rhetorical and poetic analysis too far. The sets of parts do not fit each other exactly. While invention corresponds pretty closely to the *fictio* in a poetic plot (*fabula*), disposition, in the sense of organizing the structure of the whole work, also corresponds to Aristotle's conception of plot as the combination of the incidents, the σύνθεσις τῶν πραγμάτων, the *rerum constitutio*. And where does character (*mores*) fit the rhetorical scheme; does it correspond to invention or to disposition, or to both? Where does Thought fit? Scaliger,[64] who said that the poet must exercise invention, form, and ornament, placed character and thought under both invention and ornament. It was hardly necessary, however, to make the oratorical and poetic analyses fit each other precisely; the important achievement was the fusion of the two, with the result that literary criticism gained new terms and new aids.

Critics following Robortellus elaborated on his demonstration of the parallel between rhetorical and poetic analysis. Minturno[65] drew wordy comparisons between oratory and poetry. Of course he believed that invention, disposition, and style are required of the poet as well as of the orator. Delivery and memory, he acknowledged, are necessary to the actor rather than to the poet, and correspond to

---

[62]"In Rhetorica facultate hae quoque a Rhetoribus partes eiusmodi vocatae fuerunt, Inventio, Dispositio, Elocutio, Memoria, Pronunciatio. sic in facultate poetica, Fabula, cui annexae sunt Agnitio, Peripetia, Perturbatio, Mores, Sententia et reliquae. Sciendum vero partes has, quae formam respiciunt, in ipsa artificis mente versari; partes autem alias, quae ad quantitatem referuntur; in ipso opere. quales enim in Rhetorice sunt Exordium, Narratio, Partitio, Confirmatio, Confutatio, Conclusio. tales quoque in poetice sunt, Prologus, Episodium, Exodus, Choricum." (P. 117.)

[63]See T. W. Baldwin, *William Shakspere's Five-Act Structure* (Urbana, 1946).

[64]*Poetices* 1.11.

[65]See *De Poeta*, pp. 108-09, 111, 119.

spectacle and music, which are accessories to the art of the poet. Plot, character, thought, and diction, to be sure, correspond to invention, disposition, and style. Minturno also presented a rather elaborate discussion of the quantitative parts of poetry. First he analyzed *principium* (i.e., exordium) and *narratio*. He adopted the Platonic division of *narratio* into three classes: (1) simple—e.g., lyric poetry; (2) imitative—e.g., tragedy and comedy; (3) mixed—e.g., heroic poetry. He tried to make a distinction between rhetorical and poetic *narratio*. The rhetorical *narratio* should make known what is in the debate; the poetic *narratio* should make known what is in the plot (*fabula*). Then he proceeded to show why the poet must be able to divide, to prove, to disprove, and to conclude; in other words, the poet, like the orator, must be trained in the use of partition, proof, disproof, and conclusion.

Castelvetro, very probably influenced by Robortellus, also stated the parallel between rhetoric and poetry, and more succinctly than did Minturno:

These parts [plot, character, thought, diction, spectacle, music], which Aristotle calls the qualitative parts and which ought to be taken as qualities of tragedy, have that place in poetry that they hold in rhetoric— invention, disposition, diction, delivery, and memory, which likewise are qualitative parts of the oration (*diceria*) and so qualities of the oration, the oration making use of each of these five parts. Since, moreover, there are quantitative parts of the oration in rhetoric, exordium, *narratio*, proposition, proof, disproof, and conclusion, not otherwise there are quantitative parts of tragedy in poetry, which Aristotle has named prologue, incoming chorus, episode, stationary chorus, episode, stationary chorus, episode, stationary chorus, exode.[66]

Notice that Castelvetro was careful to make his Aristotelian quantitative parts of tragedy fit the Roman five acts; there are three episodes, preceded by a prologue and followed by the exode.

Robortellus, Minturno, and Castelvetro, all influential critics in the Renaissance, made a synthesis of the established principles of rhetorical art and the rediscovered Aristotelian principles of poetic art. As a result, the rhetorical analysis and the poetic analysis became virtually inextricable, as they formerly were in ancient times. In the seventeenth century, critics who had studied Aristotle and his sixteenth-century commentators, and all the leading critics did study them, freely mingled invention, disposition, and style with fable (plot), character, sentiment, and diction; sometimes they used the rhetorical terms, sometimes the poetic; often they combined the two sets of

---

[66]*Op. cit.*, pp. 257-58.

terms.[67] "Design," for example, might mean invention and it might be equivalent to Aristotle's "plot."[68] The rhetorical terms never outgrew their usefulness, especially in criticizing prose and non-dramatic poetry, though the Aristotelian Plot, Character, Thought, and Diction were destined to become the common scheme of analysis for novel and short story as well as for drama and epic poem.

Invention, disposition, and style, along with exordium, *narratio*, proof, and conclusion, served the theory and practice of both oratory and poetry for centuries, and these terms still live, even outside the classroom in public speaking. The addition of Aristotle's division of dramatic and epic poetry into plot, character, thought, and diction, along with the quantitative parts, (prologue, episodes, exode) and the Renaissance five-act formula, greatly enriched literary criticism during the sixteenth century. For general purposes, and for the schoolroom, the traditional rhetoric was long considered the most useful. Invention and disposition were broader terms than plot, character, and thought, and could be more generally applied.

For the majority of compositions in prose or verse, whether orations, essays, epistles, dramatic scenes, or lyric poems, the analysis into exordium, *narratio*, proof, and conclusion was the usual practice.

---

[67]Rapin, in his *Reflections on Aristotle's Treatise of Poesie* (London, 1674, pp. 23-24), as translated by Rymer, said:

"The art of poetry in general comprehends the matters of which a poet treats and the manner in which he handles them; the invention, the contrivance, the design, the proportion and symmetry of parts, the general disposition of matters, and whatever regards the invention, belong to the matters of which this art ought to treat. The fable, the manners, the sentiments, the words, the figures, the numbers, the harmony, the versification regard the manner in which the matters are to be handled."

Dryden, who knew Rapin, arranged the qualitative parts of the Homeric poem in the following approved order: "The design, the disposition, the manners, and the thoughts are all before it [the diction]." (*Preface to the Fables*, in *Essays* 2.252.) When, in the *Preface to the Fables*, Dryden compared Chaucer with Boccaccio, he examined invention and disposition. When the speakers in his *Essay of Dramatic Poesy* discussed ancient and modern drama they examined plot, character, sentiment, and diction, and spoke of protasis, epitasis, and catastrophe. When Dryden compared Chaucer with Ovid, in the *Preface to the Fables*, he combined rhetorical and poetic terms and discussed invention [i.e., design], manners, thoughts, and diction.

[68]Rapin (*op. cit.*, p. 28), for example, said: "The design of a poem must consist of two parts, of truth and of fiction; truth is the foundation, fiction makes the accomplishment. And Aristotle calls the mixture of these two the *constitution of things*, or the *fable*, which is no other than the subject of a poem, as the design or fable of the *Andria* in Terence are the loves of Pamphilus and Glycerium."

Willichius knew what he was doing when he prepared his edition of Terence. If he had been better acquainted with the *Poetics* of Aristotle—he did know the work[69]—if he had studied Robortellus' masterly interpretation of the treatise, he might have greatly enriched his criticism of Terence as, later on, Dryden enriched his criticism of Jonson, Ovid, and Chaucer. As it was, Willichius at least presented a practical method of studying dramatic poetry. Classical rhetoric was, after all, the solid basis of literary criticism in the sixteenth century, and classical rhetoric laid the foundations of the literary criticism of succeeding centuries. Modern theories of the drama, including modern theories of comedy, were shaped by the Aristotelian theory of poetry plus classical rhetorical theory, and the classical rhetoric came first.

---

[69]See his *Commentaria in artem poeticam Horatii* (Strassburg, 1539).

Chapter III: The Function of Comedy

THE MEDIEVAL distinction between comedy and tragedy was largely based upon conceptions of outcome and style, and had nothing to do with dramatic form. As all students of Chaucer know, any tale that ends in gloom was apt to be called a tragedy, any tale ending in merriment a comedy. The style of tragedy was supposed to be mainly serious and lofty, the style of comedy generally light and familiar. Dante, who offered a typical medieval summary in his letter to Can Grande della Scala, said that tragedy begins quietly but ends in horror while comedy begins harshly but ends in prosperity. Further, said Dante, "Tragedy speaks in an elevated and sublime fashion, but comedy in a lowly and humble way, according to the prescription of Horace in his *Art of Poetry*, where he grants that sometimes comic actors may speak like tragedians, and conversely:

At times, however, even Comedy exalts her voice, and an angry Chremes rants and raves; often, too, in a tragedy Telephus or Peleus utters his sorrow in the language of prose."[1]

Since medieval poets and scholars had little or no acquaintance with Aristotelian dramatic criticism, no emphasis, save by implication, was placed upon the distinctive aesthetic functions of comedy and tragedy. Speculations on the tragic *catharsis*, for example, and on the possibility of a corresponding comic *catharsis*, had to wait for the publication of the Renaissance commentaries on Aristotle's *Poetics*. Before the middle of the sixteenth century, Horace and Donatus were the principal authorities on dramatic poetry, and the common critical approach at the time was a comparison of the moral purpose and style of comedy and tragedy. Early sixteenth-century critics maintained that comedy, using fictitious plots and characters, presented a familiar image of everyday life, while tragedy, using historical plots and characters, presented an exalted image of noble life. Both comedies and tragedies, if they were properly written, provided important lessons in moral conduct, for they exhibited lively mirrors of human action for the edification of spectator or reader. The didactic function of comedy, therefore, received major attention. Medieval people, and those living in the first half of the sixteenth century, knew well enough what was ridiculous and what was sad. Apparently they were not much disposed, however, to analyze what makes man laugh

---

[1]Gilbert, pp. 203-04.

and what makes him weep. Of course they recognized the ridiculous when they met it on or off the stage, but evidently they seldom discussed *ridiculum* in any philosophical, critical fashion. Neither Horace nor Donatus, who certainly understood and appreciated manifestations of the comic spirit, tried to analyze or define the risible. Nevertheless, sixteenth-century scholars and critics sooner or later had to face this problem of critical analysis, for both Plato and Aristotle, not to mention Cicero, had indicated that the distinctive, essential quality of comedy was the risible.

While critical discussion of the *ridiculum*, then, was not prominent during the Renaissance until the middle of the sixteenth century, some conception of the risible is at least implied in any comic theory. Horace, Donatus, and their Renaissance followers in the late fifteenth and early sixteenth centuries may not have analyzed the *ridiculum*, but they doubtless knew something about the phenomenon. For one thing, as I shall soon demonstrate, they were probably familiar with the speculations of Cicero if not with those of Plato and Aristotle. Therefore I shall examine the sixteenth-century theory of the risible before turning to the traditional comparison of comedy with tragedy, which received first attention during the first half of the century. After 1550, when Aristotle's brief but profound remarks on comedy, in the *Poetics*, had been added to the Ciceronian discussion of the *ridiculum* and the remarks of Horace and Donatus, comic theory acquired the familiar pattern that appears in well-known Renaissance critics like Cinthio, Minturno, Trissino, Scaliger, Castelvetro, Sidney, and Ben Jonson.

THE RISIBLE

Attempts to formulate a theory of comedy in general have always been tenuous and elusive, but a satisfactory formula for explaining what makes people laugh has proved to be the most baffling element in the whole study of comedy. Julius Caesar, whom Cicero introduced as one of the speakers in his *De Oratore*, remarked that although witticisms were invaluable in oratory, there was no way of learning the use of witticisms from art. Caesar admitted that he had examined various Greek treatises on the laughable in the hope of learning something, but found that all who tried to formulate a theory or art merely proved themselves laughable. Nevertheless, when urged to present his views on wit and humor in speaking, Caesar proceeded with definitions and illustrations. His discussion forms the principal basis of Renaissance theories of the risible.

According to Caesar (*De Oratore* 2.58.236), "The seat or province, so to speak, of the laughable (*ridiculum*) lies in a certain ugliness (*turpitudo*) and deformity (*deformitas*); for those sayings are laughed at solely or chiefly which point out and designate something ugly in a manner that is not ugly." Quintilian (6.3.7 ff.), who was also influential in forming Renaissance theories of the ridiculous, quoted this definition and for the most part agreed with Cicero's analysis. This Roman theory doubtless goes back ultimately to Aristotle and Plato. With the revival of Aristotle's *Poetics* in the early part of the sixteenth century, the Aristotelian conception of the ridiculous gradually came to share authority with the Ciceronian; obviously there is a close connection between the two.

Aristotle's definition of comedy and the ridiculous runs as follows in Bywater's translation:

As for Comedy, it is (as has been observed) an imitation of men worse than the average; worse, however, not as regards any and every sort of fault, but only as regards one particular kind, the Ridiculous, which is a species of the Ugly. The Ridiculous may be defined as a mistake or deformity not productive of pain or harm to others; the mask, for instance, that excites laughter, is something ugly and distorted without causing pain. (*Poetics* 5.)

The Greek word for "the ridiculous" (τὸ γελοῖον) was translated into Latin as *ridiculum*; the Greek word for "ugly" (αἰσχρός) as *turpis*. Cicero made *turpitudo* the basis of the risible.

So far as I can discover, the first use of Aristotle's definition of the ridiculous in a printed book, and perhaps the first reference to the *Poetics* in a printed book, appeared in a 1499 commentary on Plautus by Pietro Valla. Pietro followed the Latin version of the *Poetics* published by his father, Giorgio Valla, in 1498. Pietro Valla's comment runs as follows:

Aristotle says that comedy is an imitation of the worse sort, not as regards every vice but rather the ridiculous part of ugliness. For the ridiculous is a certain fault and ugliness devoid of pain, as a ridiculous face is ugly without being painful.[2]

---

[2]"Comoedia inquit Aristoteles est improborum imitatio non per omne uitium; sed turpitudinis pars ridicula. Ridiculum namque est delictum quoddam atque turpitudo doloris expers uelut ridicula facies turpe quiddam citra dolorem." (*Plautinae uigenti comediae emendatissimae cum accuratissima ac luculentissima interpretatione doctissimorum uirorum Petri Vallae placentini ac et Bernardi Saraceni Veneti* (Venice, 1499), p. Aiir.)

Giorgio Valla's Latin version (p. riiv) runs as follows:

"Comoedia uero est quemadmodum diximus imitatio improborum quidem sed non usque quaque per omnem uitiositatem uerum turpitudinis etiam portio ridicula. Ridiculum namque est delictum quoddam atque turpitudo doloris expers ac minime afflictabile ueluti confestim ridicula facies turpe quiddam et peruersum citra dolentiam."

The Aristotelian conception of the ridiculous, however, may have been known to a few fifteenth-century scholars much earlier, for Averroes' paraphrase included the definition. The sixteenth-century Latin translation of the paraphrase by Jacobus Mantinus, for example, gives a fairly accurate statement:

In arte vituperandi non quaeritur imitatio secundum omne genus vitii et turpis tantum, sed eius vitii omnis, quod ridiculum est: nempe quod quidem vile est ac turpe, de quo dolendum non est.[3]
(In the art of blaming, imitation is not sought according to every kind of fault and ugliness, but only of every fault that is ridiculous: that is, what is indeed mean and ugly but not a cause of pain.)

Donatus, as I remarked earlier, was not specially interested in the theory of the ridiculous. At least the famous essay on comedy and tragedy did not discuss the laughable. Nevertheless, Donatus occasionally called attention to good examples of the risible in Terence. On the *Eunuch* 4.7.775, where the braggart-captain, Thraso, is assembling his household company and exhorting them to storm the house of Thais and carry off the girl Pamphila, Donatus wrote, "It is humorous, moreover, since ridiculous matters are derived from great matters." In other words, Donatus recognized one of the main sources of the risible, namely the belittling of the great and dignified or the incongruous contrast between the serious and the trivial. Incongruity was to become recognized as the main characteristic of the risible. Here, in the *Eunuch*, the battle-lines of the Roman legions have been reduced to a rag-tag scramble of cooks and kitchenboys, armed with household implements. Donatus particularly admired the ridiculous character of Thraso, who pompously and cautiously announces before the attack (*Eunuch* 789), "It becomes a wise man to try every means before arms."

"Notice," remarked Donatus, "how much power to confer pleasure in comedies serious sentiments have when they are uttered by ridiculous persons." Thraso's speech, according to Donatus, is even more ridiculous because he said "wise man" rather than "me." Again, I think, an unexpected incongruity is the basis for the humor.

Renaissance commentators following Donatus singled out this scene as a capital example of the risible. Willichius was particularly impressed by the comic names of Thraso's troops, such as "Ape-face" (*Simalio*), "Reed" (*Donax*), "Little Fig-Basket" (*Syricus*); he found that these names made the scene all the more remarkable for its τὸ γελοῖον.[4] These epithets, to be sure, are incongruous names for soldiers.

---

[3]Heidenhain's reprint, p. 359.   [4]Willichius on *Eunuch* 4.7.772.

Victor Faustus, whose essay on comedy (*De Comoedia Libellus*) was first published at Venice in 1511, gave a definition which, he believed, fitted Aristotle's conception of comedy as an imitation of the ridiculous in the ugly. According to Faustus, comedy is a "poem for softening the minds of men and rousing what is specially disposed to laughter."[5]

With the appearance, in 1536, of Paccius' edition of the *Poetics*, which contained the Aldine Greek text and the editor's own Latin translation, Aristotle's suggestive remarks on the ridiculous must have become better known. Until the great commentaries of Robortellus and Madius were published,[6] however, few writers ventured to meddle with the theory of laughter. For one thing, the treatment by Cicero and Quintilian was known and served well enough.

TRISSINO ON THE RISIBLE

Trissino published the first four divisions of his *Poetica* in 1529. Even that early Trissino may have had some acquaintance with the *Poetics*; at least, he referred to some of Aristotle's general ideas on poetry.[7] His discussion of comedy, however, came in the last division (VI), which was not published until 1563. It is perhaps impossible to determine whether or not Trissino's theory of comedy in general, and of the ridiculous in particular, antedated or followed the work of Robortellus and Madius. So far as I can discover, Trissino never referred to Robortellus or Madius, nor did Robortellus and Madius mention Trissino. In view of the slight acquaintanceship with Aristotle evidenced in the first part of the *Poetica*, one suspects that Trissino was indebted to the commentaries of Robortellus and Madius when he prepared the second part for publication. At all events, his theory of comedy in general, which applies the Aristotelian analysis of tragedy to comedy, is very like the scheme worked out by Robortellus in his essay *On Comedy* (1548), and his theory of the ridiculous closely corresponds in several details to the theory advanced by Madius in his essay *On the Ridiculous* (1550).

Trissino knew Cicero and Quintilian, of course, but was dissatisfied with the oratorical bias in their theory of the ridiculous; he preferred to treat the laughable in a more philosophical manner, that is, in the manner of Aristotle:

It is necessary to investigate it [the ridiculous], which we shall do according to a method other than that used by Marcus Tullius and Fabius

---

[5]Terence, *Comoediae* (1552), p. 41a.

[6]Robortellus' commentary was first published in 1548, Madius' in 1550, and Victorius' in 1560.

[7]*Poetica*, Vol. I (1529), pp. IIv, IVv.

Quintilianus, because their method was rather oratorical than philosophical. The ridiculous then, as Aristotle says, is a mild form of the ugly, and is a defect and an ugliness that is neither deadly nor painful.[8]

The pleasure of laughter, argued Trissino, is physiological; it comes from the senses, from sight, sound, touch, taste, smell, or from the memory or hope of these sensations. But all sensuous pleasure is not laughable. The sight of a beautiful woman or a fine jewel or the sound of music that praises is not laughable; such pleasurable sensations, in fact, bring admiration, not laughter. Trissino, like most critics of his generation, thought of admiration as a characteristic response to serious and dignified experiences. (I hope very shortly to show how Madius took exception to the conventional view and placed *admiratio* in his theory of the laughable.) Trissino continued with his explanation as follows:

But if the object that is presented to the senses has some mixture of ugliness, it moves laughter, as an ugly and distorted face, an inept movement, a silly word, a mispronunciation, a rough hand, a wine of unpleasant taste, or a rose of unpleasant odor moves laughter at once, and those things especially cause laughter from which better qualities were hoped, because then not merely our senses but also our hopes are slightly offended.[9]

Man by nature is envious and malicious, and, according to Trissino, delights in the mishaps of others—if these mishaps are not deadly or painful. If a man sees another find some money he does not laugh, but he laughs if he sees another fall down in the mud.

Trissino adopted a twofold classification of ugliness which goes back ultimately to Plato and which I shall consider in more detail when I come to Madius. For the time being it will suffice to say, with Trissino, that ugliness may be divided into (1) ugliness of the mind (ignorance, imprudence, credulity) and (2) ugliness of the body (deformities). The most appropriate means of ridicule, according to Trissino, is that which deceives expectation—in other words, surprise. The *Amphitryon* of Plautus, for example, is a very gay comedy because its characters repeatedly deceive themselves.[10]

MADIUS ON THE RISIBLE

The most elaborate discussion of the risible in the sixteenth century, so far as I know, is an essay, *De Ridiculis,* which Madius published with his commentary on Aristotle's *Poetics* in 1550. This essay

[8]*Poetica*, Vol. II (1563), pp. 36v-37r; Gilbert, p. 226.
[9]Gilbert, p. 227.
[10]*Poetica*, Vol. II, p. 39v; Gilbert, p. 231.

presents a synthesis of theories from Plato, Aristotle, Cicero, and Quintilian, and anticipates many features in our present-day theories of the risible. Madius went much further than Trissino; his treatment, when compared with that of Trissino, suffers only by its neglect of the drama and by its lack of any modern illustrations. Madius was content to follow the ancients and took virtually all of his examples of the risible from Cicero.

Fundamental in Madius' theory are the two definitions of the ridiculous from Aristotle's *Poetics* and Cicero's *De Oratore*. Then after referring to a passage in Plato's *Sophist* (226 ff.), he adopted the ancient philosophical, and rhetorical, division of good and evil into three kinds—namely, of the body, of the soul, and from external causes.[11] Turpitude, therefore, according to Madius, may be (1) bodily, (2) mental, or (3) external. He further divided bodily, mental, and external turpitude into three sub-heads, namely into turpitude that is (a) true, (b) feigned, (c) accidental. Thus laughable ugliness of the body may be either actual, as an inborn hump on the back; or formed, as a limp; or accidental, as when one falls down (without serious injury). True turpitude of the mind is plain ignorance or stupidity. Feigned ignorance is a common and important source of laughter.

Madius illustrated both true and feigned ignorance from an anecdote about Cato in *De Oratore* (2.69.279). A man carrying a trunk jostled Cato and then cried, "Look out!" This action was inept because of true stupidity; why warn Cato after he had already been bumped? Cato replied, "Are you carrying something else besides the trunk?" This reply is based on feigned ignorance; Cato pretended not to know whether or not the man was going to bump him with another trunk. This feigned ugliness is comparable to a picture of true ugliness. And, as Aristotle says in the *Poetics* (4.48^{b}9), man naturally takes pleasure in viewing pictures, even when they are representations of the lowest animals and dead bodies, because in so doing man is learning something. Madius held that feigned ugliness is superior to true ugliness since it involves art, that is, the creative invention of the author. In rhetoric, for example, there are two kinds of

---

[11]Cf. Plato's *Gorgias* 477, *Philebus* 48-49, *Laws* 697: Aristotle's *Nicomachean Ethics* 1.8.

The ancient rhetoricians apparently borrowed this three-fold division of good and evil from the philosophers; they applied it especially to demonstrative rhetoric, that is, to praise or blame. See Cicero, *De Inventione* 2.59; the author of the *Ad Herennium* 3.6.10. And Quintilian (6.3.37) remarked: "Laughter then will be derived either from the physical appearance of our opponent or from his character as revealed in his words and actions, or from external sources."

proof, inartificial and artificial. Inartificial proofs, such as witnesses, laws, contracts, etc., are already at hand in the subject matter; but artificial proofs, such as persuasive arguments, must be invented by the speaker.[12]

Madius found another example of feigned turpitude which forms a picture in an anecdote about Crassus, the celebrated Roman orator. Crassus was attacking a violent sort of man named Gaius Memmius (*De Oratore* 2.59.240-41), and fabricated an outrageous story, with appropriate gestures, that Memmius, while quarreling with one Largus over a courtesan, bit Largus and ate a piece of his arm. There was no truth to the story, but it made a laughing-stock of Memmius. Such buffoonery, however, was considered dangerous. Cicero (*De Oratore* 2.59.242) and Madius warned against it; the good orator will suggest mimicry rather than display it openly. And Aristotle (*Rhetoric* 3.18.7) warned that there are jests becoming a gentleman and jests that are not becoming; irony is more gentlemanly than buffoonery.

The third kind of mental turpitude, namely the accidental, is any error of the mind in word or deed that comes from ignorance. No man, remarked Madius in the best manner of Seneca, is truly wise, no mortal so faultless that his mind will not occasionally waver. Madius did not offer specific examples of this accidental turpitude of the mind, but another Roman anecdote that he liked may serve. Nero once remarked of a thievish servant: "He was the only member of the household against whom nothing was sealed or locked up." (*De Oratore* 2.61.248.)

External turpitude may also be divided into the true, the feigned, and the accidental. Madius did not illustrate this class either; but one of his earlier examples of external turpitude may serve though I am not sure whether it is true, feigned, or accidental. The illustration, also from the *De Oratore* (2.71.286), is a retort of Gaius Laelius to a low-born fellow who had told Laelius that he was unworthy of his ancestors. "But you, by Hercules," said Laelius, "are worthy of yours."

Any classification of human actions and emotions is sure to contain classes that overlap, and Madius' somewhat elaborate classification of the various human turpitudes is no exception. His theory is further complicated by his reluctance to abandon any thing inherited from the ancients. Thus, the division of the risible into things (*res*) and words (*dicta*) that characterized the theory of both Cicero and Quin-

---

[12]See Aristotle *Rhetoric* 1.2.2, 1.15. See p. 179.

tilian[13] had to be retained, though Madius seemed more interested in developing the threefold classification of turpitude. More significant, however, than his attempts to elaborate the ancient classifications of the risible was his dissatisfaction with the theory that turpitude or ugliness is the only cause of laughter. Both Aristotle and Cicero seemed to regard ugliness as the only proper basis for the ridiculous, and it must have taken some courage for Madius, who was a loyal disciple of the ancients, to seek further. But he did seek further, and found another basis for the ridiculous in *admiratio*, which I shall translate as "admiration," using the term in the old-fashioned sense of astonishment, wonder, surprise. Madius clearly thought of *admiratio* in this sense, for he coupled it with *novitas* (novelty) and with *nova* (unexpected).[14]

At first sight it is rather curious to find Madius deciding that admiration is an important factor in the risible, and therefore in comedy; for *admiratio*, in both rhetoric and poetics, was traditionally connected with the lofty, serious style, with Homeric poetry, tragedy, and political oratory.[15] Further, Madius believed that he was proceeding contrary to Cicero, who apparently thought of admiration as the opposite of laughter. In *De Oratore* 2.62.254, Caesar remarked that a play upon words is apt to arouse admiration rather than laughter: "sed admirationem magis quam risum movet." It may be recalled that Trissino also thought of admiration as opposed to laughter. Since Madius was worried by his seeming contradiction of the great Roman authority, it is strange that he overlooked several passages in Cicero which might have bolstered his argument. In *De Oratore* 2.71.288, Caesar mentioned that the Greeks included "astonishments" (*admirationes*) in their classification of witticisms. In the *Partitiones Oratoriae* (6.22), Cicero remarked, "Anything that is surprising (*admirabile*) delights." In the same treatise (9.32) Cicero came even closer to

---

[13]This division into *res* and *dicta* also governed the theory of laughter in the *Tractatus Coislinianus* and in John Tzetzes' treatment of comedy. See Cooper, *An Aristotelian Theory of Comedy*, pp. 224-89.

[14]Patet igitur ex dictis, risum ex turpitudine sine dolore proficisci, quae (ut diximus) aut corporis, aut animi, aut rerum extrinsecus contingentium est: atque horum turpitudo, aut uera, aut simulata, aut casu est, cui turpitudini, si ab ea risus excitari debet, admiratio necessario comes esse debet: quae necessario a nouitate pendet. nouitas autem aut in re, aut in exprimendi modo consistat, oportet. hoc autem tantundem ualet, ac si diceremuş turpitudinem risum mouere aptam, nouam esse debere: aut per rem ipsam turpem nouam, aut si haec noua non sit, per nouum exprimendi, atque depingendi modum. utrouis autem modo sit, risum excitare poterit. (P. 310.)

[15]See my article, "Some Neglected Sources of *Admiratio*," in *Modern Language Notes* 62 (1947) 222-26.

what Madius evolved when he said, "A statement is pleasing which has surprises (*admirationes*), suspense, and unexpected issues."

Nevertheless, Madius did not have to stand alone in his championship of admiration as an important ally of turpitude in the laughable; he found excellent authority in Horace, Plato, and Aristotle. Two or three good lines in a slovenly poet like Choerilus, said Horace, surprised him and made him laugh.[16] Madius quoted a sentence of Socrates in Plato's *Theaetetus* (154 B) that actually has nothing to do with the theory of the risible but does join together the Greek words for *admiratio* and *ridiculum*: "For now, my friend, we are easily compelled to say astonishing (θαυμαστά) and ridiculous things (γελοῖα)." Finally, Madius found that Aristotle, in his discussion of clever sayings (*Rhetoric* 3.11.6), explains that the pleasure derived from these witticisms comes from our learning something new and from the unexpected turn:

Most smart sayings are derived from metaphor, and also from misleading the hearer beforehand. For it becomes more evident to him that he has learnt something, when the conclusion turns out contrary to his expectation, and the mind seems to say, "How true it is! but I missed it."

The ridiculous, Madius argued, must need something besides turpitude (without pain). Anything ridiculous, if heard too many times, brings loathing rather than delight. Moreover, if the ugliness in ridicule persists after the surprise ceases, we do not keep on laughing; if the ugliness is no longer unexpected (*nova*) it fails to amuse, because ugliness in familiar things is not a cause for laughter. It should be clear then, Madius continued, that ugliness is not the only cause of laughter; admiration is also necessary:

Wherefore if laughter comes from ugliness and admiration, and accordingly springs from two causes, why is it extraordinary that if one of them, admiration I say, stops, laughter stops? Therefore it must be that admiration goes beyond ugliness.[17]

With this idea in mind, Madius proceeded to restate the theory of the risible, as he found it in Cicero, Aristotle, and Plato, to fit this dual basis of ugliness and admiration.

Cicero himself remarked the effectiveness, for laughter, of the unexpected turn, of which there are numerous examples.[18] Madius found that admiration in the ridiculous may arise by means of an

---

[16]Sic mihi, qui multum cessat, fit Choerilus ille, quem bis terve bonum cum risu miror. . . . (*Ars Poetica* 357-58.)

[17]Madius, p. 306.

[18]See *De Oratore* 2.70.284.

unexpected turn or by means of a turpitude that seems new. He drew several illustrations from the *De Oratore*, some of which may be worth recounting.

One day Crassus, the great orator, who was a wit but also noted for his dignified oratory, was addressing an opponent who took great pride in his family tree. Crassus spoke with mock gravity, "By your rank, by your family!" Then, suddenly stretching out his arm in a ludicrous gesture, he cried, "By your statues!"—whereat the whole assembly burst into laughter. (*De Oratore* 2.59.242.) Such a broad gesture, as Madius noted, was not customary with Crassus; it took the audience by surprise and hence evoked admiration and laughter.

Another example of admiration in laughter, according to Madius, is the saying of Nero quoted above, namely the remark about the thievish servant: "He was the only member of the household against whom nothing was sealed or locked up." Here laughter is not moved primarily because of turpitude. If Nero had said that he had a greedy, voracious servant from whom nothing could be locked up, he would merely have pointed out the ugliness but would not have raised any laughter. But the image of ugliness here is suggested by means of the ambiguous expression; therefore it is unexpected and laughable. From this unexpectedness, argued Madius, springs admiration, "which necessarily moves laughter." If Nero had said that the servant stole necklaces, clothes, and money, detestation rather than laughter would have arisen. If however, we understand, as we do, that the servant was merely a filcher of food and drink, then his ugliness is laughable and not criminal. Madius was careful to point out that three classes of people should not be laughed at: the poverty-stricken, the wicked, and the virtuous. Paupers, unless they are insolent, deserve pity rather than ridicule; the wicked merit hate; ridicule of the virtuous is contrary to good taste.[19]

Laughter then, springs from ugliness (without pain) of body, of mind, or from the outside, and this ugliness may be real, feigned, or accidental. If this ugliness excites laughter, admiration, "which necessarily depends upon unexpectedness (*novitas*)," ought to be its partner. This unexpectedness lies either in the matter itself or in the manner of expression; in other words, either in things (*res*) or in words (*dicta*). Most of the above illustrations have been based upon things. Madius tried to demonstrate that the turpitude in words must also be accompanied by admiration—if laughter is to be the result. He took his illustrations, as usual, from the *De Oratore*.

---

[19]Madius, p. 309.

One day in court (*De Oratore* 2.60.245), a very small witness came forward. "May I question him?" asked Marcius Philippus. The presiding magistrate, who was in a hurry to end the case, answered, "Only if you are short." "You will not complain," said Philippus, "for I shall be just as short as he is." Unfortunately for Philippus, but happily for the audience, one of the judges on the bench was Lucius Aurifex, who was even shorter than the witness. Consequently the laughter turned upon the judge and the jest seemed scurrilous. According to Madius, the first part of the jest depends upon the turpitude of the undersized witness, and the first laughter arises because of this turpitude coupled with admiration; the jest is expressed by a double meaning, i.e., the surprise of the play on the word for "short." There is also laughter at the undersized judge, but not because of any turpitude in Lucius Aurifex; rather because of the exposure of turpitude in the mind of Philippus, whose jest struck where he had not intended and who made himself ridiculous by this unexpected display of imprudence. A little later on, Castelvetro was to emphasize the importance of the jest which unexpectedly recoils upon its author. Since, Madius continued, turpitude of the mind surpasses turpitude of the body, more laughter was directed at Philippus than Philippus aroused at the expense of the witness.

Another example of a jest that recoiled upon its author is the story of Appius and Gaius Sextius (*De Oratore* 2.60.246). Appius, who was a wit but too apt to be scurrilous, said to one-eyed Sextius, "I will sup with you, for I see there is a vacant place." Cicero went on to explain that this joke raised little laughter because it was unprovoked and premeditated. And, in the opinion of Madius, Cicero was right, because premeditated jokes lack admiration. The retort of Sextius, on the other hand, was pat and extempore. "Wash your hands," said Sextius, "and come to supper." The implication was that Appius was unclean or dishonest. But, as Madius explained, it is admiration that brings laughter here, for Sextius did not say outright that Appius had dirty hands; he gave an unexpected picture of the man as a thief, a picture that combined turpitude with surprise. Similar is the unexpected retort of one Lucius Nasica to Cato the censor. "Are you truly satisfied," asked Cato, "that you have taken a wife?" "No, by Hercules," replied Nasica, "I am not truly satisfied." (*De Oratore* 2.64.260.)

Ironic dissimulation in the sense that an honorable epithet is substituted for a dishonorable term has always been a good source of amusement, especially when the epithet is unexpected. Madius found an example in the story of Africanus and the centurion (*De Oratore* 2.67.272). Africanus had expelled from his tribe a centurion who had

stayed in camp while a battle was being fought. The centurion's defense was that he stayed behind to take care of the camp. "I do not
like," said Africanus, "people who are too careful."

Another example of ironical dissimulation is the remark of Quintus
Fabius Maximus to Livius Salinator, who lost the town of Tarentum
but managed to hold the citadel (*De Oratore* 2.67.273). When the
town was finally recaptured Livius begged Fabius to remember that
it was owing to his efforts that Tarentum was retaken. "Why
shouldn't I remember?" said Fabius, "I could never have retaken it
if you hadn't lost it." Admiration is aroused here because Fabius'
feigned ignorance exposes the true turpitude of Livius. Another illustration of feigned ignorance or feigned stupidity, of what Caesar
called "pretending not to understand what you do understand" (*De
Oratore* 2.68.275), is the reply of Pontidius when he was asked what
he thought of a man who is caught in adultery. Said Pontidius, "He's
slow." This joke, observed Madius, "also has admiration since the
response seems to fit although it goes beyond the intention of the
question."[20]

Similar is the quip of the Sicilian whose friend was lamenting the
death of his wife. The wife, he reported, had hanged herself from a
fig tree. "I beg of you," said the Sicilian, "give me some cuttings from
that tree to plant." (*De Oratore* 2.69.278.)

Obviously Madius regarded the unexpected, which is allied with, if
not, indeed, synonymous with *admiratio*, as a very important element
in the laughable. He brought in an Aristotelian concept here which
he borrowed from the theory of tragedy in the *Poetics*:

Ridiculous matters . . . will be much more pleasant if they are brought
in contrary to expectation, since they are like the reversals of fortune
which afford a wonderful delight in plays.[21]

Cicero also furnished authority (*De Oratore* 2.70.284): "But of all
these devices nothing causes more amusement than an unexpected
turn, of which there are countless examples." One more example that
Madius retailed will suffice. A praetor had assigned as counsel to a
Sicilian, a man who was noble but rather stupid. "I pray you, Mr.
Praetor," said the Sicilian, "assign this gentleman as counsel to my
opponent and then you needn't give me any counsel." (*De Oratore*
2.69.280.)

---

[20]Madius, p. 317.

[21]Pulchra igitur erunt ridicula, quae ex pluribus turpitudinibus mixta fuerint,
quae longe magis uenusta erunt, si in contrarium eius, quod expectatur, affe-
runtur; quoniam similis sunt peripetijs, quae in fabulis miram afferunt uolup-
tatem. (P. 321.)

Madius was well aware of the difficulties attending any inquiry into the risible. In fact, he anticipated the celebrated observation of Molière when he remarked that human beings differ widely and "do not laugh alike." But it is no wonder that all do not laugh alike since all do not fear alike. Madius called upon Aristotle, and upon his commentator Eustratius, for an explanation of these differences in taste, and found an answer in the golden mean between buffoonery and boorishness. According to Aristotle (*Ethics* 4.14), the mean state of social relaxation or diversion is wittiness, which is between the deficiency of boorishness and the excess of buffoonery. A gentleman, who occupies the mean state, uses and listens to language befitting an honorable gentleman. The obscenity of the Old Comedy was an excess; the New Comedy, which merely suggested obscenity, was nearer the mean state. Therefore, Madius concluded, outright obscene expressions should be rejected and laughter in comedy should be obtained from suggestion.[22] Finally, Madius pursued his investigation beyond the classification of the various kinds of jests and witticisms. Cicero had neglected to investigate the physiology of laughter. Caesar, perhaps wisely, had passed over any discussion of the nature of laughter (*De Oratore* 2.58.235):

Now the first of these topics, the essential nature of laughter, the way it is occasioned, where it is seated, and how it comes into being, and bursts out so unexpectedly that, strive as we may, we cannot restrain it, and how at the same instant it takes possession of the lungs, voice, pulse, countenance, and eyes—all this I leave to Democritus; for it does not concern the present conversation, and, even if it did, I should still not be ashamed to show ignorance of something which even its professed expositors do not understand.

Madius, apparently undeterred by this implied warning from Cicero, summoned Aristotle to his aid and proceeded to reconstruct the physiology of laughter. His method was by means of syllogism and analogy, not by observation and experiment.

The Aristotelian demonstration of the nature of thunder in the *Posterior Analytics* (2.10), as interpreted by Averroes, runs as follows:

In the clouds is fire, which is quenched. In the fire which is quenched is sound. Thus it may be concluded that the sound in clouds is by reason of the fire which is quenched in them. This, indeed, is the complete defi-

---

[22]Ex quibus Aristotelis dictis colligere debemus, in Comoediis obscoena uerba explodenda prorsus esse: et ideo in iis, non ex risum captandum esse, sed ex illorum tantum suspicione. (P. 322.)

nition of thunder: viz., Thunder is the sound in clouds by reason of quenched fire.[23]

Proceeding by analogy with this demonstration, Madius constructed a definition of laughter which included his theory of admiration:

Laughter is an involuntary motion of the rational mind, a consequent pouring out of heat, an enlarging of the heart beyond what is normally produced. A constriction of the midriff follows, and a shortening of the muscles which lead to the sides of the face. This motion of the heart, indeed, is produced by the intervention of an unexpected appearance of something ugly without pain; it is granted men by nature for the relaxation of the mind. I have said that laughter is a motion of the mind; since admiration follows learning to know (cognotio),[24] learning to know is indeed a motion perfecting the mind. That such motion is involuntary is very plainly perceived by everybody.[25]

There is nothing original in this definition unless it be the addition of admiration. Madius found his matter in Aristotle, in the *Movement of Animals*, where Aristotle pointed to the heart as one of the human organs whose movement is involuntary and observed that nearly everything painful or pleasant is accompanied by some degree of chilling or heating,[26] in *On the Parts of Animals*, and in the *Problems*. Madius' theory that laughter accompanies or follows heating of the heart and midriff is based upon *On the Parts of Animals* and upon the commentary of Michael of Ephesus. Aristotle's argument is:

Another indication that it is when heated that they [*phrenes*, i.e., diaphragm] quickly make the sensation recognizable is afforded by what happens when we laugh. When people are tickled, they quickly burst into laughter, and this is because the motion quickly penetrates to this part, and even though it is only gently warmed, still it produces a movement (independently of the will) in the intelligence which is recognizable. The fact that human beings only are susceptible to tickling is due (1) to the fineness of their skin and (2) to their being the only creatures that laugh. . . .

It is said that when in war men are struck in the part around the diaphragm, they laugh: and this is due to the heat which arises owing to the blow.[27]

---

[23]Quoted by Madius, p. 323.

[24]Cf. Aristotle, *Metaphysics* 1.1.1: "All men by nature desire to know." Cf. *Poetics* 4.48^{b}12-15: "To be learning something is the greatest of pleasures not only to the philosopher but also to the rest of mankind."

[25]Madius, pp. 323-24.

[26]See *Movement of Animals* 8-11.

[27]*On the Parts of Animals* 3.10. Translation by A. L. Peck in the Loeb Library.

Madius, though he did not quote the passage, may have gained something from the *Problems*, where we may read:

Now laughter is a kind of derangement and deception, and so men laugh when they are struck in the midriff. . . . Now that which comes unawares tends to deceive, and it is this also which causes laughter.[28]

To continue with Madius' argument, it seems that this dilation of the heart and this pouring out of heat, if too violent and too prolonged, relaxes the spirit too much and may cause pain. Pleasure causes the heart to dilate, but grief causes it to contract. The problem, then, is why do men weep from excess of joy as well as from excess of grief. Madius found some help here in the *Problems* (1.29) of Alexander of Aphrodisias, an Aristotelian commentator well known in the early Renaissance:

Those who suffer from a thickening of the pores situated in the eyes discharge a moisture which the eyes contain. Pain, indeed, cools and contracts the pores. But those who are merry and cheerful pour out moisture from the laxity of the pores.[29]

In other words, we weep from both pain and joy.

Madius went further and offered a physiological explanation that is at least ingenious if not scientific. We always weep, he argued, because of a compression of the brain that can come about in two ways. In joy, the brain dilates; but, since the parts of the skull are hard and unyielding, compression of the brain follows. This compression produces moisture which flows from the eyes in tears. In grief, the brain is also compressed, this time from the chilling and its effect of condensation, with the consequent flow of tears. According to Madius, laughter is the interplay of dilation and contraction, and this interplay, which takes the form of a struggle between the mind (*anima*) and corporeal heaviness (*gravitas*), causes the whole body to shake when the laughter is violent.

In the light of present-day physiology, Madius' explanation of the nature of laughter may seem fantastic; certainly the method of Madius will not meet approval. His results, however, are not very different from the conclusions of physiologists and psychologists of the twentieth century. According to Professor P. T. Young, writing in 1943, current theory holds that laughter is produced by deep inspirations followed by spasmodic contractions of the chest and dia-

---

[28]*Problems* 35.6. Translation by E. S. Forster in the Oxford *Works of Aristotle*.

[29]Quoted by Madius, p. 326. Cf. [Selections from Aristotle, by Theodore Gaza] Venice, 1513, p. 258r.

phragm with ensuing contractions of the facial muscles.[30] Let us recall that, according to Madius in 1550, laughter is an involuntary motion of the mind with a consequent enlarging of the heart and a pouring out of the heat, followed by contraction of the diaphragm and a shortening of the facial muscles. It would seem that man's knowledge of the physiology of laughter has not progressed very far since the time of Aristotle. The nature of laughter is still the mystery it was in Roman days when Julius Caesar wisely referred the matter to Democritus.

LATER SIXTEENTH-CENTURY CRITICS ON THE RISIBLE

Madius did make, I believe, a real contribution to the sixteenth-century theory of the risible. He brought together the theories of Aristotle, Plato, Cicero, and Quintilian in the most detailed treatment of the subject in the Renaissance. The most significant element in his theory is his coupling of the classical *turpitudo* with *admiratio*. Madius' "admiration" is virtually synonymous with the unexpected or surprise. While I can find very little direct evidence that Madius influenced later writers on the ridiculous, I suspect that he played an important part in establishing surprise as the most characteristic feature of the risible. At least one learned critic of the century acknowledged a debt to Madius' theory of comedy. In 1587, Antonius Riccobonus published a Latin version of Aristotle's *Poetics* with elaborate paraphrases and an essay entitled the *Ars Comica ex Aristotele*. One section of this essay, which, like Robortellus' *On Comedy*, attempts to reconstruct a theory of comedy from Aristotle's analysis of tragedy, is based on Madius' *De Ridiculis*. Furthermore, Riccobonus followed Madius in maintaining that comedy as well as tragedy should stir *admiratio*. Comic admiration, according to Riccobonus, is an important feature of the comic *catharsis*; for comedy also has its catharsis: "That [tragedy] by means of pity and fear; this [comedy] by means of the delight from the laughable incites a purgation of the spirits." (P. 147.) Moreover, "Just as tragedy moves admiration in pitiable and fearful matters, so comedy in ugly and ridiculous matters." (P. 151.) Riccobonus argued that comic admiration arises from deception, as, for example, Demea in Terence's *Brothers* is deceived by his sons and so brings delight to the spectators.

Whether or not Madius influenced other critics as he did Riccobonus I am not prepared to say; certainly writer after writer, from the sixteenth century to the present time, has found that the unexpected is *the* source of laughter. Some eminent critics have disagreed

---

[30]*Emotion in Mind and Animal* (New York, 1943), pp. 253-54.

and sought other sources, but the unexpected has persisted as the most satisfactory explanation of why men laugh.

Castelvetro, who never mentioned Madius, though he must have known his work on Aristotle, offered an explanation of the risible that is similar to the deductions of Madius. Starting with Aristotle and Cicero, Castelvetro[31] divided turpitude into two classes: (1) mental turpitude, which may consist of either knavery or folly; (2) bodily turpitude, which may be unpleasant or pleasant. Then he proceeded to analyze four different kinds of laughter.

The first kind of laughter is not essentially comic, but arises from affection, such as the mother's laugh when she welcomes her little children. The second kind, and a very important kind of truly comic laughter, arises from deception, i.e., the deception of some one else. Like Trissino, Castelvetro held that man by nature rejoices in the evils that befall others, and he made much of these comic deceptions, dividing them into four different varieties. Men delight in seeing another turn out ill, as in a drunken fall; or fail to accomplish something that he has boasted he will do; or fall victim to his own jest; or fall victim to mischance. The third kind of laughter arises from knavery or from physical defects. This type, said Castelvetro, is especially effective if the knavery or the physical defect is presented covertly, that is, by subtle suggestion. In other words, the element of the unexpected is important. An illustration that Castelvetro found in Boccaccio's *Decameron* contains this element of surprise. Ermino Grimaldi asked Guielmo Borsiere to give him a subject for a painting in his house, something that had never been seen before in his home. Borsiere replied, "Have courtesy painted there."[32] The fourth kind of laughter, according to Castelvetro, arises from indecencies, and Castelvetro agreed with Madius that obscenities are best presented covertly, not directly.

Sir Philip Sidney and Ben Jonson were well acquainted with the sixteenth-century theory of the risible which was based upon Cicero and Aristotle. The remarks of both Sidney and Jonson reflect a curious interpretation of the risible which seems to derive ultimately from the *Nicomachean Ethics* of Aristotle. This modification is a warning to avoid excessive laughter or to avoid laughter for the sake of a laugh. In the *Ethics*, Aristotle analyzed virtues and vices in terms of the mean and its extremes. Thus true wittiness, or the right use of the risible, is a mean between the extremes of buffoonery and boorishness:

---

[31]Pp. 92-98.
[32]*Ibid*, p. 97; in Gilbert, p. 314.

It is clear that in this matter, as in others, it is possible to go beyond or to fall short of the mean. Now they who exceed the proper limit in ridicule seem to be buffoons and vulgar people, as their heart is set upon exciting ridicule at any cost, and they aim rather at raising a laugh than at using decorous language and not giving pain to their butt. On the other hand, they who will never themselves speak a word that is ridiculous, and who are indignant with everybody who speaks so, may be said to be boorish and rude.

People whose fun is in good taste are called witty (εὐτράπελοι), a name which implies the happy turns of their art, as these happy turns may be described as movements of the character; for character, like bodies, are judged by their movements. But as it is never necessary to look far for subjects of ridicule and as an excessive fondness for fun and mockery is pretty universal, it happens that not only true wits but buffoons are described as witty, because they are amusing. But it is clear from what has been said that there is a difference, and indeed a wide difference, between the two.[33]

Sidney, who knew the *Ethics*, was careful to recommend a gentlemanly kind of laughter; for vulgar, unwitting laughter would defeat the important didactic aim of comedy. The passage on laughter in the *Defense of Poesy* is unusually interesting; in it the reader may easily recognize several familiar echoes of ancient and sixteenth-century criticism:

But our comedians think there is no delight without laughter; which is very wrong, for though laughter may come with delight, yet cometh it not of delight, as though delight should be the cause of laughter; but well may one thing breed both together. Nay, rather in themselves they have as it were a kind of contrariety; for delight we scarcely do but in things that have a conveniency to ourselves or to the general nature; laughter almost ever cometh of things most disproportioned to ourselves and nature. Delight hath a joy in it, either permanent or present. Laughter hath only a scornful tickling. For example, we are ravished with delight to see a fair woman, and yet are far from being moved to laughter. We laugh at deformed creatures wherein certainly we cannot delight. We delight in good chances, we laugh at mischances; we delight to hear the happiness of our friends and country, at which he were worthy to be laughed at that would laugh. We shall, contrarily, laugh sometimes to find a matter quite mistaken and go down the hill against the bias, in the mouth of some such men as for the respect of them one shall be heartily sorry, yet he cannot choose but laugh; and so is rather pained than delighted with laughter. Yet deny I not but that they may go well together. For as in Alexander's picture well set out we delight without

---

[33] In Welldon's translation, here used, this passage appears in 4.14. In most editions the passage is in 4.8.

laughter, and in twenty mad antics we laugh without delight, so in Hercules, painted with his great beard and furious countenance, in woman's attire, spinning at Omphale's commandment, it breeds both delight and laughter. For the representing of so strange a power in love procures delight; and the scornfulness of the action stirreth laughter. But I speak to this purpose, that all the end of the comical part be not upon such scornful matters as stir laughter only, but mix with it that delightful teaching which is the end of poesy. And the great fault even in that point of laughter, and forbidden plainly by Aristotle, is that they stir laughter in sinful things, which are rather execrable than ridiculous; or in miserable, which are rather to be pitied than scorned. For what is it to make folks gape at a wretched beggar or a beggarly clown; or against law of hospitality to jest at strangers, because they speak not English as well as we do? What do we learn? since it is certain

> Nil habet infelix paupertas durius in se,
> Quam quod ridiculos homines facit.

But rather a busy loving courtier, a heartless threatening Thraso, a self-wise-seeming schoolmaster, a wry transformed traveler—these if we saw walk in stage names, which we play naturally, therein were delightful laughter, and teaching delightfulness; as in the other, the tragedies of Buchanan do justly bring forth a divine admiration.[34]

Did Sidney mean to imply, at the conclusion of the above passage, that there is a corresponding "admiration" (not divine) present in good comedy, in the comedy of Terence, for example? Unfortunately there is no evidence, so far as I can see, that he had read Madius' essay. It seems likely, however, that he had read Trissino on comedy, and he certainly thought of laughter as arising from disproportion or incongruity.

Ben Jonson, in his *Discoveries*, stated this objection to unwitting laughter so strongly that he misrepresented Aristotle on the risible. It should be pointed out, however, that here he was following Daniel Heinsius' essay on Plautus and Terence.[35] The passage on laughter runs as follows:

The parts of a comedy are the same with a tragedy, and the end is partly the same. For they both delight and teach; the Comics are called διδάσκαλοι of the Greeks no less than the Tragics.

Nor is the moving of laughter always the end of comedy, that is rather a fooling for the people's delight, or their fooling. For, as Aristotle says rightly, the moving of laughter is a fault in comedy, a kind of turpitude that depraves some part of a man's nature without a disease. As a wry face without pain moves laughter, or a deformed vizard, or a rude clown

---

[34]*Elizabethan Critical Essays* 1.200-201.
[35]See Heinius, *Ad Horatii de Plauto et Terentio judicium dissertatio.*

dressed in a lady's habit, and using her actions, we dislike, and scorn such representations; which made the ancient philosophers ever think laughter unfitting in a wise man. And this induced Plato to esteem of Homer as a sacrilegious person; because he presented the gods sometimes laughing. As, also it is divinely said of Aristotle, that to seem ridiculous is a part of dishonesty, and foolish.[36]

But Jonson did not mean that laughter was always inappropriate in comedy. On the contrary, he evidently believed that there is a kind of comic *catharsis* effected by laughter. Jonson's theory of the risible was evidently the traditional Ciceronian-Aristotelian theory as interpreted by Italian and Dutch scholars of the sixteenth and early seventeenth centuries. In the prologue to the revised version of *Every Man In His Humor*, he remarked of comedy:

> When she would show an image of the times
> And sport with follies, not with crimes.

Cordatus, one of the interlocutors in *Every Man Out of His Humor* (3.1), subscribed to the Ciceronian definition of comedy—*imitatio vitae, speculum consuetudinis, imago veritatis*[37]—and added, "a thing throughout very pleasant and ridiculous, and accommodated to the correction of manners." Asper, in the Induction of the same play, proclaimed:

> We hope to make the circles of your eyes
> Flow with distilled laughter.

The Boy, an interlocutor in the *Magnetic Lady* (Act 1), promised the following result:

> Give our springs leave to open a little, by degrees; a source of ridiculous matter may break forth anon, that shall steep their temples, and bathe their brains in laughter, to the fomenting of stupidity itself, and the awaking any velvet lethargy in the house.

Although he disapproved, theoretically at least, of scurrilous laughter, Jonson also recognized, with the help of Heinsius, that the unexpected, or surprise, plays an important part in raising laughter. He remarked in the *Discoveries*:

> Perverse and sinister sayings (and the rather unexpected) in the Old Comedy did move laughter; especially where it did imitate any dishonesty; and scurrility came forth in the place of wit: which who understands the nature and *Genius* of laughter cannot but perfectly know.[38]

An examination of Jonson's comic practice at once reveals that he often employed incongruity attended by surprise. His amazing pa-

---

[36]*Discoveries*, p. 99.   [37]See p. 60.   [38]P. 100.

rades of clowns, gulls, coxcombs, parasites, malcontents, with their warped judgments and affected humors, which usually arise from incongruous affectation, furnish classic examples of the risible. According to Henry Fielding, who was himself a master of comic incongruity and of ridiculous surprise, Jonson, better than any other man, understood the true nature of the risible. In his Preface to *Joseph Andrews*, Fielding wrote:

From the discovery of this affectation arises the Ridiculous, which always strikes the reader with surprise and pleasure; and that in a higher and stronger degree when the affectation arises from hypocrisy than when from vanity; for to discover any one to be the reverse of what he affects is more surprising, and consequently more ridiculous, than to find him a little deficient in the quality he desires the reputation of. I might observe that our Ben Jonson, who of all men understood the Ridiculous the best, hath chiefly used the hypocritical affectation.

In the main, the theory of the risible, from Aristotle and Cicero through the sixteenth century to the present day, has been an intellectual theory. Aristotle's suggestive remarks in the *Poetics* and *Rhetoric*, coupled with his observations in the the *Ethics*, were not calculated to encourage the belly laugh; they pointed to an intellectual type of humor. Cicero also had in mind a gentlemanly kind of laughter, the kind that the aristocratic Roman orator might use with propriety. Further, the sixteenth-century critics pretty consistently disapproved, in theory, of the broad Aristophanic humor of the Old Comedy and preferred, in theory at least, the intellectual comedy of Terence to the slapstick of Plautus. Consequently the nearest approach to common ground among the many theories of the risible that have appeared in Western Europe during the past four centuries lies in the element of surprise or the unexpected.[39] As Professor Lane Cooper, whose amplification of the *Tractatus Coislinianus* offers numerous illustrations of the risible from a variety of writers ancient and modern, says, "Deception and surprise are, strictly considered, *the* sources of laughter *par excellence*, and underlie all others."[40]

GENERAL COMPARISONS OF COMEDY WITH TRAGEDY

Before the middle of the sixteenth century, Horace and Cicero were the principal classical authorities on both comedy and tragedy. It was Donatus, however, who provided the details of formal criticism. It was Donatus who taught the sixteenth century what the pat-

[39]See my article on *The Laughable* in *Quarterly Journal of Speech* 35 (1949), 1-16.
[40]*An Aristotelian Theory of Comedy*, p. 249.

tern and function of both comedy and tragedy ought to be. It was Donatus who transmitted, among other classical matter, the Ciceronian definition of comedy and who established a critical eulogy of Terentian methods. Included in Donatus' famous commentary on Terence are two essays, one entitled *De Fabula* and now ascribed to Evanthius, the other entitled *De Comoedia*. In the sixteenth century, these two essays were usually combined under the title of *De Comoedia et Tragoedia* and ascribed to Donatus. The chief factors, then, in forming the theory of comedy in the sixteenth century were scattered remarks of Horace and Cicero, the theory set forth under the name of Donatus, and, by the middle of the century, a reconstructed Aristotelian theory. Since the influence of Donatus took root in the sixteenth century before the Aristotelian theory became familiar, I shall summarize the Evanthius-Donatus preface first.

Evanthius-Donatus

Tragedies and comedies, argued Evanthius, originated in ancient religious rites after harvest. Tragedy sprang up first as society slowly progressed from a rude, pastoral culture to an urbane way of life. Thespis was the founder of tragedy. Eupolis, along with Cratinus and Aristophanes, fathered ancient comedy.[41] It was Homer, however, the greatest source of all poetry, who provided models for both —the *Iliad* for tragedy, the *Odyssey* for comedy. Ancient comedy, like tragedy, was formerly a simple poem consisting of a chorus, but first one actor emerged from the chorus, then another, then a third. The plots (*argumenta*) of the early poets were not as now altogether fictitious, but used actual events (*res gestae*) and real names.

There was another kind of play, a satyr-play, in which satyrs portrayed gods in wanton jest. This satyr-play became suspect and was replaced by a more general kind of drama, New Comedy, dealing with middle-class people, using closer-knit plots, more familiar manners, wholesome sentiments, pleasing jokes, and careful meter. Menander and Terence were the masters of this New Comedy. The use of the chorus, which originally was all important in Old Comedy, was gradually curtailed as plays passed from control of the singers to that of the actors. The Greek prologues are not like those of the Latins. Some Latin poets use "gods from the machine" for narrating plots, but Terence does not, though he does make use of "protactic characters," i.e., characters who introduce the action but are otherwise outside it.

---

[41]Cf. Horace *Sermones* 1.4.1.

No one has more carefully preserved the rules of characterization as to manners, age, and occupation than Terence. Although he sometimes goes against the comic rules when he introduces courtesans who are not naughty, he nevertheless gives cause why these are good courtesans. With admirable art, Terence restrains his comic characterizations and so tempers the emotions that he never swells to tragic heights or descends to farce. He is always clear, while Plautus is often obscure. Moreover, Terence is mindful of plot and style; he so knits the middle part with the beginning and end that no extraneous matter is present, but the whole composition appears compact and of one body. He keeps his various characters distinct, and, unlike Plautus, never lets them digress from the play itself. Another praiseworthy feature of Terence is that he enriches his plots with double actions, for with the exception of the *Mother-in-law*, in which there is only the one love affair of Pamphilus, the other plays have two young lovers.

According to Evanthius, the Latins added many types of plays to New Comedy, among these, *togatae* (native Roman), *praetextatae* (historical and Roman), *Atellanae* (named for the town in Campania and emphasizing debates), *tabernariae* (with humble plots and style), *mimi* (long-established representations of low matter and wanton characters).

Evanthius found several differences between comedy and tragedy. In comedy there are ordinary human affairs, containing petty onsets of danger and cheerful outcomes. In tragedy everything is the opposite: distinguished personages, great fears, lamentable outcomes. The first part of comedy is turbulent, the last part peaceful. The reverse order obtains in tragedy; for tragedy ought to express the abandonment of life, and comedy the commencement of life. Every comedy has a feigned plot while tragedy often borrows a true story.

Evanthius divided Terentian comedies into three general types: (1) lively (*motoriae*), (2) quiet (*statariae*), (3) mixed, containing both kinds of action. A comedy has four parts, *prologue*, *protasis*, *epitasis*, and *catastrophe*:

The prologue is the preface to the play, in which something over and above the plot may be presented or something to do with the author, the play itself, or the actor. The protasis is the first act and the beginning of the play proper. The epitasis is the rising of the forward progress of turmoils, or, as I have said before, the knot of the whole uncertainty. The catastrophe is the reversal (*conuersio*) of affairs preparatory to the cheerful outcome; it reveals all by means of a discovery (*cognitio*).

So much, then, for the main ideas in Evanthius' *De Fabula*. I have presented a rather detailed summary because all these ideas were influential in shaping the theory and practice of comedy during the Renaissance.

Much of the material in the second essay, *De Comoedia*, is repetitious, and I can present a briefer summary. This second essay contains a Greek definition of comedy from Diomedes: "Comedy is a treatment of private and civil station that is without danger to life.[42] Donatus added a definition attributed to Cicero: "the imitation of life, the mirror of custom, the image of truth." Livius Andronicus, who invented Roman comedy and the *togata*, called comedy the "mirror of everyday life." (In the sixteenth century, Cicero's statement on comedy in *Pro Sexto Roscio Amerino* (16.47) was often quoted. In this famous speech, Cicero remarked: "I think, indeed, that these fictions of the [comic] poets are made so that we may see our own manners represented in other characters and a lively image of our own daily life.") Donatus emphasized the didactic function of comedy, whose models of various public and private feelings teach us what is useful in life and what must be avoided. He emphasized the difference in social rank between comic and tragic characters; comic characters "live in villages because of moderate circumstances, not in royal palaces as do tragic personages." Finally, Donatus devoted some attention to the theatrical production of Roman comedy, and discussed costume, scenery, and musical accompaniment. (Virtually all this theatrical information was incorporated by Robortellus in his essay *On Comedy*, which I have placed in the Appendix.)

SERVIUS

Another Terentian commentator, and therefore an authority on comedy, was Servius, whose commentary was well known in the Middle Ages and early Renaissance. Servius apparently followed Donatus, and added very little to the account I have just summarized. "Comedy," he said, "is a certain kind of poem in common, humble language, fashioned from trifling matter."[43] He assigned comedy to the plain (*humile*) style of writing; the other two styles were, of course, grand (*grave*), and middle (*mediocre*). Comedy, said Servius, should employ fictitious material, for actuality (*res gesta*) has no

---

[42] The corresponding definition of tragedy in Diomedes is: "Tragedy is a treatment of heroic station in misfortunes." See Keil, *Grammatici Latini* 1.487-88.

[43] For Servius I have used the Latin text in a doctoral dissertation, as yet unpublished, by Professor Kenneth M. Abbott, namely, *Prolegomena to an Edition of the Pseudo-Servian Commentary on Terence*, Urbana, 1933.

Professor T. W. Baldwin has translated several sections of Servius in his *William Shakspere's Five-Act Structure*, pp. 66 ff.

place in it. *Argumentum*, the proper term for comic story, is fictitious, something which could happen, i.e., something verisimilar. *Fabula* is matter that is neither true nor verisimilar. History is actual deed (*res gesta*).

Servius maintained that comedy should accommodate itself to character (*moralitas*); it should characterize ages, sexes, ranks, as youth and old age, men and women, servants and freemen, matrons, courtesans, etc. The intent of the comic author in his characterization is to enable us to fashion good character for ourselves. He aims, moreover, at delight so that he may bring both utility and delight to the people.

ARISTOTLE

Aristotle had relatively little to say about comedy in the *Poetics*, thought what he did say was eagerly seized upon during the sixteenth century and incorporated with the traditional accounts based on Horace, Donatus, and Servius. Robortellus, in 1548, successfully combined all these materials in both his commentary on the *Poetics* and essay *On Comedy*.

Aside from a brief sketch (*Poetics* 3-4) of the evolution of comedy and tragedy in the Greek world, Aristotle made four important statements about comedy. The first of these is that Homer was the father of both tragedy and comedy (*Poetics* 4.48^{b}34-49^{a}2):

Homer's position, however, is peculiar: just as he was in the serious style the poet of poets, standing alone not only through the literary excellence, but also through the dramatic character of his imitations, so too he was the first to outline for us the general forms of Comedy by producing not a dramatic invective, but a dramatic picture of the Ridiculous; his *Margites* in fact stands in the same relation to our comedies as the *Iliad* and *Odyssey* to our tragedies.

The last part of this statement contradicts Donatus (Evanthius), who said that the *Iliad* was the model for tragedy, the *Odyssey* for comedy, and sixteenth-century scholars puzzled for some time before they finally resolved the contradiction in favor of Aristotle. The decision in favor of Aristotle was based on the types of characters in the drama, not on the kind of ending. Thus Jason Denores said: "[Homer] imitated the better, more excellent sort in the *Iliad* and *Odyssey*, the worse sort, indeed, in the *Margites*."[44] Jacobus Grifolus, another important commentator on Horace, remarked: "I wonder why Donatus wrote that Homer made the *Odyssey* in the image of

[44]Denores on *Ars Poetica* 129. Cf. Robortellus, Commentary, p. 38; Castelvetro, p. 81.

comedy, because judged by the nature of events and characters, and according to the authority of Aristotle, this is false."[45]

The second important statement of Aristotle on comedy is his distinction between the characters proper to tragedy and comedy *Poetics* 2.48ª17-18:

This difference it is that distinguishes Tragedy and Comedy also; the one would make its personages worse, and the other better, than the men of the present day.

Paccius' in 1536, translated the Greek word for "worse" as *humiliores*, the Greek word for "better" as *praestantiores*. Furthermore, Aristotle himself, in the *Problems* (19.48), had said that characters in tragedy imitate heroes since the leaders in olden times were heroes. Aristotle accepted the common practice of using stories from ancient legend for tragedy, and the characters in these legendary tales were usually heroic. Consequently the sixteenth-century commentators and critics assumed that Aristotle recommended men of noble rank, especially kings and heroes, for tragedy, and men of humble rank for comedy. This distinction fitted the definitions from Diomedes and the general remarks on the subject by Horace and Donatus. Thus Aristotle's statement was used to bolster the traditional view inherited from classical and medieval times.

In *Poetics* 5.49ª32-34, Aristotle repeated this distinction between comic and tragic characters, incorporating it with his definition of the ridiculous:

As for Comedy, it is (as has been observed) an imitation of men worse than the average; worse, however, not as regards any and every sort of fault, but only as regards one particular kind, the Ridiculous, which is a species of the Ugly. The Ridiculous may be defined as a mistake or deformity, not productive of pain or harm to others; the mask, for instance, that excites laughter, is sometimes ugly and distorted without causing pain.

As I have indicated earlier in the chapter, this celebrated definition exerted relatively little influence on dramatic criticism before the middle of the sixteenth century, though all literary men of the Renaissance were doubtless familiar with a parallel definition of the ridiculous in Cicero's *De Oratore* and a few scholars may have met the Aristotelian *ridiculum* in Averroes' paraphrase.

In *Poetics* 9.51ᵇ11 ff., Aristotle pointed out that while tragic poets commonly used historic stories and characters, comic poets in time came to the use of fictitious incidents and names:

---

[45]On *Ars Poetica* 136.

In Comedy this has become clear by this time: it is only when their plot is already made up of probable incidents that they give it a basis of proper names, choosing for the purpose any names that may occur to them, instead of writing like the old iambic poets about particular persons.

It was easy enough to harmonize this statement with the prescription of Donatus and Servius, that actuality (*res gesta*) is not proper for comedy, which is altogether feigned. Plots and characters in the New Comedy, with the notable exception of Plautus' *Amphitryon*, were always fictitious.

The Terentian commentators, from Donatus on, attached great importance to the names of comic characters. "The names of the characters in comedies," said Donatus (on the *Brothers* 26), "ought to have reason and etymology." In other words, the names of comic characters, which are created by the author, should be fitting and descriptive, and in accord with verisimilitude. Donatus and other commentators[46] found that Terence admirably illustrated the proper use of comic names. Servius, for example, remarked of the *Brothers*: "The names, therefore, are suitably fitted, so that as Micio because he was soft (*mitis*) should be thus named, so the unreasonable (*demens*) should be Demea." Aristotle's observation on the universal nature of comic names was welcomed as additional support for the established rule. Robortellus, in his comment (p. 92) on the passage from the *Poetics* quoted above, pointed out that one important sign of the universal quality of poetry is the made-up names given comic characters. These made-up names should be in accord with probability (*verisimile*) or necessity. Robortellus cited as good illustrations Micio and Demea in the *Brothers*, Phaedria (beamish) and Thraso (bragging) in the *Eunuch*. Castelvetro (p. 192), commenting on the same passage, called attention to such Terentian names as Chremes (cough), Pamphilus (all-loving), Philumena (worthy to be loved), and added that Boccaccio, in his *novelle*, also made up names to fit actions, countries, and seasons. The names of Shakespearian characters, such as Benedict and Beatrice, Hotspur and Pistol, readily come to mind. Most of Ben Jonson's comic characters are excellent illustrations of the long-established tradition. English comic drama, and English prose fiction as well, has long provided an abundant supply of comic characters whose names are reasonable and etymological, universal, descriptive, and in accord with probability or necessity.

Finally, Aristotle, in commending the unhappy ending for tragedy, remarked that a happy ending for the chief personages, as in the

---

[46]Ioannes Theodoricus Bellovacus wrote an essay on comic names which was reprinted several times during the sixteenth century. See the 1552 (Paris) edition of Terence, pp. 47-48.

double outcome of the *Odyssey*, "belongs rather to Comedy, where the bitterest enemies in the piece (e.g., Orestes and Aegisthus) walk off good friends at the end, with no slaying of any one by any one." (*Poetics* 13.53^{b}36-39.) This observation was interpreted as authoritative support for the traditional pattern of tragic and comic actions. (It may also have furnished some support—was it a source?—for the disputed tradition, appearing in Donatus, that the *Iliad* is the model for tragedy, the *Odyssey* the model for comedy.)

While these somewhat fragmentary remarks of Aristotle in the *Poetics* became influential, the most important contribution of Aristotle to the formation of the Renaissance theory of comedy was his method of criticizing tragedy. This systematic analysis of tragedy was adapted, in the middle of the sixteenth century, to the analysis of comedy; it was added to, and fitted to, the prescriptions of Horace, Cicero, Donatus, and Servius, most notably and most thoroughly by Robortellus in his essay *On Comedy* (1548).

TERENTIAN COMMENTATORS ON COMEDY AND TRAGEDY

The formation of comic theory in the first half of the sixteenth century, then, was largely an elaboration of the theories I have summarized above. While the significant contribution of Aristotle had to wait for Paccius' Latin version of the *Poetics* in 1536, and more especially for the great commentaries of Robortellus, Madius, and Victorius in 1548, 1550, and 1560, there was some earlier use of the *Poetics* by editors and commentators working on the comedies of Plautus and Terence. There was the essay, *De Comoedia*, by Pietro Valla, which I mentioned previously in connection with the *ridiculum*.[47] Pietro Valla's essay, published in a 1499 edition of Plautus, and making use of Giorgio Valla's Latin version of the *Poetics* (1498), borrowed some features of Aristotle's historical sketch of comic drama and incorporated the Aristotelian definition of comedy. But there is very little from the *Poetics* in Valla's account—he made more use of Horace and Donatus—and his introduction of Aristotle into the discussion of comic theory apparently won few followers. The next reference to Aristotle's remarks on comedy, so far as I can discover, is in Victor Faustus' essay *De Comoedia*, first published at Venice in 1511. Faustus referred to Aristotle's conception of the "ridiculous in ugliness" and to the statement in the *Poetics* that the Sicilian Epicharmus was the earliest comic dramatist.[48]

---

[47]See p. 38.

[48]*Libellus de comoedia*, in *P. Terentii comoediae* (Mainz, 1522), p. 389; also in the 1552 (Paris) edition of Terence, p. 41a.

Meanwhile the late fifteenth- and early sixteenth-century commentators on Terence were developing the comic theory found in Horace, Cicero, and the grammarians. Some of Donatus' comments on specific scenes and lines in Terence are quite as valuable as the formal statements in the introductory essays on comedy and tragedy; these comments were repeated and expanded by Renaissance scholars.

DONATUS

From the time of Plato and Aristotle, considerable emphasis was placed upon the fictitious quality of comedy. Aristotle carefully noted the change that had come about following the political satire of Aristophanic comedy, the change that transformed comedy from personal invective or lampooning to a universal, impersonal imitation of everyday human actions. In other words, the Old Comedy of Aristophanes gave way to the New Comedy in which plots and characters were feigned by the poet, who nevertheless was obliged to preserve an air of truth, a convincing verisimilitude. Consequently verisimilitude by means of fiction became the rule for comedy. A gloss by Donatus on the *Eunuch* 1.2.104 offers about as ingenious a summary as one could find of the difference between "counterfeit" (*falsum*), "lie" (*vanum*), "fiction" (*fictum*), and "fact" (*factum*). Donatus said:

Counterfeit is the dissembling of fact, a lie is what cannot happen, a fiction is what is not fact but could happen. A counterfeit is a feigned untruth similar to the truth, a lie is neither possible nor verisimilar, a fiction is wholly without truth but verisimilar. To utter a counterfeit is deceptive, a fiction clever, a falsehood stupid. To utter a counterfeit is a fault, a fiction an ingenuity, a lie a folly. We are deceived by counterfeits, we are delighted by fictions, we despise lies.

Thus the fiction of comedy, which presents matter wholly untrue but like the truth, does no harm since it deceives no one. On the contrary, comic fiction delights.

Donatus and his Renaissance followers found that Terence was a master of delightful, verisimilar fiction. Two illustrations will perhaps suffice.

The only fantastic escapade in all the Terentian comedies, which usually stick pretty close to everyday happenings, is young Chaerea's entry into the house of Thais. Parmeno, the clever slave, knows that Chaerea's older brother, Phaedria, has bought a eunuch for his mistress, and he suggests that Chaerea disguise himself as a eunuch and thereby gain entrance to the household wherein Chaerea's own flame, Pamphila, is a maid. At first sight it is incredible that Chaerea could deceive Thais and her whole household, for he is a near neighbor and his brother has long been an ardent suitor of Thais. But Terence, as Donatus noted, was careful to make the incident credible and verisimilar. When Parmeno explains the situation to Chaerea, that Phaedria is planning to present Thais with a eunuch and that the courtesan lives close by, Chaerea exclaims, "Hang it, why haven't I ever seen her? Tell me now, is she the beauty she is said to be?" It seems that Chaerea never happened to meet Thais or she him. Therefore Donatus (on *Eunuch* 2.3.360) could maintain that verisimilitude is preserved here; Chaerea could pass as a eunuch with Thais since he was unknown to her.

In the *Mother-in-law* 5.1 (756), the courtesan Bacchis appears in a role that was considered rare for one of her profession; she generously agrees to tell Philumena and her mother that Pamphilus has never visited her since his marriage. This extraordinary behavior in a courtesan called for special comment by Donatus, who felt obliged to justify it as verisimilar though contrary to custom. (Comedy, we must remember, is the "mirror of custom.") Bacchis agrees to explain the truth to the respectable married women, remarking, "Upon my word, I'll do what I'm sure no other member of my profession would do—show herself before a married woman for such a purpose." Donatus judiciously observed:

The poet himself vigilantly anticipates the reader lest it not seem verisimilar that any courtesan would do this. And so Terence generally manages in everything that is unusual or that varies from custom.

Any departure from custom in a comedy must be made probable. Many centuries after Donatus, Rapin was upholding the same principle; he was emphasizing the necessity of keeping comedy close to nature so that probability, or verisimilitude, could be preserved: " 'Tis only by adhering to Nature, that the *probability* can be maintain'd, which is the sole infallible guide that may be followed on the Theatre."[49]

Both Donatus and Servius stressed the didactic function of comedy, which mirrors everyday life and so teaches us what is useful and what must be avoided. The Renaissance followers of Donatus and Servius agreed. All three types of Roman comedy afforded both profit and delight, but apparently the first type (*motoria*) aimed principally at delight and the second type (*stataria*) at profit. Donatus found that the third kind (*mixta*), such as the *Mother-in-law* of Terence, "is a mixture of lively and quiet actions." He added, "The style as a whole comprises many sentiments and figures. Therefore, as it delights very

---

[49]*Reflections on Aristotle's Treatise of Poesie* (1674), p. 127.

much, so it affords no less profit to the spectators."[50] Very early, critics of the drama as well as antagonistic clergymen warned the public against exaggerated, farcical action in comedy and recommended the use of profitable sentiments. Whether or not Donatus knew Plato at first hand I cannot determine. Later on, however, by the beginning of the sixteenth century, Terentian commentators like Petrus Marsus and Adrianus Barlandus found strong support for the didactic aim of "right rhetoric" in the *Republic, Gorgias,* and *Phaedrus.*

While Donatus had little to say about tragedy in his commentary proper, many of his scattered observations on comedy are either direct or indirect comparisons with tragedy. He repeatedly illustrated from Terence the dividing line between tragic and comic deed and word. Sometimes this dividing line is rather subtle; but Terence, according to Donatus, had an infallible sense of artistic propriety and never stepped over the line. Cicero, in his treatise *On the Best Style of Orators,* had said that "in tragedy anything comic is a defect, and in comedy anything tragic is out of place." Nevertheless, there might be some overlapping of the two genres in a play. Comic characters, as Horace (*Ars Poetica* 93-96) said, might occasionally raise their voices in passion, and grievous troubles might be introduced in comedy, but the comic author should avoid the representation of any lasting pain.

For example, Sostrata, the mother-in-law in the play of that name, gets into serious difficulty with her husband, but Terence is careful to show that she is actually blameless. "The duty of the good comic poet," said Donatus (on *Mother-in-law* 2.2.274), "is not to wrong any class of mankind." Near the close of the *Andrian* (5.2.865), Simo orders the deceitful slave Davus bound hand and foot, but, as Donatus remarked, proceeds no further—"Lest he bring the tragic into comedy, his wrath proceeds no further than fetters, nor does he try anything more extreme." Later, to be sure, Davus is pardoned and released. The *Brothers* 4.5 is an emotional scene in which Micio maneuvers his nephew Aeschinus into a full confession of his love affair with Pamphila, and thereupon rebukes the young man. Micio's rebuke, however, as Donatus observed, is not harsh but friendly; Aeschinus' fault is not made a crime. The effect of the scene, therefore, is kindly and not painful. Micio's severest censure is that his nephew has been careless. Donatus (on 4.5.684) commented as follows:

Therefore Aeschinus is not unkind but heedless, not heedless but careless (*indiligens*); he has offended not another but himself. It is a wonderful

[50]Preface to the *Mother-in-law.*

sort of clemency either to forgive altogether or to lighten the reproach. For even so the whole reproof is friendly so that it differs little from a blandishment and brings more profit to the audience, as Terence wishes.

In the *Mother-in-law* 3.1.281 ff., young Pamphilus, who is married to the estranged Philumena, laments his unhappy situation in bitter terms. He has been placed in a dilemma that is common enough in tragedy: whatever he does will bring grief to some one, to his wife, to his mother, or to himself.

In Sargeaunt's translation, Pamphilus says:

Was ever a man that met with more bitternesses from love than I have? Distraction! was this the life for which I was so careful to save myself? Was this the reason that made me so eager to return home? Bah! how much better to live in the worst hole in the world than to come back here and learn to my misery that things were like this! If our path ahead is blocked with any trouble, all the time before we find out is always pure gain.

After an interruption by Parmeno, who tries to comfort him, Pamphilus continues:

Why try to comfort me? Is anyone in the wide world as wretched as I am? Before I married this girl, my heart had a devotion elsewhere: still I couldn't bring myself to refuse the wife that my father thrust on me. That's an affair in which anyone can see without my telling him how wretched I must have been. I had hardly weaned myself from the old love and cleared my thoughts of that entanglement, hardly given my heart to my wife, when, behold, up turns a new calamity to drag me clean away from her. Yes, I expect to find either my mother or my wife in fault here, and when I do, what is left but further misery? To bear with wrongs from my mother, Parmeno, is prescribed me by filial duty: on the other hand I owe much to my wife, who in the first days had the patience to bear with me, and never at any time breathed a word of all my affronts.

These two speeches are in the tragic vein, but they remain proper to comedy for one reason; the griefs of Pamphilus all arise from love. According to Donatus, "The griefs in this scene would be too elevated, too tragic, not comic, were it not that he [Pamphilus] added 'from love' (*ex amore*)." Barlandus repeated Donatus' criticism. Willichius added a further refinement; he labeled the scene "pathetic," but agreed that it was yet comic: "For if he [Pamphilus] had said, 'Would to God I had perished at sea,' it would have been more tragic."

Pain, suffering, death, especially violent death, were the traditional components of tragedy. Death might enter into the comic plot, but it should do so indirectly or at a distance, preferably outside the action. In the exposition of the *Mother-in-law* (1.2.171 ff.), Parmeno explains that young Pamphilus was packed off to Imbros because an old man, a relative of the family, had died and left some property. In the *Andrian* 1.1.105, Chrysis, the courtesan who protected the girl Glycerium, is reported dead. Donatus commended Terence for the way in which he introduces these deaths, which are necessary to the plot but must not be tragic. Terence, argued Donatus, was careful to make Pamphilus' relative an old man and Chrysis a courtesan. In comedy, it seems, a troublesome courtesan, an old man, or one of two wives may die and cause no grief; in fact, their deaths may be very convenient.

Although Donatus apparently had no direct acquaintance with Aristotle's definition of the proper function of tragedy—i.e., the arousal and relief of pity and fear—he had good classical authority for his insistence upon the kindly effect of comedy as opposed to the grievous effect of tragedy. For example, Quintilian (6.2.8 ff.) presented a rather detailed explanation of the distinction between *ethos* and *pathos*:

Emotions, however, as we learn from ancient authorities, fall into two classes; the one is called *pathos* by the Greeks and is rightly and correctly expressed in Latin by *adfectus* (emotion): the other is called *ethos*, a word for which in my opinion Latin has no equivalent: it is however rendered by *mores* (morals) and consequently the branch of philosophy known as *ethics* is styled *moral* philosophy by us. But close consideration of the subject leads me to think that in this connection it is not so much *morals* in general that is meant as certain peculiar aspects; for the term *morals* includes every attitude of the mind. The more cautious writers have preferred to give the sense of the term rather than to translate it into Latin. They therefore explain *pathos* as describing the more violent emotions and *ethos* as designating those which are calm and gentle: in the one case the passions are violent, in the other subdued, the former command and disturb, the latter persuade and induce a feeling of goodwill. . . . The emotion of love and longing for our friends and connections is perhaps of an intermediate character, being stronger than *ethos* and weaker than *pathos*. There is also good reason for giving the name of *ethos* to those scholastic exercises in which we portray rustics, misers, cowards, and superstitious persons according as our theme may require. For if *ethos* denotes moral character, our speech must necessarily be based on *ethos* when it is engaged in portraying such character.

The *pathos* of the Greeks, which we correctly translate by *emotion*, is of a different character, and I cannot better indicate the nature of the difference than by saying that *ethos* rather resembles comedy and *pathos* tragedy. For *pathos* is almost entirely concerned with anger, dislike, fear, hatred, and pity.

That this rhetorical distinction described by Quintilian was long an important influence upon dramatic theory is indicated by repeated references to it throughout the sixteenth and seventeenth centuries. In his *Essay of Dramatic Poetry* (1668), Dryden wrote: "In their New Comedy which succeeded, the poets sought indeed to express the πάθος as in their tragedies the ἦθος, of mankind."[51] Nevertheless pathetic speeches and scenes, as I have indicated above, were not barred from ancient comedy. Occasionally, according to Donatus, the comic poet may even adopt the order of tragedy. In the *Brothers* 3.1.(288 ff.), Sostrata is anxiously awaiting the outcome of her daughter's confinement. The situation is certainly serious. Donatus remarked: "This scene keeps the order of tragedy, for tragedy is divided into three: the expectation, the events, the outcome."

The borderline between comedy and tragedy was always uncertain. The chief determining factor was the outcome, though the social rank of characters also weighed heavily. (Certainly after the dramatic form became clearly recognizable in the early Renaissance, and the medieval notion of comedy and tragedy was pushed into the background, the social rank of characters in a play was a major factor in determining its kind.) Donatus evidently believed that whatever *pathos* might enter a comedy its *exitum* must be cheerful. In the *Mother-in-law* 4.1.563, Phidippus forbids his wife to remove Philumena's newborn child from the house. (Philumena, the daughter of Phidippus, is the estranged wife of Pamphilus.) Donatus explained that the child could not be removed, and perhaps done away with, lest "tragedy grow out of comedy." The happy ending of the play needed the child, who was actually the son of Pamphilus, to patch up the breach between the two families. And so the play, thanks to the child, ends with a complete reconciliation of all the people in both families. If events had gone the wrong way, if the child had been done away with, then the inevitable outcome would have been tragic.

LATE FIFTEENTH- AND EARLY SIXTEENTH-CENTURY COMMENTATORS

Early Renaissance commentators on Terence followed Donatus pretty faithfully; they adopted the theory of comedy set forth in the prefatory essays and they took careful account of Donatus' comments on individual scenes and lines. The first complete commentary on Terence in the Renaissance was the work of Guido Juvenalis, first published in 1492 and many times reprinted, often with added notes

---

[51]*Essays* 1.85.

of another prominent scholar, Iodocus Badius Ascensius. Guido Juvenalis[52] was no bold inovater; he quoted Horace, the definitions of comedy and tragedy from Diomedes, the Ciceronian definition of comedy, and summarized the historical development of comedy as recorded by Donatus. Guido also presented one of the early statements of the five-act formula, which he borrowed from Landinus' commentary on the *Ars Poetica* of Horace.[53] Badius Ascensius, whose own commentary on Terence appeared in 1502, also went over familiar ground. He was devoted to Horace and he was content to follow Diomedes and Donatus. Didactic, as were all the Renaissance commentators, Badius injected a Senecan note in his interpretation of tragedy that was acceptable to several generations of western Europeans; he remarked that tragedy primarily exhibited the "frailty of human affairs."[54]

Petrus Marsus, who first published on Terence in 1503, was perhaps the most didactic, the most philosophical of all the commentators, the most zealous to find moral lessons in every scene. He found moral lessons, to be sure, in tragedy as well as in comedy. In his gloss on the *Andrian* 5.5.980, Marsus wrote:

The end of comedy is cheerful, and employs a quieting of the emotions, which do not increase to a tragic perturbation or to mischiefs that are immoderate. Therefore Tragedy ends in extreme perturbations, teaching us with reason to shun that which, by its depravity, drags us into misery and breeds the most violent hatred. Truly we have not been born for strife and discord, but for peace and harmony. . . . Comedy employs those emotions that are easily reduced to a middle state which is called strength of character. This is not a purifying strength, but a step on the way; for, by long practice, it sets human desires in order, so that they may beget heroic strength (*Heroicum virtutem*). Surely we cannot proceed from extreme to extreme without some mean.

Marsus also recognized that the dividing line between comedy and tragedy cannot be rigidly drawn. He found a fine lesson in the *Brothers* 3.4.447 ff., wherein the elderly Hegio, who is mistaken, tells Demea, also misinformed, that his city-bred son, Aeschinus, has been behaving like a rascal. "This scene," said Marsus, "teaches how many tragedies error and wrongly understood matters can encourage." But

[52]*Guidonis Juvenalis . . . in Terentium familiarissima interpretatio, cum additionibus* (Lyon, 1498), pp. aiv-aiir. The additions are by Badius.

[53]See Landinus on *Ars Poetica* 196; Baldwin, *William Shakspere's Five-Act Structure*, pp. 120-23. Professor Baldwin believes that this statement is not Guido's but an addition by Badius. So far as I can determine, however, it is Guido's.

[54]*Prenotamenta* iv.

this particular scene, as Marsus well knew, is not actually tragic, though it makes use of tragic error and misunderstanding. The errors and misunderstandings in the *Brothers*, as in all true comedies, are happily cleared up before the end of the play.

Benedictus Philologus (Benedetto Ricardini), another early commentator on Terence, was important in the development of the five-act formula. His essay on comedy was reprinted several times during the first half of the sixteenth century and was sometimes mistakenly ascribed to Melanchthon.[55] Benedictus was a pretty slavish follower of Donatus. Comedy, he said, describes "slaves and humble folk, satyr-drama rustics, tragedy wealthy folk and kings." One statement of his, if indeed it is his own, proved popular:

In comedy love-affairs and the rapes of virgins are generally introduced, in tragedy sorrows, exiles, and slaughters. In comedy the endings are nearly always joyful, in tragedy sad.[56]

MELANCHTHON AND OTHERS

Melanchthon, whose work on Terence appeared at least as early as 1528, perhaps as early as 1524, was one of the famous scholars of the century and exerted a major influence on educational methods and practice. His own attitude toward comedy was primarily didactic; he was most concerned about the benefits that schoolboys might derive from the study of Terence. He was equally interested in logic and rhetoric, to be sure, and his criticism of Terence was largely philosophical and rhetorical. His contribution to the development of dramatic theory was relatively slight, but his remarks on Terence were reprinted many times and consequently must have been as well known as the work of Donatus.

Melanchthon was content to follow the account of the origin and evolution of comedy that he found in Donatus. Yet he knew the *Poetics* of Aristotle and made some use of it. Donatus (Evanthius) had explained the origin of the word comedy as a derivation from κώμη (village) and ᾠδή (song). Melanchthon[57] quoted, without comment, a different explanation from *Poetics* 3.48ᵃ37-38, where Aristotle remarks that comedians "got the name not from their *comoe* or revels, but from their strolling from hamlet to hamlet, lack of appreciation keeping them out of the city." Why did not Melanchthon, who could quote the Greek of Aristotle, make more use of the *Poetics*

---

[55]See *Corpus Reformatorum* (Brunswick, 1853) 19.681.

[56]*Terentius in sua metra restitutus* (Venice, 1506), p. aiiir; *Comoediae* (Mainz, 1522), p. 371.

[57]*In Andriam.*

here? The University of Illinois copy of the 1499 edition of Plautus, which contains Pietro Valla's quotations and paraphrases from Giorgio Valla's Latin version of the *Poetics*, was at one time in Melanchthon's hands; the book has several marginal notes in his own handwriting. It is true that there is little on comedy in the *Poetics*, and nothing on Terence. The great Renaissance commentaries on the treatise had not yet appeared. Perhaps the most reasonable explanation is that Melanchthon was not specially interested in the criticism of comedy itself; he viewed the plays of Terence primarily as lessons in moral conduct.

The most concise statement of Melanchthon on the content and function of comedy appears in his remarks on the *Eunuch*:

As comedies imitate the life, the chances (*casus*), and counsels of men, they contain dangers, because there is most occasion for counsels and fortune in dangers. Therefore, since the characters endeavor to discuss danger rationally, various counsels are feigned, some of which are mistaken and others successful. Chance prevails more often than reason. Fortune generally rules affairs.

It looks as though the philosophy of Seneca, Roman essayist and tragic dramatist, had entered the criticism of comedy. Melanchthon's more elaborate remarks on the first play of Terence, the *Andrian*, best illustrate his didactic attitude and, indeed, his whole method of dramatic criticism:

Authors of comedies wish to show examples of familiar manners and events by which we may be admonished and so the more prudently judge of human affairs and enrich our manner of speaking. . . . In recounting the argument of the plays, the chief care of the poet should be to set forth counsel. . . . The arguments of all plays, according to the ancient manner, are divided into *protasis*, *epitasis*, *catastrophe*, so that the young folk may more readily understand the parts. Moreover, the plays generally contain some danger, for there is no occasion for counsel save in doubtful matters. Nor, indeed, is comedy anything other than an image of human counsels and events. In the *Andria*, Pamphilus is put to the test, so that he may make good his plighted troth to Glycerium, inasmuch as through an error he has been promised to another, is about to fall under his father's control, and to wed his father's choice. This is as it were the *stasis* of the play. All counsels, all quarrels, all arguments ought to be brought to this end. And the whole play is like the persuasive type of oration; for old men, young men, and servants deliberate on the whole matter in various ways. But in order that the boys can more conveniently understand the argument let us record the separate parts in order.

Then Melanchthon proceeded to explain the events and counsels of protasis, epitasis, and catastrophe; and he followed this procedure for all the other plays of Terence.

In the first volume of Stephanus Riccius' elaborate edition of Terence (1566) there are several prolegomena by various scholars. One of these prefaces, dated 1528, is attributed to Ioannes Stigelius (1515-62), prominent neo-Latin poet, rhetorician, editor, professor at Wittenberg and Jena. If the date 1528 is correct, a doubtful supposition —1548 seems more likely—then Johann Stigel must have been a precocious youth. His "what comedy is," however, was not a startling performance since it merely reproduced the familiar routine of the century. There is one interesting feature in the brief account that deserves mention; the Plutarchian aphorism that poetry is a speaking picture was here incorporated with the traditional comic theories of Donatus, Horace, *et al.* So far as I know, this was the first time that this celebrated aphorism was specifically applied to comedy. Stigelius, who was a poet in his own right, expressed himself very well, and a few of his remarks are worth quoting, even in my inadequate translation:

Comedy, to be sure, is nothing other than an image of daily life and a speaking picture of human actions and counsels, by which one may become acquainted with the *mores* of life and govern his own. The learned finely call it a mirror of life. Just as we may discern in a mirror the beauty of a face and also its blemishes, so we may likewise perceive in comedy what ought to be imitated, what ought to be shunned, what is appropriate to an honorable life.[58]

The castigations on Terence by Ioannes Rivius first appeared at Cologne in 1532, and were many times reprinted. Like Melanchthon, Rivius was a staunch exponent of the didactic purpose of comedy. He found an admirable example of moral conduct in the *Andrian* 5.3.896-97. Here Pamphilus proves himself a dutiful son as well as a faithful lover; he says to Simo his father: "I confess that I love Glycerium. If that is a fault, I confess that also. I put myself in your hands, father; put any burden on me, command me." Rivius considered this, with the lines that follow, a fine speech, as indeed it is, and he hoped that boys in the sixteenth century would emulate Pamphilus in yielding to paternal authority. As Solomon justly said, a soft answer turneth away wrath. Pamphilus' conduct, as Rivius remarked, is worthy of a Christian. Then Rivius proceeded with some eloquence to describe the lessons contained in Terentian comedy:

---

[58]Riccius' edition of Terence 1.6.

Although these things are feigned by the poet, we may see our own manners represented in other persons and the image of daily life set forth, as Cicero says in *Pro Roscio Amerino*. Comedy is truly the mirror of human life, and accordingly comedies are read so that we may thenceforth make our own life better and correct our own behavior. We learn what in life is useful and to be followed, what, on the other hand, is useless and to be shunned, what is done right and otherwise. In comedy, "as in a mirror," the manners of men and their daily life are set forth to view, the vices of youths and servants are portrayed to the life, the guiles of strumpets are shown; pernicious pleasures, shameful allurements, the follies of lovers are placed before the eyes, to the end that well-bred youths may detest the wanton loves of courtesans, may be urged toward virtue by the fairest examples, and may be kindled by the most wholesome admonitions. In short, they learn from others what is useful and honorable for themselves.

It was not difficult to find edifying speeches in Terence, and most of the commentators were looking for edification. Even Bartholomaeus Latomus, whose terse analyses of Terentian scenes are remarkably free from moral digressions and always hold steadily in view the dramatic structure of the play, upon at least one occasion pointed out the moral lesson in a scene. (The annotations of Latomus first appeared in 1534.) Latomus remarked of the *Brothers* 5.4, a soliloquy by Demea:

Moved by these examples, Demea alters the course of his life, and from a rough, uncivil man endeavors to become a kind one. This scene, as he knows, is suitable for instructing the audience, which is the purpose of the play.

Obviously a favorite argument of the Renaissance commentators on Terence was that comedy can be a highly successful means of instructing youth. Illustrations of this belief are legion. Some of the most interesting may be seen in the work of a German associate of Melanchthon, Ambrosius Berndt Iuterbocensis (d. 1542), one-time professor of Latin at Wittenberg. Numerous prefaces to the plays of Terence were ascribed to Ambrosius by Stephanus Riccius. One of these, a preface to the *Andrian*, dated 1537, contains an eloquent expression of the popular Renaissance contention that the poet is the most delightful of all teachers. Ambrosius anticipated in particular the famous defense of poetry by Sir Philip Sidney, who argued that the poet is superior in teaching to both historian and philosopher since he combines the specific examples of the former with the abstract precepts of the latter. Ambrosius confined his argument to the comic poet, but his conclusions were almost identical. (Such conclusions, to be sure, had become commonplaces in the sixteenth century.) Ambrosius believed that Terence was a superior teacher of moral conduct:

The chief utility is that since many examples and sentiments are presented, which refer to that most excellent branch of philosophy, ethics, even so these often contain a wholesome disputation. And there is this beauty in comedies; they contain much in few words that other writings are wont to unfold in long-winded disputation.[59]

In a preface to the *Brothers*, Ambrosius repeated this idea:

Much that Aristotle, Xenophon, Plato, Cicero, and others have written at great length is wisely and usefully transmitted in the plays of Terence by means of brief sentiments and fictitious characters.[60]

Following the preface to the *Andrian* quoted above there is a short catechism on comedy, which may also be by Ambrosius, possibly by the editor, Stephanus Riccius. Two of the questions and answers provide excellent illustrations of the conventional theory of comedy in the sixteenth century:

1. What is Comedy?

Comedy is properly a poem containing the image of human counsels and events. Cicero rightly defines it to be an "imitation of life, a mirror of custom, and an image of truth," and moreover it belongs to moral philosophy (*ethice*). Thus Cicero on comedy in the oration *Pro Roscio Amerino:* "I think, indeed, that these fictions of the poets are made so that we may see our own manners in other characters and a lively image of our own daily life."

4. How do Comedy and Tragedy differ?

The special difference is this, that comedy comprises plebeian characters of moderate fortune and also counsels and dangers, but with a cheerful ending. Tragedy, however, has noble characters, great dangers, and lamentable endings.[61]

About the middle of the century there appeared an essay "On the Origin of Plays," by Petrus Menenius. Evidently this essay was considered important; Willichius included it in his edition of Terence (1550). Menenius drew upon a variety of classical writers, including Aristotle, but his main sources were Donatus and Horace. For the most part, he merely embroidered the conventional groundwork of the century. Thus he distinguished between tragedy and comedy:

In tragedy lofty matters, fiery passions, grievous mischiefs, and great dangers are treated. Hence τραγῳδικά are marvelous, pitiful, incredible, grand; and τραγῳδεῖν or ἐπιτραγῳδεῖν is to amplify tragically, to speak tragically, i.e., to speak in stately words. . . . The char-

---

[59]Riccius' edition of Terence 1.10r.   [60]*Ibid.*, 2.Y6r.   [61]*Ibid.*, 1.10v-11r.

acters of kings, princes, emperors, and wealthy people are brought into tragedy; the urban and civil life of middle-class, private agents in comedy. Finally, tragedians wear the cothurnus, comedians the sock.[62]

WILLICHIUS AND WAGNERUS

Willichius himself had a first-hand knowledge of Aristotle's *Poetics*, but made little use of it in his commentary on Terence. He repeatedly referred to the *Rhetoric* of Aristotle, though he was evidently more at home with Cicero, Quintilian, and Hermogenes. So far as I can discover, he incorporated just two ideas from the *Poetics* in his edition of Terence; in the foreword to the *Eunuch* he connected the traditional concept of comedy with the Aristotelian *mimesis* and with Aristotle's definition of the ridiculous:

It is sufficiently clear in the commentaries of many that comedy is chiefly a pattern of civil life. Also, Aristotle has very wisely called it *mimesis*, because it is a kind of imitation or representation of the manners and actions of domestic life. Aristotle separates comedy from tragedy by means of persons and manners, in so far as comedy is an imitation of humbler persons and leaner fortunes. Then it is clear that comedy is not subject to just any vices, but needs jokes, witticisms and the ridiculous, which nevertheless is not altogether averse to ugliness. For the ridiculous is a kind of fault, but this ugliness, it is supposed, is without pain, harm, or misfortune.

Willichius' comment on the *Mother-in-law* 4.1.516 also dealt, by implication, with the proper functions of tragedy and comedy. In this scene, Myrrina, the mother of Philumena, is greatly distressed over her daughter's unhappy state. Philumena, estranged from her husband, has given birth to a child. Myrrina's speech is a lament in the tragic manner, and Willichius commented as follows:

The proposition is from a querulous and disturbed mind. It is a depicting of trouble and grief, in which the understanding, and so both counsel and judgment, is darkened, since the heart itself is contracted. So, on the contrary, as gladness, light, and fair weather cheer minds, the sun dispels grief from the mind.

The thought here suggests Seneca, whose tragic characters repeatedly express the notion that sorrow darkens the mind.[63]

Willichius, in his edition of Terence, published a long prefatory letter by one of his relatives, Gregorius Wagnerus, who had evidently adopted the same dramatic theories. The letter was addressed to Willichius' son, and contains many moral admonitions. Wagnerus

---

[62]*De origine fabularum*, in Willichius' edition of Terence, p. 30.
[63]See *Troades* 902-03, 545-46; *Hercules Oetaeus* 1402-03; *Octavia* 52-54.

was a rhetorician and a stout defender of the moral usefulness of Terentian comedy. Needless to say, Terence for all his great prestige had not wholly escaped the attacks of reforming poet-haters. Wagnerus quoted the Ciceronian definition of comedy and added:

It praises virtues and censures vices, and exhibits the substance of virtue in whatever age, sex, or condition. The image and pattern of nearly all domestic actions are here made manifest. To this end let one consider that of Demea in the *Brothers*. I charge that he look upon the lives of men as in a mirror and from others choose an example for himself.[64]

Then, after adducing several illustrations of useful moral examples in Terence, he proceeded:

Therefore it is wholesome to inscribe the beauty of virtue in the mind, to represent by means of imitation, to expel the stench of vice from the mind and forever to hate it. To become acquainted with these things is health for young lads. Is there any lad so lumpish, stupid, and witless who will not choose and follow something for himself from a reading or acting of comedies, as for instance from a public reading of this comic poet [Terence] there will appear, I honestly and eagerly predict, what is best and most worthy for praise?

Wagnerus was preparing the way for the most difficult part of his defense, namely the defense against the charge of eroticism in Terence. Calling upon the aid of Horace, who stated that poets should both profit and delight, Wagnerus cited an erotic incident in the Bible. He asked where could one find a more grievous instance of incestuous love than the story of Ammon's violation of his sister Thamar. Terence, he argued, shows the miseries and tortures of love in his young lovers, so that his readers may learn to avoid these evils. Nor does Terence, as some allege, countenance the evil of wenching. Micio (in the *Brothers* 1.2.101 ff.) does say that it is no great crime for a young man to wench and drink, but later in the same scene (after his brother Demea has left) he admits, "Not that these matters are not painful to me, but I do not wish to show my vexation before him [Demea]." No, Wagnerus would not allow that there was anything in the good Terence but the worthiest lessons in right conduct. And Wagnerus made about as good a defense of the poet as did more celebrated defenders.

Willichius also included in his edition the annotations of Marcus Antonius Muretus, another well-known commentator. Muretus corrected the misleading statement in Donatus, that the *Iliad* is the prototype of tragedy and the *Odyssey* the prototype of comedy. He referred to Aristotle, "whose authority certainly outweighs the opinion

---

[64]Willichius' edition of Terence, p. 12.

of this grammarian";[65] he quoted the Greek of *Poetics* 4.48^{b}34-49^{a}2, wherein Aristotle calls the *Margites* of Homer, not the *Odyssey*, the protoype of comedy, both *Iliad* and *Odyssey* being tragic poetry. By the middle of the century the authority of Aristotle had successfully challenged the long rule of Donatus in comic theory.

SIXTEENTH-CENTURY CRITICS ON COMEDY AND TRAGEDY

The sixteenth-century commentators on Aristotle and Horace and the literary critics in general also discussed comedy and tragedy. Some of these men, such as Scaliger and Castelvetro, became well known throughout Europe. Others, while less prominent, offered substantial contributions to the development of comic theory.

ROBORTELLUS

Robortellus, in 1548, first brought the full force of Aristotle to bear upon the traditional theories of comedy. In his commentary on the *Poetics* and in an appended essay *On Comedy* (*Explicatio eorum omnium quae ad Comoediae artificium pertinent*), he utilized every statement of Aristotle on comedy. He did not neglect other authorities, to be sure, but made use of Horace, Donatus, Plutarch, Julius Pollux, Vitruvius, and others. His chief contribution, however, was the thorough adaption to comedy of Aristotle's detailed analysis of tragic drama. He firmly established in comic theory the Aristotelian terms, plot, character, thought, diction, spectacle, and music, simple and complex plot, complication and denouement, discovery and reversal of fortune, unity of action and limited time. Since I have included a complete translation of Robortellus' essay in the Appendix, and since I shall have to refer to him again when I come to the discussion of plot, character, sentiment and diction, I shall not discuss the details of his contribution here. Robortellus exerted a major influence in formulating the Renaissance "rules of comedy." Some years later, at the beginning of the seventeenth century, Lope de Vega would have us believe that Robortellus was the leading modern authority on the art of comedy. Lope himself made fun of the classical rules, but his reference to Robortellus may be taken as serious evidence:

If it is art that you desire, I implore you, men of genius, to read the learned Robortello of Udine, and you will see in his *On Aristotle* [the commentary] and in the part where he has written *On Comedy*, as much as is scattered through many books; for everything today is confusion.[66]

[65]*Ibid.*, p. 732.

[66]*The New Art of Making Comedies* (1609), in Gilbert, pp. 543-44.

CHYTRAEUS

Robortellus' synthesis of comic theories became the accepted standard whether later critics followed Robortellus directly or indirectly. Thus, for example, the "Propositions on Comedy" for an academic disputation at Rostock in November of 1574 closely parallel the dicta of Robortellus' *On Comedy*. These "propositions" at Rostock were the work of a German schoolmaster and poet, Nathan Chytraeus, and were printed in his edition of Terence's *Brothers* in 1576.

Chytraeus shared the views of fellow schoolmasters and commentators; he had studied the same authorities, ancient and modern. He tried, for example, to dispose of the charge of eroticism in Terence in the same way that Wagnerus tried. It seems likely, in fact, that he knew the letter of Wagnerus; he included Willichius in his imposing list of learned authorities. Aristotle is on this list, and while Chytraeus, in his commentary on the *Brothers*, depended upon the *Rhetoric* rather than the *Poetics*, the propositions on comedy embody the Aristotelian analysis of a play. The propositions show a characteristic blend of Horace, Donatus, Aristotle, and Melanchthon. In fact, outside Robortellus' essay *On Comedy* I do not know where one may find a clearer, more concise summary of comic theory in the Renaissance. Consequently I feel justified in translating and quoting a number of Chytraeus' propositions.[67]

XII. The parts of tragedy, in the qualitative reckoning of Aristotle, are defined as six, which are in common with comedy, to wit "plot, character, diction, thought, spectacle, and music."

XIII. "Plot" ($\mu\hat{v}\theta os$), or *fabula*, in comedy is the imitation, in the proper sequence and arrangement of material, of any action having a just magnitude; or the well-managed comic argument itself.

XIV. "Character" ($\mathring{\eta}\theta\eta$), or *mores*, is a seemly representation of natures, dispositions, inclinations, actions, emotions, and endeavors according to the diversity of persons.

XV. Character, moreover, is in a fourfold diversity of persons, who vary as regards emotions, habits, age, and fortune. Aristotle has accurately explained this in the second book of his *Rhetoric*.

XXII. "Diction" ($\lambda\acute{\epsilon}\xi\iota s$), or *dictio*, is the interpretation of the mind by means of words, which in comedy is by means of measured speech.

XXIII. "Thought" ($\delta\iota\acute{a}\nu o\iota a$), or *sententia*, is the way in which a speaking character designates that something is or is not, proves or does not prove something, or makes some general observation.

XXIV. "Spectacle" ($\mathring{o}\psi\iota s$), or *apparatus*, comprises everything that is set before the eyes of the spectator, such as the *décor* of the scene,

---

[67] P. *Terentii comoedia Adelphi* (Rostock, 1576), pp. Bb3-Cc2.

costumes of the actors, and the rest, which add much to the understanding of the matters that are acted.

XXV. "Music" ($\mu\epsilon\lambda o\pi o\iota\iota a$) is the artistic management of melody fitted to the decorum of the proposed argument.

XXVI. Although spectacle and music can be regarded as non-essential to comedy, since even when stripped of these, and read in private, a comedy retains its name, nevertheless these were regarded by Aristotle as parts in order to distinguish a play from an epic poem.

XXVII. The parts of comedy in the quantitative reckoning are *protasis, epitasis, catastrophe.*

XXXII. Faults, counsels, manners, actions, dangers, unexpected accidents have afforded, in their kind, matter for comedies.

XXXIII. Or, as we might actually indicate something of a particular kind: the contents of comedies are the peevishness or indulgence of parents, the goodness or knavery of children, the harmony or discord of married couples, the fidelity or deceits of servants, the diligence or meddlesomeness of citizens, marriages and divorces, prodigality and niggardliness, and very many others of such kind.

XXXIX. The end of comedy in general, as likewise with other common forms of poetry, is to imitate aptly and to teach with delight.

XLI. Tragedy is akin to and sister as it were of Comedy. Both, in fact, bring in persons acting; both present nothing from the person of the poet; both usually finish their action in a short interval of time; both usually use iambic meter.

XLII. Comedy and Tragedy, however, differ from one another, first in the rank of personages, who in comedy are of less account and plebeian, in tragedy noble and royal.

XLIII. Second, in the quality of employments and affairs, which in comedy are everyday and often merry, in tragedy truly weighty, difficult, dangerous, and lamentable.

XLIV. Third, in the manner of the beginning, which in comedy is usually turbulent, in tragedies quiet.

XLV. Fourth, in the manner of the ending, which in comedy is joyful, in tragedy dreadful.

XLVI. Fifth, in the manner of style, which in comedy is humble and popular, in tragedy serious and removed from vulgar diction.

XLVII. Sixth, comedy is more expressive of character (*morata*), tragedy more passionate (*pathetica*).

XLVIII. Seventh, comedy makes use of the affairs and the names of fictitious persons; tragedy, in truth, chooses the affairs and the principal names of its persons from histories.

GIRALDI CINTHIO

By the middle of the sixteenth century the reconstructed Aristotelian theory of comedy began to appear not only in the commentaries on Aristotle and Terence but in more general critical writings as well. Thus Giraldi Cinthio, whose discourse on comedy and tragedy was written in 1543, published in 1554, was heavily indebted to Aristotle. Cinthio's summary of comedy was similar to many that I have quoted. As did virtually all critics of his generation, he emphasized the fictitious quality of comedy:

Comedy deals with actions that occur in the ordinary life of citizens while tragedy deals with famous and regal deeds, for comedy presents private men and tragedy is concerned with kings and great persons; hence it would not be true to life, since great men are in the eyes of the world, that any strange deed could be done by them which would not, as soon as it is performed, come to the ears of everyone. Therefore, since tragedy deals with illustrious acts, by treating of persons who perform them, it does not appear that such acts can be brought on the stage without their having been known before. But private actions can properly be feigned because for the most part they do not get beyond private houses and in a short time are forgotten. Hence the poet has a large field for feigning what he wishes in order to bring new comic plots on the stage.[68]

But Cinthio, taking advantage of a statement in Aristotle's *Poetics*, went on to argue that the plot of a tragedy may also be feigned:

I hold nonetheless that the tragic plot can be feigned by the poet as well as the comic. Aristotle, judicious here as everywhere, conceded it in more than one passage of his *Poetics*, . . . though saying that comedy feigns its fables and tragedy usually takes them from history, shows that it is not always necessary to take them from history. It appears to me also that reason is able to present the same truth to us with sufficient probability, because the power of moving tragic feelings depends only on imitation which does not depart from probability, and facts do not move the feelings without words fitly and poetically joined together. Therefore it seems to me that it is in the power of the poet to move at his wish the tragic feelings by means of a tragedy of which he feigns the plot, if that plot is in conformity with natural habits and not remote from what can happen and often does happen. And perhaps the feelings are moved to the adoption of good morals the more in proportion as by coming anew into the minds of the listeners the feigned plot gains for itself the greater attention.[69]

---

[68]*Discorsi* (Venice, 1554), pp. 208-09; quoted by Gilbert, pp. 252-53.

[69]Gilbert, p. 253.

Aristotle, in *Poetics* 9.51^{b}19-26, did grant that fictitious tragedies were proper. Tasso, however, did not agree with Cinthio; he maintained that Aristotle distinctly preferred true stories in tragedy and epic poem. See Tasso's "Discourses on the Heroic Poem," in Gilbert, pp. 471-72.

Cinthio had a personal motive in trying to broaden the conventional limits of the tragic plot; his own *Orbecche*, which he hoped was a proper tragedy, had a feigned plot. I should say that the theory here expressed by Cinthio led rather to tragicomedy than to tragedy. By the end of the century playwrights were feigning plots for tragicomedies, but tragedies proper were usually based on historical events.

MINTURNO

Minturno, whose *De Poeta* (1559) was a great Renaissance clutter-hole of literary theories, tried to follow everybody and to include everything, and he almost succeeded. His elaborate discussions included the history of comedy, definitions of comedy, classifications of comedy, comparison of comedy with tragedy, and analyses of classical comedies. His principal authorities were Plato, Aristotle, Horace, and Donatus, and he repeated nearly every theory and observation that I have hitherto mentioned. Since his criticism became widely known, he cannot be ignored.

Minturno subscribed to the Athenian's argument in Plato's *Laws* (2.658-59), that children prefer puppet shows, the bigger boys comedy, young men and educated women tragedy, and the older men heroic poetry. In other words, he professed to believe that comedy was on a somewhat lower plane than that of tragedy and the epic poem. He also accepted the feigned plots and humbler characters of comedy. Nevertheless, Minturno may have contributed to a recognition of the respectable element in comedy; at least he objected to any overemphasis on low characters. He maintained that comedy uses not only servants, parasites, and clowns, but kindly, respectable, middle-class folk as well, and he found good support for his argument in the characters of Terence.[70] Like Robortellus, whose work he probably knew, Minturno adapted the Aristotelian analysis of tragedy to comedy. His remarks on comic plot are of some importance, and I shall make use of them in a later chapter. For the present, a typical quotation from *De Poeta* (pp. 280-81) will illustrate his general attitude and the general background of his conception of comedy. Notice the blend of Cicero, Diomedes, Donatus, and Aristotle:

[Comedy] is an imitation of life, mirror of custom, image of truth, or that which treats of civil and private affairs devoid of danger, or what I think Aristotle most approves; it is an imitation for representing, in pleasant, plain speech, some action of civil or private matters, not renowned, not serious, but certainly cheerful and ridiculous, and truly suited to the amendment of life, and comprehending a perfect whole of

---

[70]See *De Poeta*, pp. 24, 50, 280-81.

just magnitude, introducing characters who do not arouse grief or horror but, as it were, amuse and delight by their acting.

TRISSINO

The dramatic theories of Trissino, who published the first four divisions of his *Poetica* in 1529, the last two divisions appearing in 1563, provide another good illustration of the modifications that the study of Aristotle brought to literary criticism in the sixteenth century. Trissino showed only a slight acquaintance with the *Poetics* in 1529; the second volume in 1563, however, was in large part a restatement of Aristotelian theory. In this second volume (p. 31r), Trissino helped to clear away the last vestige of the medieval conception of tragedy and comedy. He explained why Dante called his own great poem a comedy although it is better classified among the heroic poems. Dante called the poem a comedy because it ended in bliss and was written in the middle style, between the grand and the humble styles. But Dante, argued Trissino, although a very learned and gifted man, was the victim of the unpolished, barbarous age in which he lived and did not know the arts of rhetoric and poetry; meaning, of course, that Dante could not have understood the arts of rhetoric and poetry as the sixteenth-century scholars understood them. By implication, certainly, Trissino meant that Dante did not know the *Poetics* of Aristotle.

Trissino not only made a careful study of Aristotle's *Poetics*, but tried to expand and particularize the ideas he found in that treatise. As a result, his discussion of comedy, as well as his discussions of tragedy and epic poetry as well, was primarily based on Aristotelian theory. Like Robortellus, and perhaps influenced by that great commentator, he adapted Aristotle's analysis of tragedy to comedy and yet retained many of the traditional conceptions. "Comedy," he said, "has the same fundamental parts as tragedy, that is, the plot, the manners, the thought, the words, the presentations, and the music."[71] He retained the traditional social distinction between tragic and comic characters, and he continued to emphasize the fictitious basis of comedy. The following quotation from the *Poetica* pretty clearly indicates the Aristotelian framework of his theory:

Comedy, then, imitates worse actions with speech, rhythm, and harmony, as does tragedy; and it imitates an action single, complete, and large, which has a beginning, a middle, and an end. But in this it differs from tragedy, that as tragedy carries on its teaching by means of pity and fear, comedy teaches by deriding and censuring things ugly and vile. . . .

---

[71]*Poetica* 2.30v. Cf. Gilbert, p. 224.

The comic fable, then, is made up of actions diverse from those of tragedy, and as it were contrary to them, because tragedy produces the effect of its teaching with pity, with tears, and with fear, which are sad things, while comedy does it with jokes and with laughter, which are pleasant things; hence as for tragedy are sought out piteous acts of great and illustrious men, so in comedy it is necessary to use jocose acts of persons of low rank and unknown, and as in tragedy there come about sorrows and deaths and it almost always ends in unhappiness, so in comedy, though there are some disturbances, they do not involve wounds and deaths, and all terminate in good, as weddings, peaceful agreements, and tranquility. . . . So he who wishes to compose a comedy well should first arrange the fable, that is, find the action and write a summary of it, and put it before his eyes, and consider well the moral traits, and see what is fitting and what is contrary and repugnant, and then put in the names, and insert the episodes, and treat it with excellent sententious sayings, and with words familiar, ornate, and suitable, as we have said about tragedy.[72] But comedy will differ from tragedy in that while in tragedy the actions and names are true, either all or the greater part, in comedy the actions and names are all invented by the poet, though Plautus in his *Amphitryo* did not do it, whence it is called a tragi-comedy.[73]

SCALIGER

Julius Caesar Scaliger, who liked to scold the grammarians, found fault with the traditional definitions of comedy, and while he actually suggested few changes in theory, these few changes were significant. He quarreled with the emphasis on imitation in poetry and scoffed at Diomedes' statement that comedy is "free from the suggestion of danger, dealing with the life and affairs of the private citizen." Scaliger said, "Our definition would be:

Comedy is a dramatic poem full of action, happy in its outcome, and written in a popular style."[74]

In the next chapter of his *Poetices* (1.6), he repeated the conventional similarities and differences between comedy and tragedy, i.e., the common dramatic genus of the two forms, the common pattern of real life, the differences in social rank of the characters, in style, in action, and in outcome. But Scaliger, like Cinthio, did help to broaden the accepted view of comedy. Robortellus,[75] for example, following Plutarch and Donatus, had slighted Aristophanes and Old Comedy. As I have tried to show, comic theory during the first half

[72]And as Aristotle said about tragedy. See *Poetics* 17.
[73]Gilbert, pp. 224-25.
[74]*Poetices* 1.5.
[75]See *On Comedy* in the Appendix.

of the sixteenth century was overwhelmingly Terentian. Scaliger helped to restore Aristophanes to his rightful position in comic drama, and he helped to extend the rather narrow limits of comedy imposed by the grammarians' devotion to Terence. Scaliger (3.97), in fact, while recognizing the importance and the popularity of Terence, found the Roman poet rather tame: "If Apollodorus and Menander were like their imitator Terence, they certainly were too tame." He did not join with Robortellus and others in recommending a faithful copying of the Terentian manner. "There was not just one manner of comedy," he proclaimed, "for so long as comedies won laughter they needed nothing else."

Since Scaliger enjoyed great prestige as a critic, his tolerant attitude toward comic technique must have been an important influence. At all events, the theory and practice of our great English playwrights at the close of the century reflect the same freedom. Ben Jonson, for example, who began writing comedies as a pretty faithful imitator of Roman comedy soon turned to more complex plots and characterizations. The plots of Jonson's early comedies, the *Tale of a Tub* and the *Case is Altered*, more or less followed the classical intrigue established by Plautus and Terence, but thereafter his comedies, from *Every Man In His Humor* to *Bartholomew Fair*, departed from the relatively simple classical structure and became more and more complicated and multiform.[76]

CASTELVETRO

While both Minturno and Scaliger gave about as much attention to comedy as to tragedy, the third famous critic of the Italian Renaissance, Castelvetro, left only incidental remarks on comedy. Castelvetro's scattered references indicate a reactionary view; he emphasized more strongly than did any other prominent critic of his day the sharp dividing line between tragic actions and characters and comic actions and characters. "The private action of a private citizen is the subject of comedy, as the actions of kings are the subject of tragedy."[77] Since Aristotle's fragmentary remarks on comedy emphasized the ridiculous, Castelvetro limited his conception of comedy to the ridiculous, and he made some contribution to the theory of the risible, as I have indicated earlier in the chapter.

The grammarians and the Terentian commentators built up a neat and relatively narrow conception of comedy which was generally

---

[76]See Freda L. Townsend, *Apologie for Bartholmew Fair*, (New York, 1947).

[77]Quoted by Charlton, p. 135.

accepted in theory if not always in practice during the first half of the sixteenth century. In the second half of the century, Giraldi Cinthio and Minturno somewhat relaxed the limits of comic theory, and Scaliger extended these limits to include almost anything that aroused laughter. While the dividing line between tragedy and comedy was sharply drawn by most Renaissance critics and commentators, in practice, this line was often blurred, sometimes nearly obliterated when a new type of drama became fashionable. The ups and downs of tragicomedy at the close of the sixteenth and beginning of the seventeenth centuries, the theories of Guarini,[78] the practice of Tasso, Guarini, Fletcher, and Shakespeare constitute an important chapter in the history of Renaissance drama, but it is not a chapter that I am prepared to elucidate here. Furthermore, the growth of tragicomedy, as students of the drama know, was vigorously opposed by conservative critics and poets. The neoclassical pattern of comedy, with Terence as the principal model, the pattern that I have tried to describe, was firmly established and did not quickly lose its shape. Sir Philip Sidney, one of many who termed tragicomedies gross absurdities, subscribed to the Terentian model of comedy and the Senecan model of tragedy:

Comedy is an imitation of the common errors of our life, which he [the comic poet] representeth in the most ridiculous and scornful sort that may be, so as it is impossible that any beholder can be content to be such a one. Now, as in geometry the oblique must be known as well as the right, and in arithmetic the odd as well as the even, so in the actions of our life who seeth not the filthiness of evil wanteth a great foil to perceive the beauty of virtue. This doth the Comedy handle so in our private and domestical matters, as with hearing it we get as it were an experience, what is to be looked for of a niggardly Demea, of a crafty Davus, of a flattering Gnatho, of a vainglorious Thraso,[79] and not only to know what effects are to be expected, but to know who be such, by the signifying badge given them by the comedian. . . . So that the right use of Comedy will (I think) by nobody be blamed, and much less of the high and excellent Tragedy, that openeth the greatest wounds and showeth forth the ulcers that are covered with tissue; that maketh kings fear to be tyrants and tyrants manifest their tyrannical humors; that, with stirring the affects of admiration and commiseration, teacheth the uncertainty of this world, and upon how weak foundations gilden roofs are builded, that maketh us know,

---

[78]See the selections from Guarini's "Compendium of Tragicomic Poetry" in Gilbert, pp. 505-33.

[79]Characters in the *Brothers*, the *Andrian*, and the *Eunuch* of Terence.

> Qui sceptra saevus duro imperio regit,
> Timet timentes, metus in auctorem redit.[80]

This condemnation of tragicomedy was fairly typical of Elizabethan critics, but not of the practicing playwrights, with the notable
exception of Ben Jonson. English playwrights of the late sixteenth
and early seventeenth centuries continued to mingle "compassion
with mirth."[81] In comic theory, however, Elizabethan critics never
deserted the standards set by Terence and the Terentian commentators. Richard Bernard, theologian and writer, whose *Terence in English* first appeared in 1598, well expressed the conventional attitude of
his generation toward comedy in general and toward Terence in particular:

I offer you here, that which Fortune hath vouchsafed to favor me withal,
a Latin author taught to speak English, a comical poet, pithy, pleasant,
and very profitable: as merry as Eutrapelus, as grave as Cato, as ethical as
Plato, he can play craftily the cozener and cunningly the clown: he will
tell you the nature of the fraudulent flatterer, the grim and greedy old
sire, the roisting ruffian, the mincing minion, and beastly bawd; that in
telling the truth by these figments men might become wise to avoid such
vices and learn to practice virtue: which was Terence's purpose in setting
of these comedies forth in Latin, mine in translating them into English;
and this end I desire you to propound to yourselves in reading them, so
shall you use them and not, as most do such authors, abuse them. Accept
of him, Gentlemen, read him, as you may, with pleasure and no small
profit.

---

[80]Seneca *Oedipus* 705-06. For the passage from Sidney see *Elizabethan Critical Essays* 1.176-77.

[81]It is true that English drama in the second half of the seventeenth century,
owing in large part to the influence of neoclassical French drama, became
more conventional. Dryden, for example, in his *Essay of Dramatic Poesy*
(1668), defended tragicomedy, but later took a more conservative position.
In a late essay, the *Parallel of Poetry and Painting* (1695), he condemned
tragicomedy, including one of his own successful plays:

"The Gothic manner, and the barbarous ornaments, which are to be avoided
in a picture, are just the same with those of an ill-ordered play. For example,
our English tragicomedy must be confessed to be wholly Gothic, nothwith-
standing the success which it has found upon our theater, and in the *Pastor
Fido* of Guarini; even though Corisca and the Satyr contribute somewhat to
the main action. Neither can I defend my *Spanish Friar*, as fond otherwise I
am of it, from this imputation; for though the comical parts are diverting,
and the serious moving, yet they are of an unnatural mingle; for mirth and
gravity destroy each other, and are no more to be allowed for decent than a
gay widow laughing in a mourning habit." (*Essays* 2.146-47.)

Chapter IV: The Conception of Plot
in the Sixteenth Century

OUR MODERN term Plot, when applied to a play or a narrative, has various meanings. It may mean the outline of the action, the theme, the gist of the story. It may carry the broader meaning of arrangement of incidents, the over-all structure, the form of the whole, the design of the whole. In contemporary dramatic criticism, plot usually means the highly artificial scheme of action wrought by makers of the "well-made" play, by such nineteenth-century playwrights as Scribe, Sardou, Dumas *fils*, and many others, including Ibsen in his early realistic plays. The "well-made" plot, with its neatly wrought complications rising to a denouement by means of discoveries, has no loose ends; every incident is closely fitted into the main pattern of action, and the final resolution clears up everything. This "well-made" plot is directly descended from the neoclassical plot, which in turn was modeled upon the classical intrigue of Roman comedy, in particular upon the carefully wrought intrigue of Terentian comedy.

When contemporary dramatic critics say, as many of them do, that the naturalistic plays of Chekhov and Gorki have no plot, they must mean that the *Cherry Orchard* and the *Lower Depths* do not have "well-made" plots that are descended from the *Andrian* or the *Mother-in-law* or *Phormio*. Otherwise, any statement that artists like Chekhov and Gorki ignored plot is nonsense, for both Chekhov and Gorki well understood the importance of form, of a preconceived, unified design of the whole composition. Chekhov several times spoke of the necessity of a preconceived design in any literary composition. In a letter to Souvorin, for example, he said, "In doing a story, one first of all, even involuntarily, gets busy on its framework."[1] When Souvorin and Chekhov decided to collaborate on a play the plot was to be Chekhov's special task.

What I am concerned with in this chapter is the "well-made" plot, or rather with the progenitor of the "well-made" plot, the classical intrigue of Roman comedy. While the plot of a Terentian comedy is relatively simple by comparison with the more complicated actions

---

[1] *The Life and Letters of Anton Tchekhov*, translated and edited by Koteliansky and Tomlinson (New York, 1925), p. 127.

of longer Elizabethan and contemporary comedies, the history of comic plot in sixteenth-century dramatic criticism is far from simple, complicated as it is by the various authorities, ancient and modern, that helped to build up what neoclassical critics called *Fable*.

TERMINOLOGY

Terminology offers a major preliminary problem. *Fable*, which came to be the favorite neoclassical term for plot in comedy, tragedy, and epic poem, was not the common term for plot at the beginning of the sixteenth century. When Donatus was still the principal authority on the drama, *fabula* meant either a play or a mythical tale (e.g., a "fable" of Aesop). Donatus, in *De Comoedia*, remarked: "*Fabula* is the general name; its two principal divisions, tragedy and comedy." In a comment on the Prologue to the *Brothers* (7), where Terence speaks of a play by Plautus as *fabula*, Donatus said, "As among the Greeks *drama*, so among the Latins it is generally called *fabula*; its species are tragedy, comedy, *togata, tabernaria, praetextata, crepidata, Atellana, mimus, Rinthonica*." *Fabula* had long been identified with the Greek *myth* (μῦθος), but it was not until Aristotle's use of the term in the *Poetics* became familiar that *fabula* came to mean plot.

That *fabula* usually meant a mythical tale may be seen in a popular anthology of the early sixteenth century, the *Polyanthea*, edited by Dominicus Nanus Mirabellius. The 1507 edition of the *Polyanthea* defines the term as the Latin equivalent of the Greek μῦθος: "A fable is matter indeed that is feigned for the utility or delight of men, as are the fables of the poets and the fables of Aesop." The ancient authorities here include St. Paul, Augustine, Seneca, and Aristotle of the *Metaphysics*,[2] not of the *Poetics*. Terence, although he used *fabula* to mean a comedy, also used it in the more general sense of a feigned tale. In the *Andrian* 4.4.747, Davus, upon seeing a baby on the doorstep and Mysis standing by, exclaims, "How now, what old wives' tale (*fabula*) is this?" In the same play (5.4.925), when Crito from Andros begins his story of the girl Glycerium, Simo sneeringly remarks, "Now he begins a yarn (*fabula*)." In his comment on this line, Donatus explained that *fabula* may mean either a comedy or a mocking tale such as the story of the country mouse and the town mouse in Horace.[3]

---

[2]*Metaphysics* 1.2.982ᵇ18-19: "The lover of myth is in a sense a lover of wisdom, for the myth is composed of wonders."

[3]*Sermones* 2.6.79 ff.

The classification of the three types of *narratio* in the *Ad Herennium* is typical of the rhetorical view at the beginning of the sixteenth century:

Fabula is that which contains neither true nor verisimilar deeds, like those deeds that are written in tragedies.

Historia is performed deed, but far off in memory from our own time.

Argumentum is feigned deed which nevertheless could happen, like the arguments of comedies.[4]

This conception of tragedy is not in agreement with the common Renaissance notion that tragedy should be based upon legendary matter, but the identification of *argumentum* with comedy is conventional.

ARGUMENTUM

Argumentum, the sum and substance of a discourse, was applied to rhetorical proofs and themes and to poems as well, especially to dramatic poems, particularly to comedies. As Quintilian (5.10.9) said, "But argument also has more meanings; for plays that are composed for acting on the stage are called arguments." Servius applied the term specifically to comedy:

The matter consists of feigned deeds which are called argument: for the actual deed (*res gesta*) has no place in comedy. . . . Argument is a feigned deed which could happen, fable containing matter neither true nor verisimilar; history is actual deed. Therefore the name of this matter is argument; the name of the writing comedy.[5]

In dramatic criticism, then, argument meant plot in the sense of gist of the story. Terence so used it in his Prologue to the *Andrian* (9-12):

Menander wrote the *Lady of Andros* and the *Lady of Perinthus*. Know one and you know the other. They are not very different in plot (*argumentum*), but they are different in sentiment (*oratio*) and style (*stilus*).

Donatus commented on this passage: "They say that *oratio* is in the sentiments, *stylus* in the words, *argumentum* in the matter." Richard Bernard, in his *Terence in English* (1598), translated *argumentum* here as "subject-matter." Evanthius used argument in the sense of plot; in praising the New Comedy of Menander and Terence he called attention to its "well-made (*concinnum*) argument."

By the beginning of the sixteenth century *argumentum* was well established in the sense that Terence and Donatus used it; that is, it

---

[4]*Ad Herennium* 1.8.13. Cf. Trapezuntius, *op. cit.*, p. 10r.
[5]Servius, *op. cit.*, Part II, p. 7.

usually meant the sum and substance of the play, the whole action reduced to a brief statement. Thus Benedictus Philologus defined it: "The argument is the statement of the whole play about to be performed, which is feigned but nevertheless could happen."[6] *Argumentum* was apparently synonymous with *periocha* (summary of the play). In Stephanus Riccius' edition of Terence, *periocha* is defined as follows: "It is the compass, the brief statement, or argument of the play, *der Inhalt der Fabel.*"[7] *Argumentum* in the drama meant about the same thing that Aristotle in the *Poetics* (17.55^{b}16-23) meant by *logos*:

The argument (λόγος) of the *Odyssey* is not a long one. A certain man has been abroad many years; Poseidon is ever on the watch for him, and he is all alone. Matters at home too have come to this, that his substance is being wasted and his son's death plotted by suitors to his wife. Then he arrives there himself after his grievous sufferings; reveals himself, and falls on his enemies; and the end is his salvation and their death. This being all that is proper to the *Odyssey*, everything else in it is episode.

Curiously enough, however, it was not until Victorius' edition (1560) of the *Poetics* that Aristotle's *logos* here was translated as *argumentum;* Giorgio Valla (1498) used *oratio,* Paccius (1537) *sermo.*

Aristotle used several terms for plot since plot had several meanings, such as story, action, form, structure. The usual term for plot in the *Poetics* is μῦθος, which was naturally translated into Latin as *fabula*[8] by Valla, Paccius, and Victorius. Occasionally, when he wished to express the idea of brief outline of action, Aristotle used *logos,* which Victorius, for one, translated as *argumentum.* When he wished to express the broader meaning of plot as the arrangement of the whole action in orderly fashion, Aristotle used the phrase "combination of the incidents":

Now the action (that which was done) is represented in the play by the Fable or Plot. The Fable, in our present sense of the term, is simply this, the combination of the incidents (σύνθεσις τῶν πραγμάτων), or things done in the story.[9]

---

[6]*Terentius in sua metra restitutus,* p. a [v] v.

[7]*Op cit.* 2.B4v.

[8]Benedictus Philologus, who wrote a preface to an early edition of Seneca's tragedies, spoke of the six parts of tragedy, according to Aristotle, as *Fabula, Mos, Dictio, Sententia, Visus,* and *Melopoeia.* But, so far as I can discover, Benedictus never spoke of plot in Terence as *fabula.* See *Senecae Tragoediae* (Florence, 1513), p. aiiiiv. This edition first appeared in 1505, but I have not seen so early a copy.

[9]*Poetics* 6.50^{a}3-5. A similar phrase, σύστασις τῶν πραγμάτων, seems to mean about the same thing.

This "combination of the incidents," from the time of Giorgio Valla and Paccius, was translated as *rerum compositio* or *rerum constitutio*. After the *Poetics* became more familiar to students of the drama, *fabula* began to be used for plot in general and its meaning of play or comedy dropped out. In time *argumentum* also came to be identified with μῦθος or *fabula*. The commentators on the *Poetics*, and the commentators on Horace and Terence as well, contributed to the establishment of Fable as the common term for plot, and more often than not it meant the arrangement of the incidents, the form, the structure of tragedy, comedy, or epic poem.

To Robortellus (p. 96), plot meant the arrangement of action: "I call the action itself the plot (*fabula*), or the arrangement of the incidents (*constitutio rerum*)." In a later passage of his commentary (p. 164) he said, "Tragic plot indeed is no other than the arrangement of action." The same thing, to be sure, could be said of comedy. Georgius Fabricius, whose castigations on Terence first appeared in 1548, identified *argumentum* with μῦθος. In a comment on the Prologue to the *Andrian* (11-12), where Terence speaks of his borrowing from two plays of Menander, Fabricius said, "That is, they had a common plot (*hoc est, habuisse* τὸν μῦθον *communem*)." Lambinus, one of the most influential sixteenth-century commentators on Horace, also identified *argumentum* with μῦθος; in his note on the first line of the *Ars Poetica*, where Horace begins his discussion of poetic unity, he remarked: "This admonition pertains to the argument of the work, what Aristotle calls μῦθος ."

Victorius, who translated Aristotle's poetic *logos* as *argumentum*, usually used *fabula* for plot. In his commentary on the *Poetics* (p. 189) he thus defined plot: "Plot is properly the very joining together of the incidents which are then acted, without the episodes." Victorius (p. 136), in fact, offered a good explanation of the difference between Aristotle's and Terence's use of *fabula*:

Moreover, Aristotle signifies another meaning than that made plain by Terence, because our master speaks of plots (μύθοι) as that part of tragedy which is properly called by this term, that is, the joining together of the incidents. The Latin comic poet in truth understands by that word [*fabula*] a comedy.

While Victorius' explanation did not mark the end of the confusion of terms for plot, it must have aided in clarifying the terminology. Minturno adopted *fabula* for plot. Scaliger called attention to Aristotle's use of *fabula* and of σύστασις, both words meaning the sum of tragic incidents. More often than not Scaliger used *fabula* to mean a

play. Gradually, however, the terminology settled down to a general
acceptance of Fable as the first qualitative division of a play or of a
story. Chytraeus, in his thirteenth proposition on comedy, said,
"μῦθος, or *fabula* . . . or the well-managed comic argument itself."
Daniel Heinsius, the great Dutch scholar, who directly influenced
Ben Jonson's theory of drama, offered a very clear statement on plot,
and his statement may be taken as representative of the best neoclassical usage at the beginning of the seventeenth century. In his essay
on Horace, Plautus, and Terence, Heinsius said:

Μῦθος indeed, as generally everywhere in Aristotle, is not the drama
but the action from which the drama is constituted, "the action, the combination of the incidents." Thus he explains when he says, "The unity of
a plot does not consist, as some suppose, in its having one man as its
subject." And he himself calls those diverse events that are brought together as going on simultaneously, and not as one and the same event,
"polyplots" (πολυμύθοι). Therefore to select a plot (*fabula*), and to
arrange this chosen plot right and in order is the first merit, and so the
first and most important task.[10]

Heinsius also identified *argumentum* with μῦθος. In the same essay,
he said:

The principal part of tragedy is the *argumentum*. Aristotle is wont to call
it sometimes μῦθος and sometimes the "combination of the incidents";
and he frequently demonstrates that he who excels in this part, even if he
fails in others, can be called a dramatic poet.

Dryden's *Essay of Dramatic Poesy* (1668) offers further evidence
of the final settlement of this terminology:

Next for the plot, which Aristotle called ὁ μῦθος, and often τῶν πραγμάτων
σύνθεσις, and from him the Romans *fabula*.[11]

DISPOSITIO

By the end of the sixteenth century, *argumentum* of the grammarians had been identified with the Aristotelian *fabula*, and plot
was taken to mean the sum and substance of the action or the combination of the incidents. But there were several other terms inherited
from the rhetoricians that played a part in the development of the
neoclassical theory of dramatic plot. These rhetorical terms, which
were familiar to commentators on Terence long before the rediscovery of Aristotle's *Poetics*, were *dispositio*, *ordo*, and *oeconomia*, all

---

[10] *Ad Horatii de Plauto et Terentio judicium, dissertatio.*
[11] *Essays* 1.46.

three nearly synonymous, all meaning essentially the orderly disposal of the various parts of a discourse, all applicable to a dramatic poem as well as to an oration. Since *dispositio* was perhaps the most familiar, I shall discuss it first.

Fundamentally, disposition was a qualitative part of logic that was borrowed by the rhetoricians. Abraham Fraunce expressed a common sixteenth-century view in the second book of his *Lawyer's Logic* (1588):

What precepts soever the common rhetoricians put down for ordering exordiums and framing and disposing of the whole course of their speech fitly, and according to cause, auditors, time, place, and such like circumstances; all those, I say, are altogether logical, not in any respect pertaining to rhetoric, but as a rhetor may be directed by logical precepts of judgment and disposition.[12]

"Disposition," according to Cicero in the *De Inventione* (1.7), "is the orderly distribution of the invented materials." In the *De Oratore* (2.76.307 ff.), Cicero emphasized the importance of disposition, which demands the highest professional skill; for many arguments occur to the speaker, but he must be able to choose between the important and the unimportant ones and then arrange his selected arguments in the order best calculated to move, delight, and persuade his audience. The arguments best calculated to win the audience should come first, provided the strongest appeal is reserved for the end. Matter of moderate appeal and importance belongs in the middle of the discourse.[13] In the *Partitiones Oratoriae* (4.12), the two Ciceros, senior and junior, discuss disposition. The father has just explained that the arrangement of a particular speech must be adjusted to the specific purpose at hand:

C.JUN. How so pray?

C.SEN. Because in speeches the purpose of which is to give pleasure there are various methods of arrangements. For we either keep to chronological order or to arrangement in classes; or we ascend from smaller matters to larger, or glide down from larger ones to smaller; or we group these with complete irregularity, intertwining small matters with great ones, simple with complicated, obscure with clear, cheerful with gloomy, incredible with probable—all of these methods falling under the head of embellishment.

Such methods are applicable not only to orations but to many types of discourse, including the drama. A little later I shall discuss the chronological order of nature and the inverted order of art.

[12]*Lawiers Logike* (1588), p. 115r.
[13]Cf. *Ad Herennium* 3.10.18; Farnaby, *Index Rhetoricus*, p. 17.

In the Preface to his seventh book, Quintilian defined the general purpose of disposition. (Butler has translated *dispositio* here as "arrangement.")

I think that enough has been said on the subject of invention. For I have dealt not merely with the methods by which we may instruct the judge, but also with the means of appealing to his emotions. But just as it is not sufficient for those who are erecting a building merely to collect stone and timber and other building materials, but skilled masons are required to arrange and place them, so in speaking, however abundant the matter may be, it will merely form a confused heap unless arrangement (*dispositio*) be employed to reduce it to order and to give it connection and firmness of structure. Nor is it without good reason that arrangement is treated as the second of the five departments of oratory, since without it the first is useless. For the fact that all the limbs of a statue have been cast does not make it a statue; they must be put together; and if you were to interchange some one portion of our bodies or of those of other animals with another, although the body would be in possession of all the same members as before, you would none the less have produced a monster. Again even a slight dislocation will deprive a limb of its previous use and vigor, and disorder in the ranks will impede the movement of an army. Nor can I regard as an error the assertion that order is essential to the existence of nature itself, for without order everything would go to wrack and ruin. Similarly if oratory lack this virtue, it cannot fail to be confused, but will be like a ship drifting without a helmsman, will lack cohesion, will fall into countless repetitions and omissions, and, like a traveler who has lost his way in unfamiliar country, will be guided solely by chance without fixed purpose or the least idea either of starting-point or goal.

Quintilian's highly figurative explanation, which squares with what both Horace and Aristotle had to say about the arrangement of a poem, was well known; even during the Middle Ages, when invention and disposition were overshadowed by declamation and the colors of rhetoric, his figures of unified composition remained alive. Geoffrey of Vinsauf, for example, in his thirteenth-century *Poetria Nova*, called attention to the importance of carefully planned, architectural arrangement in a poem.[14] Chaucer restated this important principle, and also practiced it, in his *Troilus* (1.1065-69):

> For every wight that hath an hous to founde
> Ne renneth nought the werk for to beginne
> With rakel hond, but he wol byde a stounde,
> And sende his hertes lyne out fro with-inne
> Alderfirst his purpos for to winne.

---

[14]See Atkins, *English Literary Criticism: the Medieval Phase*, p. 99.

This architectural figure was popular with critics for centuries. Fenelon, in his *Letter to the French Academy* (1714), used it when he wished to illustrate the unity of a true oration. Fenelon's argument was based primarily upon the advice of Horace in the *Ars Poetica*, but there are doubtless echoes here of Quintilian, Plato, and Aristotle as well:

He who perceives not the beauty and force of this unity and order has never seen any thing in its full light. He has only seen shadows in Plato's cavern. What should we say of an architect who could see no difference between a stately palace, whose apartments are adjusted with the exactest proportion so as to make one uniform structure, and a confused heap of little buildings which do not compose one regular plan, tho' they be all placed together? What comparison is there betwixt the Colisaeum and a confused multitude of irregular houses in a city? There can be no true unity in any composure unless there be nothing taken from it without spoiling it. It never has a right order but when we cannot displace any part without weakening, obscuring, and disordering the whole.[15]

Quintilian's conception of organic unity in a speech doubtless reflects similar conceptions in Plato's *Phaedrus* (264C) and in Aristotle's *Rhetoric* and *Poetics*. Certainly it fitted very well Aristotle's dicta on the unified structure of a speech and on the unified plot of a poem. Trapezuntius echoed this classical demand for organic unity in a speech. He compared successful *dispositio* with the harmony of a well ordered human body:

Likewise, though the parts of the human body may be robust, nevertheless if they are hindered by diverse efforts, or if one hand works while the other rests, they accomplish little; and if all the limbs work together in one and the same effort, even though they be weaker, they attain whatever is attempted without much difficulty. It is so with all the parts of a speech; if they are not neglected in the beginning and if they are brought together in a final agreement, the speech will have great force."[16]

Trapezuntius was probably following Quintilian (7.10.16), who said:

And disposition of the parts is not enough, but each several part has its own internal economy, according to which one thought will come first, another second, another third, while we must struggle not merely to place these thoughts in their proper order, but to link them together and give them such cohesion that there will be no trace of any suture; they must form a body, not a congeries of limbs.

---

[15]*Op. cit.*, pp. 234-35. Fenelon then quoted the passage on *lucidus ordo* in the *Ars Poetica* 40-44.

[16]*Rhetoric*, p. 112v.

Gregorius Wagnerus (1550), in his discussion of the dispostion of a Terentian comedy, used both figures of organic unity, namely the figure of the human body and the figure of the well-planned house. Part of his advice to his nephew is worth quoting:

An architect, when he erects a building, would be ridiculous if he put together stones, timbers, cement, and other things necessary for the construction, without making use of art in ordering and arranging these materials. So an orator or a writer would be judged no expert, even though he had goodly words, grave sentiments, and strong arguments impromptu, if he did not dispose every part in its place and the whole course of the discourse "in an orderly fashion (εὐκόσμως)." I assure you, and I am surer than sure, that the whole body of the discourse, however excellent, will lose your reputation and be made "to no purpose" if the commendation of *dispositio* is not added.[17]

Dispositio, as I mentioned above, was about the same thing as *ordo* and *oeconomia*. Sturm commonly used the Ciceronian term *collocatio* for disposition, though he was perfectly familiar with *dispositio*, *ordo*, *oeconomia*, and other terms to boot. In his dialogues on the *Partitiones Oratoriae* of Cicero, he defined *collocatio* as follows:

B. What do the Greeks call *collocatio*?

S. τάξις (arrangement). And Hermogenes writes about the *collocatio* of epicheiremata.[18] But *collocatio* is the artificial order (*ordo*) of invented matter and an apt and well-made *dispositio*. . . . Certain Greeks, moreover, have not improperly given the name of οἰκονομία (*oeconomia*) to *dispositio*.[19]

Sturm, in distinguishing between two kinds of order, the natural and the artificial, was merely restating a commonplace that goes back to classical rhetoric. The orator may use his own judgment, said Sturm, in altering the natural (e.g., the chronological) order, if by so doing he can better move his audience. Specifically, the orator is not strictly tied to the normal sequence of parts in a speech, namely, exordium, *narratio*, proof, disproof, peroration. An inverted order is often very effective in exciting the emotions.[20]

For the sixteenth century the main sources of theory on natural and artificial order, or disposition, lay in Cicero, Quintilian, and Horace, and popular illustrations of the artificial order were the *Aeneid* of Virgil and the *Odyssey* of Homer. In the *Ars Poetica*, Horace recommended a "lucid order" and particularly the order practiced

[17] Willichius' edition of Terence, pp. 4-5.
[18] Epicheiremata are similar to syllogisms. See Quintilian 5.14.14.
[19] *In paritiones oratorias Ciceronis dialogi duo*, p. 75.
[20] Ibid., pp. 78-79. Cf. Cicero *Partitiones Oratoriae* 4.12; *Ad Herennium* 3.9.

by Homer. The good poet, like Homer, does not begin a tale of the Trojan war *ab ovo* (i.e., with the birth of Helen) but hastens into the midst of the story; in other words, the good poet does not tell his story in simple, chronological order: he begins as it were in the middle and then cuts back; he employs the order of art rather than the order of nature. This artificial order was specially prominent in poetry and was called the poetical order to distinguish it from the historical and from the normal logical and oratorical order. Since I have elsewhere given a fairly detailed account of the sixteenth-century notion of poetical order,[21] I shall illustrate here with a single quotation from an early and famous commentator on Horace. Landinus, in his comment on the *Ars Poetica* 42, said:

In linking incidents together a duplex order is used, either the natural or the artificial. The natural is when whatever comes first is placed first in the disposition. For the most part this is to be seen in an oration, because when the audience or the judges are more unlearned or, being much occupied, slower in understanding the matter, every thing ought to be clear in the narrating. The artificial order is when, contrary to the usual reckoning of time, we very often begin at the end and then return to earlier events. For the most part, therefore, we see the natural order in the oration. The artificial order belongs chiefly to the poets; for we approach poets as more learned or more leisurely readers, and if something is not intelligible upon one reading we may repeat this same passage many times. Wherefore the poets make use of the artificial order, as we may see in Virgil.

In Cicero's *De Oratore* (2.76.307-09) two methods of arranging the divisions of a speech are mentioned: first is the natural order of exordium, *narratio*, proof, disproof, and conclusion; second is a re-arragement of this natural order at the discretion of the speaker. Quintilian (7.10.10-15) also admitted that no fixed procedure in arrangement of a speech can be established, that the speaker himself must be the judge of what comes first and what comes next:

For the most effective, and what is justly styled the economical *dispositio* of a case as a whole, is that which cannot be determined except when we have the specific facts before us. It consists in the power to determine when the exordium is necessary and when it should be omitted; when we should make our statement of facts continuous, and when we should sub-divide it; when we should begin at the very beginning, when, like Homer, start at the middle or the end; when we should omit the statement of facts altogether; when we should begin by dealing with the arguments advanced by our opponents, and when with our own; when we should place the strongest proofs first and when the weakest; in what cases we

---

[21]See Herrick, *op. cit.*, pp. 16-20.

should prefix questions to the exordium, and what preparation is necessary to pave the way for these questions; what arguments the judge will accept at once, and to what he requires to be led by degrees; whether we should refute our opponent's arguments as a whole or in detail; whether we should reserve emotional appeals for the peroration or distribute them throughout the whole speech; whether we should speak first of law or of equity; whether we should first advance (or refute) charges as to past offences or the charges connected with the actual trial; or, again, if the case is complicated, what order we should adopt, what evidence or documents of any kind should be read out in the course of our speech, and what reserved for a later stage. This gift of arrangement is to oratory what generalship is to war. The skilled commander will know how to distribute his forces for battle, what troops he should keep back to garrison forts or guard cities, to secure supplies, or guard communications, and what dispositions to make by land and by sea.

Renaissance commentators and critics drew upon Cicero and Quintilian as well as upon Horace for their conception of natural and artificial order. For that matter, the art of logic also offered illustrations of this duplex order. Alexander Richardson, for example, who closely followed his master Ramus, discussed the use of the "cryptical" method or the inverted order of discourse:

Ramus hath showed us what method is, and that it is but one. . . . If a man be to deliver an art, he must exactly observe this method in every point: but many times it falls out in discourses that disorder must be used, not for the doctrine's sake, but because of the perversity of the hearers, for they often go out of their way by reason of their weakness; now this way is especially when we reject homogenies, as orators use much to do, and draw in heterogenies, knowing that variety doth delight. . . .

This *crypsis* is more often in poets than in orators, or history, though it be used much in history: now "he offers it in order to teach the people, i.e., cattle fodder for the many," but indeed he deceives them, yet it is only for delight. This order is very usual in poetry, and very pleasant in a tale, or fables, because when we read them we cannot rest quiet till we come to an end of them. "So (as Horace says) Homer disposes the *Iliad: nec gemino bellum Trojanum orditur ab ovo, etc.*" He doth not begin the Trojan war from two eggs, in one of which eggs Helena was, and Castor and Pollux in another: *Semper ad eventum festinat, etc.* For in the first book of his *Iliads* one would think that he brought in the history of ten years, but indeed thereby he takes occasion to bring in the history of the years before. So Virgil fetcheth Aeneas from Sicily, which is a little from Carthage, *etc.* "So the comic poets, *etc.*"[22]

The quotation from Ramus that Richardson cut short runs as follows: "So the comic poets, albeit they divide comedies into acts and

---

[22]Richardson, *op. cit.*, pp. 348-49.

scenes with great judgment, nevertheless make it appear that everything happens by chance."[23]

Ramus' discussion of the natural order and the irregular "cryptical" order in a discourse is similar to an earlier discussion in Rodolphus Agricola's book on dialectical invention. Agricola was well known to the Terentian commentators of the sixteenth century, who often incorporated his ideas in their remarks on comedy. In the *Andrian,* Terence unfolds the story of the girl Glycerium in the inverted, artificial order. The audience first learns about Glycerium's love affair with Pamphilus. During the action of the play she bears a child. In the last act, Crito from Andros gives an account of her birth and childhood. By the end of the play the audience knows the whole story of Glycerium from birth through shipwreck to marriage, but has received this story piecemeal and in inverted order. Barlandus (on the *Andrian* 5.4.923) commented:

Rodolphus Agricola, in the third book of *De Inuentione Dialectica,* chapter 7, writes on the difference between the poetical order and history. It is, he says, like that in comedy and tragedy. If we consider the face of the matter, what is carried out in action, which is portrayed by means of imitation of people, the order seems natural. As regards the whole compass of the play (*fabula*), since writers very often begin with what is near the end, and what goes before is explained at a convenient time by speeches of the characters, and what comes first is sometimes joined with what comes last, thus in the *Andria* of Terence the shipwreck of Phania is disclosed at the same time the marriage of Pamphilus and Glycerium is prepared. Any one who observes this will readily understand that this order is established by means of the author's art, not by the nature of the events.[24]

Long familiarity with the use of inverted order in the plots of comedies and tragedies prepared Renaissance critics for the ready acceptance of Aristotle's recommendation of the complex plot, which I shall discuss very shortly.

OECONOMIA

The Terentian commentators, Donatus included, did not favor the term *ordo* though they were familiar with the conception of natural and artificial order. Willichius, for one, had discussed poetical order in his commentary[25] on the *Ars Poetica* of Horace, and he often analyzed narrative passages in Terence in terms of natural and artificial

---

[23]*Dialecticae* 2.20.

[24]Cf. Agricola *De Inuentione Dialectica* (Strassburg, 1521), p. 122r.

[25]See *Commentaria in artem poeticam Horatii* (Strassburg, 1539), pp. 52-54. Willichius, like Barlandus, was indebted to Agricola.

order. The commentators, however, preferred the third rhetorical term, *oeconomia*, which they used to express the orderly, unified disposition of scenes in a comedy. They had good classical authority in Quintilian (1.8.9), who used the term to express "structure":

They [the older dramatists] are, too, more careful about *oeconomia* than the majority of moderns, who regard *sententiae* as the sole merit of every kind of literary work.

Quintilian (3.3.9) explained that *oeconomia* is a "Greek word meaning the management of domestic affairs which is applied metaphorically to oratory and has no Latin equivalent."

In connection with the *oeconomia* in Terentian comedy, the commentators paid special attention to παρασκευή, meaning preparation, specifically the artful linking of scenes together, what Corneille later called *la liaison des scènes*. Donatus and his followers, in fact, were apt to restrict the use of *ordo* to short passages. In the *Mother-in-law* 3.1.291, for example, Parmeno gives Pamphilus some good advice: "You will learn the facts, free them from anger, and restore them to kindliness." Donatus remarked, "A three-fold sentiment and well ordered (*bono ordine*)."

In the *Brothers* 3.3.408-09, Syrus hoodwinks and mocks the rustic Demea with a cock-and-bull story about his favorite son, Ctesipho, who is actually a rather sly but timid fellow. Syrus tells Demea that Ctesipho tried to stop Aeschinus from buying the slave girl. (Actually Aeschinus stole the girl for Ctesipho.) According to Syrus, Ctesipho protested, "O Aeschinus, you are doing such wicked things! You to bring such shame to our family!" Demea is delighted that his pet Ctesipho has behaved so righteously; Demea is completely taken in by the account, for everything fits so well together. Donatus was moved to admiration by the skillful ordering of Syrus' false argument: "Wherewith, by the wonderful art of the poet, beginning, middle, and end come together and fit."

Ordo, then, usually meant the arrangement of a particular speech. *Oeconomia*, on the other hand, was larger than individual speeches, larger than the *argumentum* of the play. Latomus, who concentrated upon dramatic structure in his commentary, was perhaps most fond of the term *oeconomia*. Apparently he thought of it as the combination of incidents, as the skillful manipulation of all the parts of a play.

For example, in the *Andrian* 1.4.228 ff., Terence introduces Mysis, a maidservant attending Glycerium. Mysis enters talking to herself and incidentally explaining to the audience that she has been sent to fetch a midwife for Glycerium. In the midst of her monologue she runs into Pamphilus, the lover of Glycerium, and later informs him of the impending event. Mysis has some connection with the main action, to be sure, but her speech here is somewhat of a digression. If she were in an Elizabethan comedy, some critic would be pretty sure to call her a "humorous" character, inserted to add atmosphere. Latomus clearly recognized that Mysis is not in the main track of the plot but that she does contribute something to the whole play:

This scene serves the *oeconomia*, i.e., the management of events, rather than the argument of the play. For the maidservant is introduced so that she may presently meet Pamphilus and so that the midwife may be summoned to Glycerium, who is in labor.

In other words, *oeconomia* is very like Aristotle's "synthesis of the incidents"; it is plot in the larger meaning of the term. And, as I mentioned above, *oeconomia* was often used in connection with the device of *paraskeue*, i.e., preparation.

A fine example of *paraskeue*, according to Donatus, is to be found in the *Brothers* 2.3.263, an incident that precedes the passage in the third act that I cited above. Here, in the second act, Ctesipho, the timid, rustic young man, praises the generous behavior of Aeschinus, who has stolen a music-girl for him and agreed to shoulder all the scandal this action will doubtless bring on the family. This scene is a preparation, of course, for the scene in the next act wherein Syrus hoodwinks Demea and makes out that Ctesipho is a good boy, that Aeschinus is a rascal. "An excellent *paraskeue*," remarked Donatus, "by means of which Sostrata [the future mother-in-law of Aeschinus] will be mistaken about Aeschinus and likewise Demea will err because he believes that the strumpet is loved by Aeschinus." The clever lying of Syrus in Act 3, when he further complicates the troubles involving the family, would hardly be possible, certainly not so effective, without this preceding scene in Act 2.

Another good example of comic *paraskeue* may be found in the *Eunuch* 2.3.298. Parmeno, the faithful slave, has been scheming to save his young master Phaedria from the toils of the courtesan Thais. Now he sees Chaerea, Phaedria's younger brother, in hot pursuit of a girl. Parmeno knows the family well. He has had trouble enough with Phaedria, but he knows that Phaedria's infatuation for Thais is nothing compared with the extravagances to be expected from the madcap Chaerea. Parmeno already feels sorry for the father of the two young men: "Oh, the unlucky old father!" This exclamation is prophetic; the old man is in for a very rough time before all the troubles brought on the family by Phaedria and Chaerea are cleared up. As Donatus justly observed, "In this saying he has prepared for the end of the play, the *catastrophe*."

Latomus, following a suggestion in Donatus, called attention to a good example of *oeconomia* in the *Eunuch* 3.1.439. Here Gnatho, the parasite, proposes a scheme whereby Thraso, the soldier, may be able to undermine Thais' interest in his rival Phaedria. Gnatho counsels that every time Thais mentions Phaedria the man of war should counter with praise of the slave girl Pamphila. Thraso accepts this advice and acts accordingly. Thus the audience is prepared for the coming quarrel between Thais and Thraso. As Latomus said, "This counsel of Gnatho concerns the *oeconomia* of future strife between the soldier and Thais, and will be the occasion of the Epitasis of this part [the main action] of the play."

Later in the same act (*Eunuch* 3.2.501), Thais, upon leaving her house, orders one of her maids to watch for young Chremes and, if he calls, to hold him in the house or have him call again. Chremes is a key figure in the plot, for he is the only person who can discover the true identity of Pamphila. Donatus, and Latomus after him, seized upon this incident as an important illustration of *oeconomia* and *para-skeue*. Donatus said, "*oeconomia* for future strife and for the outcome of the play"; Latomus, "*oeconomia* and preparation for the following scene."

Any device for connecting scenes, anything that contributes to further turmoil or misunderstanding, anything that later contributes to the final resolution, any movement, any speech that prepares the audience for future movements and speeches and so fits into the overall pattern of action represents the poet's use of *oeconomia*. Sometimes the unifying device consists of a character who serves as a link between the actions of other characters. Such a character is Parmeno in the *Mother-in-law*. Parmeno is kept busy from the first act to the last, scurrying to and fro, carrying messages, summoning people; he knows everybody and brings them all together. Donatus (on the *Mother-in-law* 5.3.809) remarked how wonderfully the whole play is contrived with Parmeno on the run. Latomus (*ibid.*) said that Parmeno the messenger is part of the *oeconomia* of the play. Davus in the *Andrian* and Syrus in the *Brothers* are better schemers and actually contribute more to the plot than does Parmeno in the *Mother-in-law*. Ben Jonson's Brainworm in *Every Man In His Humor* is a classic example in the modern drama of the clever servant who acts as the connecting link between all the groups of characters, and Brainworm outschemes the best efforts of Davus and Syrus.

Terence was considered a master of dramatic structure as well as a master of sentiment and style. Donatus, Latomus, and Willichius repeatedly praised his mastery of *oeconomia*. As Willichius (on the *Andrian* 3.4.605) said, "The poet is always mindful to connect the scenes of his act by some preparation." Apparently Willichius regarded *paraskeue* as a special device of the comic poets. In the *Brothers* 4.4.635, there is an obvious use of preparation. Aeschinus hears someone coming out of the house. He says, "Someone is coming out? I'll stand aside." Then Micio comes on and an important scene ensues. Willichius said of Aeschinus' speech: "Fashioned and used by comic poets, it specially forms a connecting link with the next scene." In the *Mother-in-law* 4.3.620-22, old Laches, who has finally come to realize that the meddling of old folks has not mended his son's unhappy marriage, admits, "We, Pamphilus, belong only in the play, 'Old Man and Old Woman.' But here comes Phidippus in the nick of time. Let us meet him." Willichius observed: "Finally, in the comic manner, he connects the next scene with this one by means of *paraskeue*."

Of course there is *oeconomia* in tragedy, which also employs the *liaison* of scenes. Evidently the critical recognition of this technique, however, first appeared in the study of comedy, in Donatus' study of Terence; and here we have a good illustration of the art of comedy contributing something to dramatic art in general. When the Aristotelian theory of tragic plot became familiar it was easily harmonized with the rhetorical *dispositio* and *oeconomia* that the Terentian commentators favored. Robortellus (p. 82), for example, in calling attention to Aristotle's praise of Homer, said, "He praises Homer, who best taught *oeconomia*, that is, the disposition and order of his poem." Robortellus (p. 144) used the term *oeconomia* in discussing the structure of tragedy:

In tragedies a careful *oeconomia* or *dispositio* is necessary, in prologue, episodes, and exode; for these parts ought not to be spoken by characters who are often absent from the action but by those who are closely connected with the action, or who immediately precede or follow the event, so that the whole action is consistent and has nothing contradictory or only slightly consonant.

Ordo, however, was not used by Robortellus as synonymous with *dispositio* and *oeconomia*. *Ordo*, according to Robortellus in his essay *On Comedy*, is a quality of plot; order together with magnitude characterize the good plot:

The Plot ought to have magnitude and order. Magnitude distinguishes it from extemporaneous poems and from short ones. Order makes all the parts fit together; on the one hand, it should not be ended just anywhere, as though thoughtlessly, nor should it begin just anywhere. There is a very definite rule for fixing the limits of magnitude in any plot, namely, that in managing the single action it extend just so far as is meet, that is, so long as it seems to be pleasing, and as I shall briefly describe. The right magnitude of a comic plot is whatever is necessary to make plain the change and interchange of disturbances and quarrels. All the parts of the plot, indeed, ought to be so joined together that no part can be taken away or transplanted without ruining or disjoining the whole plot.[26]

Aristotle's Plot or Fable, in the sense of "combination of the incidents," largely displaced *dispositio* and *oceonomia* in the vocabulary of dramatic criticism. Nevertheless, as I have indicated in an earlier chapter,[27] *dispositio* continued to be used in the seventeenth century. *Oeconomia* also continued in use long after the sixteenth century. Ben Jonson, who did not subscribe to the sixteenth-century praise of Terentian structure, wrote in his *Discoveries*:

In the Greek poets, as also in Plautus, we shall see the oeconomy and disposition of poems better observed than in Terence and the later, who thought the sole grace and virture of their Fable the sticking in of sentences, as ours do the forcing in of jests.[28]

Milton in the Preface to *Samson Agonistes*, wrote of his own tragedy:

Of the style and uniformity, and that commonly called the plot, whether intricate or explicit, which is nothing indeed but such oeconomy or disposition of the fable as may stand best with verisimilitude and decorum, they only will best judge who are not unacquainted with Aeschylus, Sophocles, and Euripides, the three tragic poets unequaled yet by any, and the best rule to all who endeavor to write tragedy.

DRAMATIC STRUCTURE

The rhetorical divisions of *dispositio* are *exordium, narratio, proof,* and *conclusion*. As I have shown in the first chapter, this rhetorical analysis was used by the commentators on Terence. There was another scheme, however, inherited from Donatus, that went hand in hand with these conventional rhetorical divisions and that was the division into *prologue, protasis, epitasis,* and *catastrophe*. Fundamentally, this division of comedy was threefold,[29] for the prologue in both Plautus and Terence is not an integral part of the plot. The *protasis* is the statement of the argument, the exposition, and the beginning of the action; the *epitasis* is the complication of incidents; the

---

[26]See p. 232.   [27]See p. 34.   [28]*Op. cit.*, p. 70. Cf. Quintilian 1.8.9.

[29]Aristotle, in the *Rhetoric* (3.13.4), said that there are only two necessary parts of a speech: namely, the statement of the case ($\pi\rho\delta\theta\epsilon\sigma\iota\varsigma$) and the proof. At most there are four parts: exordium, statement, proof, epilogue.

catastrophe is the final resolution. Donatus, in his preface to the *Andrian* said: "The protasis is brisk, the epitasis stormy, the catastrophe almost tragic, yet suddenly these troubles become calm." Barlandus (on the *Andrian* 4.5.796) said: "Every play, according to Donatus, is divided into three parts, protasis, epitasis, catastrophe. We call the first growing tumult the protasis, the warmest bustle the epitasis, the sudden change of events the catastrophe."

During the first half of the sixteenth century this threefold division of a comedy was integrated with the five acts prescribed by Horace. According to Professor Baldwin,[30] the typical "regular" integration of the five-act formula with protasis, epitasis, and catastrophe was made by Willichius and his kinsman Wagnerus. In the scheme of Willichius and Wagnerus, the protasis extends through Acts 1 and 2; the epitasis through Acts 3 and 4, rising to the *summa epitasis*, which usually comes in Act 5; the catastrophe in Act 5. This formula was not absolutely rigid, for all the plays of Terence, upon which it is based, do not follow exactly the same pattern of action. A brief summary of the *Andrian* will perhaps make the "regular" comic plot clear.

Protasis:

ACT 1: Simo tells how he found out that his son Pamphilus is in love with a slave-girl Glycerium and how he plans to rescue the youth and marry him to Philumena, the daughter of neighbor Chremes. Davus, a clever slave, determines to help young Pamphilus while pretending to help old Simo. Pamphilus determines to remain true to Glycerium and to resist the match proposed by his father. (Thus far we have exposition of the main action.)

ACT 2: Another young man, Charinus, appears on the scene. Charinus wants to marry Philumena, and he receives Pamphilus' assurance that he (Pamphilus) will not stand in his way. (Here we have the exposition of the subordinate action.) Simo's plan to make his son marry Philumena strikes a snag, for Chremes does not approve of Pamphilus as a son-in-law. Consequently, when Davus finds out that the match between Pamphilus and Philumena is breaking down, he advises Pamphilus to pretend to yield to Simo's demand. Pamphilus then promises his father that he will dutifully marry Philumena. Whereupon Charinus, misinterpreting Pamphilus' intention, believes that his friend has double-crossed him. Thus misunderstandings and turmoils begin as the protasis ends.

---

[30]See *William Shakspere's Five-Act Structure*, pp. 228-51.

Epitasis:

ACT 3: Simo hears that Glycerium has borne a child to Pamphilus, but believes that this report is a hoax engineered by Davus to stop the match between Pamphilus and Philumena. Davus encourages this belief though he knows that Pamphilus is actually the father of the child. Thereupon Simo tells Chremes that his son has broken with Glycerium, and tries to persuade him to allow the match between Pamphilus and Philumena. Davus backs up Simo, feeling sure that Chremes will not change his mind. Then, to the consternation of Davus, Chremes does change his mind and consents to the match. Pamphilus turns upon Davus in a rage, and Davus has to concoct another scheme to thwart Simo again. How can Davus extricate Pamphilus this time? The hubbub is on.

ACT 4: Davus proceeds to execute a new plan. Having put off the enraged Pamphilus and the equally enraged Charinus, he cleverly arranges matters so that Chremes sees the new baby and learns that it is the offspring of Pamphilus and Glycerium. Chremes decides, naturally enough, to call off the match between his daughter and Pamphilus. In the last scene of the fourth act, Crito from Andros appears. As Donatus observed, Crito is the person who is to bring about the catastrophe—*persona ad catastrophen machinata.*

ACT 5, SCENES 1-3: Although the means contrived for the catastrophe is introduced at the close of the fourth act, the epitasis continues into the fifth act. In other words, while the remedy for the misunderstandings is at hand, there still remain some difficulties; suspense will be maintained. Simo will not yet give up his plan to persuade Chremes to allow the match between Pamphilus and Philumena, and Chremes is not a man of strong will. There is still danger that Pamphilus, and also Charinus, will lose out. Even when Davus brings news that Glycerium is not a slave but an Athenian citizen, Simo refuses to yield; he won't believe a word of the story; he orders Davus put in chains and threatens to disinherit his son. At this point (5.3), the action reaches the final crisis, the *summa epitasis.*

Catastrophe:

ACT 5, SCENES 4-5: Although Simo stubbornly holds out against Crito, whom he calls a false witness, Chremes recognizes the old Andrian and, by comparing information with him, discovers that Glycerium is not only an Athenian citizen but his own long-lost daughter. Consequently all misunderstandings and troubles are cleared away. Pamphilus may keep Glycerium, of course, and Charinus can now marry Philumena. Davus is released from his bonds. Everybody is happy and satisfied.

During the second half of the sixteenth century the five-act formula more or less absorbed protasis, epitasis, and catastrophe, and five acts came to be spoken of as a structural pattern. For a long time, however, Donatus' division hung on, and was likely to come up whenever ancient drama was discussed. When Eugenius, in Dryden's *Essay of Dramatic Poesy* (1668), discussed ancient practice he described the division into protasis, epitasis, catastasis,[31] and catastrophe. The truth seems to be that many early commentators on Terence, Donatus included, were not sure of just what acts were; they were only sure that Horace had prescribed five of them. Donatus, in his preface to the *Andrian*, admitted that it was difficult to distinguish the act-divisions in Latin plays. "No character," he said, "who has left the stage five times can exit any more." It looks as though acts (*actus*) were divisions of the histrionic actions on stage rather than the poet's structural divisions of his plot. In other words, acts were originally divisions of the theatrical production rather than structural elements of playwriting.

For some time, long after the five-act formula had become well established, critics and playwrights continued to think of acts as more or less arbitrary divisions of the stage action. Jason Denores (1553), for example, in his comment on the *Ars Poetica* 129, spoke of *actus* as the "actions of the characters." Scaliger (1.9) somewhat ambiguously remarked: "An act is so called from general actions, because the whole genus is δραματικόν. It is a part of the play containing diverse actions." Cordatus (1570) was more specific; in his introductory essay (*Fabula, Comoedia, et Tragoedia*) he said: "In tragedy and comedy there are five acts, that is, the divisions named from the movements (*gestus*) of the actors, in Greek 'actions' (πράξες)."

At all events, the fundamental division of a dramatic plot, comic or tragic, was tripartite; it consisted of protasis, epitasis, and catastrophe. And generally the protasis extended through Acts 1 and 2; the epitasis through Acts 3 and 4, sometimes into Act 5; the catastrophe was Act 5, or the concluding scenes of Act 5. Ben Jonson, for example, used this arrangement in his comedies, and twice called attention to it. In his summary of the action of the *New Inn*, he wrote:

Act III. Here begins the Epitasis, or business of the play. . . .
Act V. Is the catastrophe, or knitting up of all. . . .

---

[31]Scaliger added *catastasis*, meaning the full development of the action, the counterturn which stirs up added difficulties, such as Simo's persistent efforts to match Pamphilus with Philumena. See p. 119.

Master Probee, an interlocutor throughout the *Magnetic Lady*, remarks at the conclusion of Act 2:

Let us mind what you come for, the play, which will draw on to the epitasis now.

At the conclusion of Act 4, the Boy, another interlocutor, says:

Stay, and see his last act, his catastrophe, how he will perplex that, or spring some fresh cheat, to entertain the spectators, with a convenient delight, till some unexpected and new encounter break out to rectify all, and make good the conclusion.

When the Aristotelian analysis of tragedy became familiar to students of the drama, critics squared Aristotle's quantitative division into prologue, episodes, and exode with the five-act formula.[32] More important for the actual construction of the play, however, was the harmonizing of Donatus' protasis, epitasis, and catastrophe with Aristotle's "beginning, middle, and end," and with the Aristotelian division of the plot into Complication (δέσις) and Denouement (λύσις). In the *Poetics* (18.55ᵇ24-29), Aristotle said:

Every tragedy is in part Complication and in part Dénouement; the incidents before the opening scene, and often certain also of those within the play, forming the Complication; and the rest the Dénouement. By Complication I mean all from the beginning of the story to the point just before the change in the hero's fortunes; by Dénouement, all from the beginning of the change to the end.

Robortellus, in *On Comedy*, applied these Aristotelian terms to the comic plot:

In the art of writing Comedy it is important to recognize that its duration is limited by two goals, namely dénouement (*solutio*) and complication (*connexio*). All that extends from the beginning of the play to the point where the bustle of affairs (*turbae rerum*) turns and a change takes place is called the complication. . . . That part which extends from the beginning of the change to the end of the play is called dénouement.[33]

Minturno[34] discussed the division of plot into *colligatio* (δέσις) and *solutio* (λύσις), and gave as illustrations the *Andrian, Oedipus Rex*, and the *Aeneid*. Scaliger (3.97), in speaking of the tragic plot, called δέσις the *turbatio negotiorum*, i.e., the "bustle of affairs," a phrase usually ascribed to the comic plot.

The application of the Aristotelian complication and denouement to comedy brought with them the Aristotelian conception of complex and simple plots. As Robortellus said in his essay *On Comedy:*

---

[32]See p. 33. [33]See p. 234. [34]*De Poeta*, pp. 127-33, 187, 283-84.

There are two kinds of comic plots: some are simple, others complex (*implexae*); and such, morever, are the actions which they imitate. Simple actions are those which have nothing unexpected and contain no Discovery. Complex actions contain either one or both of these devices. Discovery occurs when we are led from ignorance to knowledge of some matter, out of which springs either joy or grief, nearly always joy, for Discoveries are, with good reason, placed in the last part of a comedy, where the disturbance in affairs begins to subside. An example of this sort can be drawn from the *Andrian* of Terence, and from many others in which there is Discovery.[35]

Not only the *Andrian* but all the other plays of Terence make use of both Discovery and reversal of fortune (Peripety), and consequently the Terentian plot may be called complex. In the *Andrian*, Chremes discovers from evidence submitted by Crito that Glycerium is an Athenian citizen and his own long-lost daughter, and this revelation brings about a change in the fortunes of all the principal characters, a change from misunderstanding and grief to joy. In the *Self-Tormentor*, Antiphila, the maidservant, turns out to be the long-lost daughter of Chremes and so can be married to her lover, Clinia, son of Menedemus. The discovery here is made by means of the ancient device of a ring.[36] In the *Eunuch*, Pamphila, a slave girl, turns out to be an Athenian citizen and sister to young Chremes, who arranges her marriage with Chaerea. Discovery here is by means of an old nurse who recognizes certain tokens in possession of the girl. In the *Brothers*, Demea finally discovers that his favorite country-bred son, Ctesipho, is the rake rather than the city son, Aeschinus, and consequently Demea reforms his own harsh, puritanical way of life. In the *Mother-in-law*, it is discovered by means of a ring that Philumena, the estranged wife of Pamphilus, is the very girl he ravished months ago. Consequently Philumena's child must be the offspring of Pamphilus. In *Phormio*, Chremes recognizes Sophrona as the nurse to his daughter by a second wife. From the nurse he learns that this daughter is the same girl who has already married his nephew. This revelation leads to a happy resolution of the whole family squabble.

The early commentators on Terence did not know about the Aristotelian "simple" and "complex" plots, but they were well aware of the importance of recognition and reversal of fortune. Evanthius, in *De Fabula*, said: "The catastrophe is the reversal (*conuersio*) of affairs preparatory to the cheerful outcome, and revealed to all by means of a discovery (*cognitio*)." The sixteenth-century commen-

---

[35]See p. 232.

[36]Robortellus, in *On Comedy*, carefully analyzed Aristotle's five types of Discovery, all of which are found in comedy as well as in tragedy and epic poetry.

tators from Badius Ascensius on were familiar with these devices and often called attention to recognitions and reversals of fortune in the plays.

Terence himself had spoken of "simple" and "double" plots. In the Prologue to the *Self-Tormentor*, he explained how he had transformed his Greek sources from two simple (i.e., single) plots to one *duplex argumentum*. The commentators generally interpreted *duplex* to mean two closely related actions involving two sets of characters—two young lovers engaged in two love affairs, and two old men engaged in two intrigues. Donatus (on the *Andrian* 2.1.301) called attention to what was later termed the "sub-plot"; he called the entrance of Charinus (the second young man in the play, who wants to marry Philumena) the disclosure of "another part of the play," and pointed out that this use of two love affairs was the common practice of Terence, since only the *Mother-in-law* employs just one lover. Donatus admired the skill of Terence in contriving a double action in the *Andrian:* "He has boldly and very artfully devised the double love affairs of the two young men and the double marriage in the one play."[37] Other commentators accepted this criticism and usually repeated Donatus' observation. Latomus, for example, who was a stickler for close-knit dramatic structure, found no fault with Terence's double plot; he said of the *Andrian* (2.1):

The disquiet of the youth Charinus is caused by the rumor of Pamphilus' marriage [to Philumena]. It is another part of the protasis, and is a new affair as it were, outside the plot (*argumentum*) of Pamphilus, by means of which there is more hubbub in the play.

Willichius remarked of the same scene: "And since this play has a double plot (*argumentum*), a certain *antithesis* as it were of youths and servants becomes wonderfully illuminating."

Since the double plot was the common practice of Terence, it became standard practice in Renaissance comedy, and persisted even after the strict interpretation of the single action recommended by Horace and Aristotle became established. Horace had said in the *Ars Poetica* (23), "In a word, be the work what you will, only let it be simple (*simplex*) and uniform"; Aristotle had insisted upon unity of action.[38] Giraldi Cinthio (1554) defended the use of double plot in tragedy as well as in comedy:

And hence it should be understood that though double tragedies are little praised by Aristotle (though some think otherwise) double structure is nonetheless to be much praised in comedy and has made the plays of

---

[37]Donatus on the *Andrian* 5.5.977.
[38]See Herrick, *op. cit.*, pp. 73-78.

Terence succeed wonderfully. I call that plot double which has in its action diverse kinds of persons of the same station in life, as two lovers of different character, two old men of varied nature, two servants of opposite morals, and other such things, as they may be seen in the *Andria* and in the other plots of the same poet, where it is clear that these like persons of unlike habits make the knot and the solution of the plot very pleasing. And I believe that if this should be well imitated in tragedy by a good poet, and the knot so arranged that its solution will not bring confusion, double structure in tragedy will not be less pleasing (always remembering the reverence due to Aristotle) than it is in comedy. If there have been those who have favored this method and held an opinion unlike that of Aristotle, they are not, I think, to be blamed, especially if the tragedy has a happy end, for this kind of end is much like that of comedy, and therefore such a tragedy can be like comedy in its imitation of the action.[39]

Guarini (1599), who was defending tragicomedy as a legitimate form of drama, presented a detailed defense of the Terentian double plot:

It now remains to defend this grafting in of subordinate stories. In order to do this I shall consider four agents indispensable to the plot of the *Andria*, the first, not merely in date but in beauty, of the comedies of Terence: Pamphilus the first, Glycerium the second, Philumena the third, and Charinus the fourth; the love of Pamphilus and Glycerium is the chief thing, and that of Charinus and Philumena is episodic and grafted to the other. That this is so, he who has but a little understanding of the dramatic art cannot doubt, since all the difficulties arise because of Pamphilus and Glycerium. With the person of Glycerium is concerned the recognition through which the plot is turned in an opposing direction, and in her marriage it has its happy end. Concerning the marriage of Charinus there is but a little sport at the end, and that with admirable artistry. Hence the principal subject is nothing else than the love of Pamphilus and Glycerium, not interrupted by that of Charinus, but greatly aided. And if that love alone had been represented, with the pregnancy of Glycerium and the displeasure of Simo, the father of Pamphilus, how insipid the story would have been! A young man fallen under the displeasure of the father because he had married a woman of no standing, who at last, when she is discovered to be a free woman, is given to him as his wife—what is there in that to make a plot? The plot might indeed have been pathetic and have displayed character, but there would have been no activity, which is the strength of the dramatic art. How would the plot have come to a crisis? From the indignation of the father and the love of the son strong feelings could have resulted, but not intrigues. The knot is tied by the marriage that Simo arranges, for it causes Pamphilus a great deal of trouble in his need for escaping it, since

[39]Gilbert, p. 254.

he has pledged his faith to Glycerium that he will take her as his wife, and causes the astute Davos to set about his clever plans. If this marriage then is so necessary that without it the drama would have little or no action, how can the person of Philumena be passed over? Pamphilus would not have believed his father when he said that he wished that day, all of a sudden, to give him a wife, if the wife had not been selected, named, and known by Pamphilus, and if the marriage had not a little before been negotiated. So the necessity of the third agent is obvious. Now that girl who was going to be that day a wife and who had been announced as such in the house of her father, was she then to remain disappointed because of the marriage of Glycerium? Was she to be all that day in the belief and hope of being a wife and then to be left high and dry? It would be very unwise and unfitted to a comic poem that, whenever there is introduced a person so necessary to tying the knot and to such an extent an accessory in untying it, no account should be made of her at the end of the story and she should not share in the common rejoicing. Hence it was necessary to prepare her a husband and to make him her lover, that he might be dearer to her and the end of the story might be more joyous, and—what is still more important—that there might be more intrigue and continual enrichment of the subject with new incidents. This makes clear the necessity of the fourth agent and the second love.[40]

The Italian critics of the sixteenth century were careful to point out that the subplot in Terence is always closely grafted to the main action so that the result does not violate the classical demand for unity of action. Elizabethan practice, Jonson's plots excepted, sometimes made use of a subplot that is virtually a separate action and but loosely tied to the main plot. English comedy in the latter half of the seventeenth century returned to the more regular practice of Terence. Dryden, who always recommended unity of action in theory, approved the Terentian duplex plot, which brought variety to the play.[41] In tragicomedy, Dryden sometimes used a loose "under-plot," but finally renounced that practice. In 1695, he acknowledged that he could not defend his own *Spanish Friar* against the imputation of an "ill-ordered" plot.[42] Congreve, in the dedication of his *Double-Dealer*, boasted of the regularity of his plot:

I made the plot as strong as I could, because it was single, and I made it single because I would avoid confusion, and was resolved to preserve the three unities of the drama.

In the dedication of his last, and greatest, comedy, the *Way of the World*, Congreve paid tribute to Terence, whose practice he reconciled to the precepts of Aristotle:

---

[40]*Ibid.*, pp. 528-29.   [41]See *Essays* 1.208.   [42]*Ibid.* 2.147.

As Terence excelled in his performances, so had he great advantages to encourage his undertakings; for he built most on the foundations of Menander; his plots were generally modeled and his characters ready drawn to his hand. He copied Menander; and Menander had no less light in the formation of his characters from the observations of Theophrastus, of whom he was a disciple; and Theophrastus it is known was not only the disciple but the immediate successor of Aristotle, the first and greatest judge of poetry.

The inheritance of Terence that Congreve traced here to Aristotle was a bequest of characterization rather than plot. Nevertheless, Congreve's plot in the *Way of the World* is a pretty faithful development of the Terentian method. The main action is the love affair of Mirabell and Mrs. Millamant. There is a subordinate affair between Fainall and Mrs. Marwood, and another subordinate affair between Lady Wishfort and the spurious Sir Rowland. In addition, there are further cross-plots in the Jonsonian manner: Lady Wishfort tries to arrange a match between Mrs. Millamant and Sir Willfull Witwoud; both Mrs. Marwood and Mrs. Fainall are in love with Mirabell; both Witwoud and Petulant are suitors to Mrs. Millamant. In other words, the principal agents have been increased beyond the four Terentian agents that Guarini recommended, but the scheme of plot is similar. Terence's method of running two parallel love affairs in comedy is doubtless a natural development; it certainly is a very common one that appears in play after play from ancient times to the present, including such widely diverse dramas, for example, as Shakespeare's *Much Ado About Nothing* and Sidney Howard's popular Freudian play, the *Silver Cord*.

The plots of Terence's plays, save that of the *Mother-in-law*, then, are duplex. As I have shown above, they are all, including the *Mother-in-law*, complex in the Aristotelian sense, though the early commentators on Terence did not call them so. Georgius Fabricius, whose castigations on Terence were first published at Strassburg in 1548, was perhaps the first Terentian commentator to express the Aristotelian concept of plot. Fabricius did not use the term *complex*, but he understood that a plot does not rise above a simple order of incidents merely because it employs two sets of characters. Fabricius had some acquaintance with the *Poetics* of Aristotle. His comment on the Prologue to the *Self-Tormentor* runs in part as follows:

He [Terence] says that this comedy is duplex not by reason of the characters, because it has two young men, even as all the others, the *Mother-in-law* excepted, have; but by reason of the unexpected recognition (*cognitio*) of Antiphila by means of a ring, but also, and especially, by reason of the time of the action. Tragic and comic actors were wont to finish their business, as Aristotle writes in the book *On Poetry*, "within a single circuit of the sun."

Fabricius went on to explain that the *Self-Tormentor* exceeds this customary time limit because it is a quiet type of comedy (i.e., *stataria*), and therefore the author could not with propriety crowd too many actions into one day. Soon after this time (1548), to be sure, the comic plot, like the tragic plot, was subjected not only to the test of unity of action but also to the other Renaissance unities of time and place.[43]

PROTASIS

The structure of the comic plot, then, was fundamentally threefold. This threefold division fitted very well Aristotle's "beginning, middle, and end," and it was easily made to fit the Aristotelian exordium, complication, and denouement. The first part, or beginning, is the protasis, which is primarily the exposition. According to both Evanthius and Donatus, the protasis is the "first act." Evanthius called it "the first act and beginning of the drama"; Donatus, "the first act of the play, in which part of the argument is unfolded and part withheld in order to hold the expectation of the audience." By the middle of the sixteenth century, Willichius had identified the protasis with Acts 1 and 2. In other words, the protasis contained not only the necessary exposition of the story and the introduction of the principal characters but also started the intrigues, the bustle of affairs. The protasis, even if interpreted as merely the exposition, was not always confined to the first act of a comedy.

As Scaliger (1.9) pointed out, the protasis (i.e., exposition) of Plautus' *Braggart Soldier* comes in the second act. Furthermore, the exposition of the subplot or subordinate action generally comes in the second act; for example, Charinus and his love affair are introduced at the beginning of Act 2 in the *Andrian*. Latomus said that Chaerea's narrative of his conquest of the slave girl, which comes well along in the third act of the *Eunuch* (3.5.549 ff.) is the "exposition of the protasis of the other part [i.e., subplot] of the play." But Latomus erred here, I think, for Chaerea is introduced in pursuit of the girl in the second act. In fact, Latomus himself remarked of this scene (*Eunuch* 2.3): "Here is a new argument and the occasion of a new movement in the play." Willichius' comment on Chaerea's narrative (*Eunuch* 3.5.563) is more judicious: "The *narratio* is just like the *protasis* of New Comedy." At all events, the main features of the protasis are the exposition of both main and subordinate actions and

---

[43]See Herrick, *op. cit.*, pp. 73-84.

the introduction of all the principal agents. Stigelius expressed it neatly when he said of the *Andrian* 1.2: "Terence begins the *protasis* with a setting forth of the argument of the play and introduces the characters through whom the play is henceforth distributed."[44] In the next century, Eugenius, in Dryden's *Essay of Dramatic Poesy*, summed it up as follows: "First, the *protasis*, or entrance, which gives light only to the characters of the persons, and proceeds very little into any part of the action."[45]

The two leading authorities in the Renaissance on the correct disposition of the *narratio* were the rhetoricians Cicero and Aphthonius. Cicero, in *De Inventione* 1.20, recommended three qualities, namely, that the *narratio* be brief, clear, and probable. He found an admirable illustration of these qualities in the first act of Terence's *Andrian*. According to Aphthonius,[46] *narratio* is divided into six parts: (1) Person (*persona faciens*), (2) Deed (*res facta*), (3) Way of doing (*modus quo pacto*), (4) Cause (*causa propter quam*), (5) Place (*locus in quo*), (6) Time (*tempus circa quod*).

Willichius, in his comment on *Phormio* 1.2, dutifully combined both the Ciceronian and Aphthonian analyses. In this scene, two servants, Geta and Davus, explain what has been going on in the families of the two brothers, Demipho and Chremes. Geta tells Davus how Chremes and Demipho left Athens for foreign parts. While the two old men were away, young Phaedria, son of Chremes, fell in love with a music-girl and young Antipho, son of Demipho, fell in love with another slave girl. Antipho was the worst smitten, for he wanted to marry the girl though he dared not marry without his father's consent. Then, says Geta, along came the parasite Phormio, who offered to set himself up as a friend of the girl and to maintain that she was a kinswoman of Antipho. Since there was an Athenian law prescribing that orphans must be married to their next of kin, Phormio could "legally" force Antipho to marry the girl. This hoax was perpetrated; the court ordered Antipho, as next of kin, to marry the girl, and he married her. Now Geta and Antipho are in a dither because Demipho, the father, is expected home at any hour.

Willichius correctly analyzed this *narratio* as follows:

1. The Person is Antipho.
2. The Business or Deed, the wife wed without a dowry.
3. The Time, because the father was absent in Cilicia.

---

[44]Riccius' edition of Terence 1.49v.

[45]*Essays* 1.45.

[46]*Progymnasmata rhetorica* (1550), p. 2v. Cf. Rainolde, *Foundacion of Rhetorike*, p. xii(v).

4. The Way, because he married advisedly and voluntarily but by means of the trumpery of Geta and Phormio.

5. The Place, Athens. Therefore the course of Attic law is observed.

6. The Cause is love; induced by which, he [Antipho] desires that the substance of the girl be made over from the old woman to himself. Here also many plausible explanations are scattered on every side so that the whole *narratio* is clear and probable.[47]

Willichius (on *Phormio* 1.2.63) also pointed out that the *narratio* here is brief as well as clear and probable; it is made brief by the use of questions and answers instead of straight narrative; Geta's account is often interrupted by lively exchange of dialogue. Long before the time of Willichius, Donatus had called attention to the artful way in which Terence breaks up the exposition of the *Mother-in-law* with characteristic pleasantries and with interjected passages of mimicry (*mimesis*) so that the audience is kept interested and held in suspense.[48] Long before Donatus, for that matter, Cicero had praised the vivid *narratio* of Terence, in particular the exposition in the *Andrian* (1.1.51 ff.). Cicero also commended the expository monologue of Micio in the *Brothers* (1.1.60-64), wherein Micio explains how his rural brother Demea disagrees with his easy-going method of bringing up a boy. Cicero, in the *De Inventione* 1.19, remarked:

But that sort of narration which is conversant about persons, is of such a sort that in it not only the facts themselves, but also the conversations of the persons concerned and their very minds can be thoroughly seen, in this way—

"He comes to me perpetually, crying 'What are you about, Micio? Why are you bringing the boy to ruin on our hands? Why this licence? Why these drinking parties? Why do you allow him expense for these things, and let him spend so much at the tailor's? It's extremely silly of you.' He himself is extremely hard, past right and sense."

In this kind of narration there ought to be a great deal of cheerfulness wrought up out of the variety of circumstances; out of the dissimilarity of dispositions; out of gravity, lenity, hope, fear, suspicion, regret, dissimulation, error, pity, the changes of fortune, unexpected disaster, sudden joy, and happy results.

Since Terence was held up as a model for the rhetorician as well as for the dramatist, his protasis naturally became a standard for the sixteenth century.

---

[47]Cf. Professor Baldwin's analysis of Armado's narrative in *Love's Labor's Lost*, in *William Shakspere's Small Latine and Lesse Greeke* 2.310-12.

[48]See Donatus on the *Mother-in-law* 1.2.104, 112, 131.

Epitasis

According to Evanthius, the epitasis is the "rising of the forward progress of turmoils, or . . . the knot of the whole uncertainty." According to Donatus, it is the "infolding of the argument." The epitasis, as Robortellus and others discovered, corresponds to the main section of Aristotle's "complication" (δέσις), the tying of the knot which later must be untied. Wagnerus, whose interpretation of comic plot was typical of sixteenth-century theory, said:

In the epitasis, the warmest bustle, the argument is entangled: mistakes, with great perturbation of all the characters, agitated gestures and countenances, are dealt with, by means of which the στάσις (main issue) of the drama is exhibited.[49]

Wagnerus, who doubtless followed Quintilian,[50] identified the Greek *stasis* with the Latin *status*.

Scaliger, in order to describe the climactic portion of the development of action, introduced the term *catastasis*, which is more or less equivalent to the *summa epitasis* of Donatus and Latomus and to what Willichius sometimes called the *extrema epitasis*. Scaliger (1.9) thus defined the term:

The catastasis is the force or issue (*status*) of the plot (*fabula*), in which the matter is caught up and mingled in the storm of fortune. Many take no notice of this part. It is nevertheless necessary.

The best explanation of catastasis that I know appears a century later in Dryden's *Essay of Dramatic Poesy*. Here Eugenius, who thought he was following Aristotle but was actually following Scaliger, described the development of the plot as follows:

Secondly, the *epitasis* or working up of the plot, where the play grows warmer, the design or action of it drawing on, and you see something promising that it will come to pass. Thirdly, the *catastasis*, called by the Romans *status*, the height and full growth of the play; we may call it properly the counterturn, which destroys the expectation, embroils the action in new difficulties, and leaves you far distant from that hope in which it found you; as you may have observed in a violent stream resisted by a narrow passage—it runs round to an eddy and carries back the waters with more swiftness than it brought them on.[51]

Sixteenth-century commentators and critics before the time of Scaliger did not use the term *catastasis*, but the phenomenon it de-

---

[49] Willichius' edition of Terence, pp. 5-6.
[50] Quintilian 3.6.3: "The Greeks call *status* στάσις."
[51] *Essays* 1.45.

scribes may be observed in the plays of Terence. In the *Andrian*, for example, although Davus succeeds in making Chremes call off the match between Pamphilus and Philumena, old Simo is far from acknowledging defeat. On the contrary, Simo orders Davus put in chains and threatens to disinherit his son Pamphilus. Davus' well-wrought intrigue has taken a serious counterturn, struck an eddy as it were, and the situation is now even more dangerous for Pamphilus, and for Davus, than it was. Then, to be sure, a new discovery (the recognition of Glycerium as Chremes' daughter) unravels the "knot of uncertainty," placating the stubborn Simo and rescuing Pamphilus, Charinus, and Davus. Similarly in the *Eunuch* (5.4), another clever slave, Parmeno, who has successfully engineered the intrigue of Phaedria with Thais and of Chaerea with Pamphila, is exulting in self-satisfaction when all his schemes seem to recoil upon him and throw him into danger of very serious punishment. But he is rescued, and his plans are happily fulfilled.

So far as I know, Ben Jonson did not use the term *catastasis*, but confined himself to the traditional protasis, epitasis, and catastrophe. Nevertheless, one may easily point out a catastasis in some of his plays. In Act 4 of the *Alchemist*, for example, Surly, disguised as a Spanish don, traps Subtle and Face into revealing their rascally schemes to hoodwink and plunder the neighbors. But these two resourceful scoundrels are far from beaten. They overpower Surly and throw him out of the house. Thus the "knot of uncertainty" is prolonged through a good part of Act 5. With Surly out of the way, Lovewit, the master of the house, who has just returned, is the only person who can expose the machinations of Subtle, Face, and Doll. Lovewit is the only person now who can untie the knot, but he seems to be no match for the wily Face. Finally, thanks to the treachery of Face, Subtle the alchemist is exposed and punished. Face makes peace with his good-natured master and escapes punishment. Examination of the epitasis of *Volpone* will disclose a comparable technique. And as Dryden said of the *Silent Woman*, "There too you will see, till the very last scene, new difficulties arising to obstruct the action of the play; and when the audience is brought into despair that the business can naturally be effected, then, and not before, the discovery is made."[52]

The *catastasis*, or *summa epitasis*, is not confined to comedy, but may be observed in tragedy as well. In Sophocle's *Oedipus Rex*, for example, the messenger from Corinth brings news to Oedipus that his "father" has died, and Oedipus believes that he is now relieved of

---

[52]*Essays* 1.88.

one of his worst fears. Since his father is dead he surely cannot now fulfill the prophecy that he would kill him. But this relief is only temporary, for further discoveries finally reveal all the terrible truth and Oedipus is plunged into hopeless despair. Students of Shakespearean tragedy have often remarked the counterturn in the hero's fortune during the fourth act. The fourth act in a Shakespearean tragedy commonly brings temporary relief to the harassed protagonist and offers him new hope, thus prolonging the "knot of uncertainty." In *King Lear*, the old king and Cordelia are happily reunited in Act 4, only to meet death in the last act. In Act 4 of *Antony and Cleopatra*, Antony beats back the troops of Octavius and enjoys a temporary success, only to meet final disaster and death later on.

One of the clearest demonstrations of how protasis, epitasis, catastasis, and catastrophe fitted in the conventional five acts of drama was furnished in 1650 by Davenant in his Preface to *Gondibert*. Davenant was explaining how he intended to use the dramatic plot in his heroic poem:

The first *Act* is the general preparative, by rendering the chiefest characters of persons, and ending with something that looks like an obscure promise of design. The second begins with an introducement of new persons, so finishes all the characters, and ends with some little performance of that design which was promised at the parting of the first *Act*. The third makes a visible correspondence in the under-walks (or lesser intrigues) of persons; and ends with an ample turn of the main design, and expectation of a new. The fourth (ever having occasion to be the longest) gives a notorious turn to all the under-walks, and a counter-turn to that main design which changed in the third. The fifth begins with an entire diversion of the main, and dependant Plots; then makes the general correspondence of the persons more discernable, and ends with an easy untying of those particular knots which made a contexture of the whole; leaving such satisfaction of probabilities with the Spectator as may persuade him that neither Fortune in the fate of the Persons, nor the Writer in the Representment, have been unnatural or exorbitant.[53]

In the comic epitasis, then, the complications, the intrigues, are developed. More often than not, dangers arise, increase, and finally become so pressing that a drastic remedy is necessary. The art of the poet is shown by his ability to weave a tangled web of threats, dangers, misunderstandings, and errors, which are then skillfully, but with an air of naturalness, happily resolved. Often a *deus ex machina* seems necessary to save the protagonists from disaster. But both Horace and Aristotle frowned upon the use of the *deus ex machina* in

---

[53]*The Authour's Preface*, p. 17, in *Gondibert: an Heroick Poem* (London, 1651).

tragedy, and the leading commentators on Terence did not favor its use in comedy. Evanthius remarked that Terence does not use the *deus ex machina*, though he occasionally makes use of *protactic* characters, i.e., characters outside the direct line of the plot. According to Donatus, Philotis and Syra in the *Mother-in-law* do not belong to the plot (*argumentum*), but merely give information. "Terence," said Donatus, "would rather do this than narrate the argument by means of a prologue or bring in a 'god out of the machine' to speak."[54]

Upon one occasion, Terence had to introduce a stranger in order to untie the knot. In the *Andrian*, Pamphilus' affair with Glycerium seems doomed to failure until Crito from Andros suddenly appears and furnishes information that sets all straight. Wagnerus observed that the intervention of Crito is "from the machine."[55]

The commentators esteemed the plays of Terence for their air of reality, for their verisimilitude. Before and after the rediscovery of Aristotle's *Poetics*, with its emphasis upon probability, they praised Terence for his fulfillment of the Ciceronian demands of comedy, that it should be an "imitation of life, mirror of custom, and image of truth." Aristotle's theory of dramatic structure merely strengthened well-established demands for verisimilitude. Robortellus (pp. 87-88), for example, and after him many other critics, argued that all drama, as imitations of human actions, is primarily *secundum naturam* although some tragedies and the Old Comedy of Aristophanes do admit gods and conversations with gods. New Comedy, however, best represented by Terence, admits nothing contrary to necessity and probability.

The comic epitasis (including the catastasis), then, sets the stage for the removal of the dangers and the untying of the "knot of uncertainty"; it prepares the way for the catastrophe, the end of the play.

Catastrophe

The meaning of *catastrophe* in comedy was clearly defined by Evanthius and Donatus. Evanthius' definition, quoted earlier, is: "The catastrophe is the reversal (*conuersio*) of affairs preparatory to the cheerful outcome, and revealed to all by means of a discovery (*cognitio*)." Notice that Evanthius said "revealed to all," for usually the discovery at the close of a comedy makes known everything to everybody. That this method was common practice is revealed by Terence himself. In the *Mother-in-law*, the main secret—namely, that Philu-

---

[54]Donatus on the *Mother-in-law* 1.1.58; cf. his comment on the *Andrian* 1.1.28.
[55]Willichius' edition of Terence, p. 7.

mena is the same young woman that Pamphilus ravished some time before—is never disclosed to any persons save those intimately concerned. Bacchis, the amiable courtesan, learns the truth by means of a ring and tells Pamphilus, Philumena, and Philumena's mother. The two fathers remain happily ignorant. Even Parmeno, the clever slave, never learns of this important detail. But such practice was evidently very unusual in comedy. Terence made Pamphilus say, "There's no need to breathe a syllable. I have no wish for it to be as in the comedies where everybody gets to know everything."[56] Donatus remarked that this incident is more like reality than comedy. Barlandus and Willichius echoed him. Willichius said, "It is wonderful that the poet should fashion not a comedy but as it were reality." In other words, the comic catastrophe is commonly the result of much artifice; for, short of violating decorum and verisimilitude, the author must somehow contrive a happy ending.

The comic catastrophe, as defined by Evanthius and Donatus, was readily harmonized with Aristotle's recommendations for the tragic plot. Robortellus (p. 103) identified Aristotle's "change of fortune" with catastrophe: "Therefore Aristotle calls the downward change (*inclinatio*) of the plot the μετάβασις, or what is called Catastrophe by some, that is, the outcome (*exitus*) of the matter." In a complex plot, tragic or comic, the catastrophe is attended, in fact, brought about, by Discovery and Peripety. Catastrophe also came to be identified with Aristotle's "unraveling" (λύσις) or denouement. Eugenius, in Dryden's *Essay of Dramatic Poesy*, described the ending of a play in terms that would have satisfied almost any Renaissance student of the drama from Melanchthon on:

Lastly, the *catastrophe*, which the Grecians called λύσις, the French *le dénouement*, and we the discovery or unraveling of the plot; there you see all things settling again upon their first foundations; and, the obstacles which hindered the design or action of the play once removed, it ends with that resemblance of truth and nature that the audience are satisfied with the conduct of it.[57]

Almost always the sixteenth-century critics identified the catastrophe with Discovery or recognition, which is usually attended by Peripety or reversal of fortune. Consequently, Discovery was considered all-important in the comic plot; it was the final step leading to the final solution. Terence himself suggested the proper use of Discovery in his term *cognitio*. In the *Mother-in-law* 5.3.831, Bacchis, the courtesan, relates how Myrrina, the mother of Philumena, had noticed a ring on her finger which looked like one her daughter had lost some months ago. Thereupon Bacchis told how she got the ring from Pamphilus, who had taken it from a girl. (This girl, to be sure, was Philumena, then unknown to him but later his wife.) "Thereupon," says Bacchis, "a recognition (*cognitio*) ensued." This speech is near the end of the play, and this recognition is the catastrophe, for it is followed by a reversal of fortune and the untying of the knot of uncertainty. Sixteenth-century scholars preferred *agnitio* to the *cognitio* of Terence and Evanthius, but both terms came to be accepted as Latin equivalents for Aristotle's "Discovery." Robortellus' statement in his essay *On Comedy* expressed the theory governing the outcome of comedy, a theory that represents a successful harmonizing of traditional Roman theory and practice with Aristotelian theory and Greek practice:

Discovery occurs when we are led from ignorance to knowledge of some matter, out of which springs either joy or grief—nearly always joy, for Discoveries are, with good reason, placed in the last part of a comedy, where the disturbance in affairs begins to subside. An example of this sort can be drawn from the *Andria* of Terence, and from many others in which there is Discovery.[58]

In his commentary on the *Poetics* (p. 113), Robortellus performed another service for dramatic criticism; he showed how the use of Discovery in rhetoric differs from its use in the drama. Discovery was a common device in both logic and rhetoric.[59] Aristotle himself indicated in the *Poetics* (11.52ᵃ34-36) that philosophically there are three forms of Discovery: (1) persons, (2) inanimate things, (3) acts or deeds. The drama makes special use of the device, and Robortellus tried to distinguish between the dramatic, or poetic, and the oratorical technique.

According to Robortellus, one important distinction between the oratorical and the poetic use of Discovery lies in the degree of ignorance when passing from ignorance to knowledge. A tragic character like Oedipus, for example, may seek to find out whether or not he killed his father and married his mother, but he is actually ignorant at first of what he has done. The orator, however, is not ignorant of what has been done though he may try to cover up the deed or evade its consequences. In judicial oratory, when someone is convicted of having done a mischief the credit goes to the cleverness of his adversary. In tragedy, on the other hand, since the mischief is done un-

---

[58]See p. 233.

[59]In the *Analytica Posteriora* (1.1), Aristotle discussed how man arrives at knowledge from ignorance, how he attains "recognition of a truth."

wittingly (as with Oedipus) it may be excused and may actually deserve commiseration. Furthermore, recognitions in tragedy are followed by reversals of fortune. In judicial oratory, however, no reversal of fortune ensues; with the recognition of what has been done or not done the whole dispute is ended and there is no need for further inquiry. Finally, orators draw their arguments from what is probable, and this generally consists of ingenious conjectures drawn from matters outside the issue, from the education, the nature, the temper of the man who is accused or defended. Or the orator merely proves what has been done or not done. Tragic poets, however, produce Discovery from signs which are in the matter itself, as, for example, in the *Oedipus* of Sophocles from a scar, from Oedipus' crippled feet, from the fork in the highways, from Laius' train of followers and from many other things. Although he did not say so here, Robortellus would have maintained that these methods of producing Discovery in tragedy are also used in comedy.

The function of the protasis is to state the argument and introduce the principal characters. The function of the catastrophe in comedy is to settle the argument and bring the principal characters together in amity. The protasis anticipates the catastrophe, and the catastrophe fulfills the promise of the protasis. The catastrophe in comedy corresponds to the conclusion in rhetoric; it is the reckoning up (*enumeratio*).[60] Thomas Wilson's definition of the rhetorical conclusion is well put, and it applies to a poem as well as to an oration:

A Conclusion is the handsome lapping up together, and brief heaping of all that which was said before, stirring the hearers by large utterance and plentiful gathering of good, either the one way or the other.[61]

By "one way or the other" the comic poet must so manipulate his characters that they all come together at the end. This traditional function of the catastrophe still obtains in the majority of comedies; the modern audience is so accustomed to it that when we see the principal characters coming together from all sides in the last act we know that the denouement is at hand, that the final curtain is poised ready to descend.

The better way to bring all the characters together for the denouement is, of course, the natural way, by means of the poet's own skill, and not by miraculous intervention of outside agents. Terence was much admired for his skill in manipulating the closing scenes. Donatus (on the *Eunuch* 5.4.941) called attention to the "wonderful artifice" of Terence in reckoning up his *Eunuch*. Pythias, maidservant to Thais, has never forgiven Parmeno for his engineering of Chaerea's

<hr />

[60]See p. 30.   [61]*Arte of rhetorique*, p. 58v.

conquest of Pamphila, and she determines to punish the rascal. Therefore she fabricates an alarming account of dire punishments awaiting both young master and slave for their crime of violating a free-born Athenian girl. Parmeno falls into the trap, from there into a funk, and decides to throw himself on the mercy of old master Laches. Thus the truth of the whole matter comes out. Thus Laches and Thais are brought together. Thus a match between Chaerea and Pamphila is arranged. Thus Phaedria wins Thais for himself, and Thais wins the protection of old Laches. Thus Parmeno is forgiven. And thus all the principal characters are brought together in cheerful union.

There is a similar solution in *Phormio*. In this play, the parasite Phormio helps to untie the knot of intrigues. It is Phormio who makes it possible for Antipho to marry Chremes' daughter. It is Phormio who secures the money to buy the music-girl for Phaedria. In the last act (5.5.829 ff.), Phormio says: "I got the money, paid off the slave-dealer, carried off the woman, and took care that Phaedria can have her for his own, for she has been set free. Now there is only one thing left to do; I must get some leisure from the old men for drinking; I shall appropriate several days for it." Thus by means of Phormio's machinations the catastrophe comes about. As Latomus observed, this scene is a "preparation for the future coming together of the characters." And Willichius said of the same scene, "It is a preparation of the *catastrophe* before the future coming together of the characters."

The catastrophes of the *Eunuch* and *Phormio* represented Terentian artifice at its best and furnished models for Renaissance critics and playwrights who approved the classical drama. Ben Jonson's artful catastrophes are generally elaborations of the Terentian. Brainworm in *Every Man In His Humor*, Mosca in *Volpone*, Face in the *Alchemist*, all engineer comic intrigues in much the same fashion as do Parmeno and Phormio, though their machinations are far more multiplex. Perhaps the most ingenious of all Jonson's catastrophes is that in the *Silent Woman*. In the last act of this play, the tortuous coil of misunderstandings, mistaken identities, turns and counterturns provides a seemingly insoluble puzzle. But the multiple threads of knotted intrigues are under the control of Truewit, the clever friend of young Dauphine. Truewit, with some help from Clerimont, has undertaken to help Dauphine outwit his uncle Morose and secure an allowance of five hundred a year plus a promise of the whole estate at the death of Morose. Truewit is eminently successful, though his success is via a tortuous series of ridiculous detours. But Truewit and Dauphine hold the key to the one discovery that will clear up all the errors and misunderstandings, namely, the discovery that Epicoene, the bride of Morose, is no bride but a youth. When every principal character, including gulls, buffoons, collegiate ladies, old Morose, and the young gentlemen, is drawn on the stage in the last scene the revelation of Epicoene's sex routs the gulls, dumfounds the collegiate ladies, restores Morose to some measure of equanimity, and rewards Dauphine with a fortune. Dryden's admiration for Jonson grew enthusiastic when he considered the masterly artifice of plot in the *Silent Woman:*

I will observe yet one thing further of this admirable plot; the business of it rises in every act. The second is greater than the first; the third than the second; and so forward to the fifth. There too you see, till the very last scene, new difficulties arising to obstruct the action of the play; and when the audience is brought into despair that the business can naturally be effected, then, and not before, the discovery is made. But that the poet might entertain you with more variety all this while, he reserves some new characters to show you, which he opens not till the second and third act. In the second Morose, Daw, the Barber, and Otter; in the third the Collegiate Ladies: all which he moves afterwards in by-walks, or under-plots, as diversions to the main design, lest it should grow tedious, though they are still naturally joined with it, and somewhere or other subservient to it. Thus, like a skillful chess-player, by little and little he draws out his men, and makes his pawns of use to his greater persons.[62]

To cite a more modern example, W. Somerset Maugham's comedy, *The Circle*, employs a similar type of catastrophe, though by no means so involved and ingenious as Jonson's. At the close of Maugham's play, following the revelation that the young mistress of the house has left her husband and run away with another man, the principal characters find themselves in precisely the same situation that obtained in the same house, in the same family, some thirty years before. In the denouement of this twentieth-century comedy we see what Dryden's Eugenius saw in the typical catastrophe of classical comedy—"all things settling again upon their first foundation." *The Circle* is professedly an attempt at the artificial comedy of manners; it has a "well-made" plot which is directly descended from the plot of classical comedy.

The comic plot that met the approval of most sixteenth-century commentators and critics was essentially Terentian. It hardly need be said that many successful comedians in the sixteenth and succeeding centuries refused to be bound by the academic rules of neoclassical drama. The living theater in every age has refused to be bound by academic rules. Occasionally a successful playwright expressed a formal protest, as did George Farquhar when he rebelled against the

---

[62]*Essays* 1.88.

bondage of Aristotle and the academic classicists. In the course of his *Discourse upon Comedy* (1702) Farquhar sketched a satiric portrait of the scholar-playwright:

So to work he goes: old *Aristotle, Scaliger,* with their Commentators, are lugg'd down from the high Shelf, and the Moths are dislodg'd from their Tenement of Years; *Horace, Vossius, Heinsius, Hedelin, Rapin,* with some half a Dozen more, are thumb'd and toss'd about, to teach the Gentleman, forsooth, to write a Comedy; and here is he furnish'd with *Unity of Action, Continuity of Action, Extent of Time, Preparation of Incidents, Episodes, Narrations, Deliberations, Didacticks, Patheticks, Monologues, Figures, Intervals, Catastrophes, Choruses, Scenes, Machines, Decorations,* etc., a stock sufficient to set up any Mountebank in Christendom.[63]

Farquhar included in his list of moth-eaten furnishings most of the neoclassical paraphernalia I have been discussing. We may agree with Farquhar, and with Castelvetro before him, that successful drama in any generation must be addressed to people in the theater, not to commentators and critics. At the same time, we may maintain that much of the theory that these commentators and critics evolved from the study of classical models holds good in any generation. There are several important features in the plot of Farquhar's own comic masterpiece, for example, that square with the comic theory evolved by Donatus and his sixteenth-century followers. Even a summary glance at the *Beaux' Stratagem* will reveal a fairly regular practice.

The *protasis* (Acts 1 and 2) of the *Beaux' Stratagem* introduces two bankrupt young gentlemen on the prowl for wealthy wives, and two young ladies ready enough to meet young gentlemen. In other words, the audience, as in the days of Terence, is prepared to witness two love affairs, one between Aimwell and Dorinda and another between Archer and Mrs. Sullen. There are added complications, to be sure, such as Mrs. Sullen's husband and a cross-plot of flirtation between Archer and Cherry, the landlord's daughter. In the *epitasis* (Acts 3, 4, and 5 through Scene 3), the two young gentlemen meet the two young ladies and soon become very well acquainted. This acquaintanceship ripens despite growing obstacles and turmoils brought on by Squire Sullen, by the French count Bellair (another suitor to Mrs. Sullen), and by preparations on the part of some local highwaymen to rob the Sullen mansion. These two love intrigues are connected with minor intrigues. Cherry, who belongs to the gang of robbers, is in love with Archer. Scrub, the incomparable major-domo of the Sullen household, is in love with a maidservant, Gipsey, but has

---

[63]*Complete Works of George Farquhar* (London, 1930) 2.328.

a formidable rival in Foigard, the Irish chaplain to the French prisoners. The attack of the robbers coincides with the crisis in the love affairs, which seem heading for disaster. Then the *catastrophe* (Act 5, Scene 4), which properly occupies the last scene of the comedy, brings a discovery and a reversal of fortune. Sir Charles Freeman, brother to Mrs. Sullen, who arrived on the scene at the beginning of Act 5, now discloses that Aimwell is no longer a penniless younger son. It seems that his older brother has just died, leaving him both title and estate. Further, Sir Charles discloses that Squire Sullen has agreed to a divorce from his unhappy wife. Thereupon a match is made between Aimwell and Dorinda and Mrs. Sullen is set free to seek a better match than the old one.

Sir Charles Freeman, in the *Beaux' Stratagem*, performs precisely the same function that Crito of Andros performs in Terence's *Andrian*. We may apply to him what Donatus said of Crito, that he is a "character contrived for the catastrophe"—*persona ad catastrophen machinata*. Farquhar's practice in this play is by no means at odds with the sixteenth-century theory of comic structure that I have tried to describe in this chapter.

Chapter V: The Conception of Comic Character in the Sixteenth Century

HORACE, in his *Art of Poetry* (309-10), directed the would-be poet to the study of moral philosophy: "The source and fount of good writing is wisdom. The Socratic pages can show you the matter." Landinus, the leading Horatian commentator at the close of the fifteenth century, remarked of this passage:

He [Horace] makes the same observation about the poet that Cicero does about the orator. In truth, no one will be distinguished for eloquence, be he orator or poet, unless he knows many and various disciplines. The poet especially should set forth his poetry adorned with all the arts and sciences. Only thus may he essay every artifice, and so express the characters (*ingenia*) of a great variety of men, observe decorum, paint the truth, and bring it before our eyes. But every discourse consists of words and sentiments. Words are obtained from the grammarian and rhetorician. Matter (*res*) ought to be borrowed from philosophy.

Franciscus Luisinus, a prominent commentator at the middle of the sixteenth century, remarked of the same passage:

He [Horace] says that invention, style, and poetic decorum flow from the founts of that philosophy which treats of morals (*mores*); for no one, indeed, can doubt that a richer invention is provided by philosophy. Nor can one doubt that this is true of style. The discourse of philosophers is more concise and more contracted; that of the poets is more fluent and ampler. Horace is of the opinion that materials for the excellent writer are provided in the books of philosophers; moreover, that the speaker fills his cheeks there, as they say, with a rich store of words whereby he may clothe and adorn the weightiest sentiments.

Luisinus also referred to Cicero; he quoted from the *Orator* (33.118):

For philosophy is essential to a full, copious, and impressive discussion and exposition of the subjects which so often come up in speeches and are usually treated meagerly, whether they concern religion, death, piety, patriotism, good and evil, virtues and vices, duty, pain, pleasure, or mental disturbances and errors.

Luisinus very properly referred also to Plato's *Phaedrus*, where Socrates argues that love of wisdom or moral philosophy is the only sound basis of true eloquence. Horace and his Renaissance interpreters, then, recommended that the poet study moral philosophy and observe *decorum*. The "learned imitator" should possess a knowledge of ethics, of human virtues, vices, emotions, and he should know how to use this knowledge with propriety in his portrayals of every human condition, rank, and age.

While a knowledge of ethics was considered valuable for every activity of the poet and orator, it seemed specially valuable for characterization. And the study of moral philosophy in the Renaissance schools went hand in hand with the study of Terence. As Professor Baldwin[1] has shown, English schoolboys in the sixteenth century read Terence while they were reading the moral essays of Cicero. Before the middle of the century, Aristotle's *Ethics*, along with Cicero and Plato, was prescribed reading. The Terentian commentator, Petrus Marsus, for example, found Aristotle's philosophical analyses of virtues and vices well illustrated in the *Brothers*. In his comment on the last scene of this comedy (5.9.958), Marsus referred to the *Ethics*. In this scene, Demea, who has now reformed his harsh, niggardly ways, good-naturedly rebukes his easy-going brother Micio for his encouragement of youthful prodigality. In the *Nicomachean Ethics* (4.3), Aristotle argues that prodigality is the opposite extreme of stinginess, that since prodigals are reckless and indiscriminate they do about as much harm as good with their generosity. At the beginning of the action in the *Brothers*, Micio and Demea fit pretty well the prodigal and the illiberal man. The outcome of the play may be interpreted, as Marsus did interpret it, as a good lesson in true liberality, which is a mean between prodigality and stinginess. When both Micio and Demea reform, as they do, they approach this golden mean of liberality; Micio has learned that his indulgence of Aeschinus has been harmful, Demea that his harsh, niggardly control of Ctesipho has also wrought harm. The *Brothers*, like the *Self-Tormentor* and the *Mother-in-law*, is a thoughtful play that emphasizes moral character, but the sixteenth-century commentators found important *ethices* in all of Terence's comedies.

While *decorum*, in the sense of artistic propriety, should govern every element in a speech or poem, it seemed specially valuable in characterization. Dramatic decorum, in the eyes of Renaissance critics, meant keeping tragic and heroic characters out of comedy and keeping plebeian characters out of tragedy; it meant assigning to every person the characteristics that properly belonged to his condition, rank, age, sex, and nationality. The theory of literary decorum, in other words, was based in good part upon moral philosophy. Sturm,

---

[1] *William Shakspere's Small Latine and Lesse Greeke* 2:591 ff.

in his *Scholae* on chapter 2 (περὶ ἤθους) of Hermogenes' *De Formis Orationum*, expressed a typical sixteenth-century view of the close relationship between *ethos* and *decorum*, both of which were admirably illustrated in Terence:

This kind of speech [*oratio morata*], and poetic decorum, belongs to the writers of comedies and tragedies. For there is one speech for Simo, another for Pamphilus, another for Charinus, another for Thais, another for Thraso, another for Gnatho; and unless this decorum is observed by the poet he is hissed from the theater.[2]

Wagnerus, in recommending the study of comedy to his nephew, said:

It commends virtues and censures vices, and exhibits the matter of virtue in whatever age, sex, or condition you please. Here may be perceived the image and lively type of nearly all domestic actions. Thereto let one consider that of Demea in the *Brothers*. I bid him view the lives of men as it were in a mirror and take from others an example for himself. Decorum and the treatment of emotions, what the Greeks called ἤθη, must be diligently observed.[3]

In order to understand how the sixteenth-century commentators approached the theory of comic characterization it is necessary to examine both *ethos* and *decorum*.

ETHOS

The Renaissance schoolmasters emphasized the study of human character, which was an important part of the training in rhetoric. Leading classical authorities on *ethos* were Cicero, Quintilian, Hermogenes, Aphthonius, and the author of the *Ad Herennium*. Quintilian gave the clearest explanation; at least his explanation throws the most light on comic characterization.

Quintilian (6.2.8-9) was careful to discriminate between *ethos* and *pathos:*

Emotions, however, as we learn from ancient authorities, fall into two classes: the one is called *pathos* by the Greeks and is rightly and correctly expressed in Latin by *adfectus* (emotion); the other is called *ethos*, a word for which in my opinion Latin has no equivalent; it is however rendered by *mores* (morals), and consequently the branch of philosophy known as *ethics* is styled *moral* philosophy by us. But close consideration of the nature of the subject leads me to think that in this connection it is not so much *morals* in general that is meant as certain peculiar aspects; for the

---

[2]*Scholae in libros duos Hermogenis de formis orationum* (Strassburg, 1571), p. 284.
[3]Willichius' edition of Terence, p. 12.

term *morals* includes every attitude of the mind. The more cautious writers have preferred to give the sense of the term rather than to translate it into Latin. They therefore explain *pathos* as describing the more violent emotions and *ethos* as designating those which are calm and gentle: in the one case the passions are violent, in the other subdued, the former command and disturb, the latter persuade and induce a feeling of goodwill.

Apparently the Roman schoolboy was exercised in the preparation of character-sketches:

There is also good reason for giving the name of *ethos* to those scholastic exercises in which we portray rustics, misers, cowards, and superstitious persons according as our theme may require. For if *ethos* denotes moral character, our speech must necessarily be based on *ethos* when it is engaged in portraying such character. (6.2.17.)

Quintilian was referring here to the *ethologiae* which declaimers used, and which were similar to the exercises in impersonation (*prosopopoeia*) that the orator had to master; they were evidently in the spirit of comic characterization:

In the case of the declaimers indeed it is of the first importance that they should consider what best suits each character; for they rarely play the role of advocates in their declamations. As a rule they impersonate sons, parents, rich men, old men, gentle or harsh of temper, misers, superstitious persons, cowards, and mockers, so that hardly even comic actors have to assume more numerous roles in their performances on the stage than these in their declamations. (3.8.51.)

Quintilian (9.2.58) thought of *prosopopoeia* as about the same thing as *ethopoeia;* both terms designated representations of manners, both were generally connected with the art of comedy, specifically with Terence:

The imitation of other persons' characteristics (*mores*), which is styled *ethopoeia* or, as some prefer, *mimesis*, may be counted among the devices which serve to excite the gentler emotions. For it consists mainly in banter, though it may be concerned either with words or deeds. If concerned with the latter, it closely resembeles ὑποτύπωσις (a vivid verbal sketch), while the following passage from Terence will illustrate it as applied to words:

"[*Phaedria*] But I don't see your drift: 'a little girl was stolen hence; my mother raised her as her own; she was called my sister; I want to rescue her and restore her to her relations.' "[4]

---

[4]See *Eunuch* 1.2.155-57.

Phaedria, in this scene, is mocking the words of Thais. Latomus called the passage a "jeering imitation."

Following the lead of Quintilian, many rhetoricians of the Renaissance illustrated *ethopoeia, prosopopoeia,* etc., from Terence. Richard Sherry, for example, in his *Treatise of the Figures of Grammer and Rhetorike* (London, 1555), designated six kinds of *prosopopoeia: Characterismus, Prosographia, Ethopoeia, Pathopoeia, Sermocination, Mimesis.* Terence provided models for *Characterismus:* "the expression or painting out, either of the body or mind. So Davus setteth out Crito; Chaerea the troublous old man." (P. xlvr.) The first of three kinds of *ethopoeia* was a "property or expression of mild manners and affections. . . . So Terence setteth out boasting, Thraso." (P. xlvv.)[5] One good reason why *ethos* was associated with comedy, and with Terence, was that it designated the gentler emotions. Quintilian (6.2.20) said:

> The *pathos* of the Greeks, which we correctly translate by *adfectus,* is different, and I cannot better indicate the nature of the difference than by saying that *ethos* rather resembles comedy and *pathos* tragedy.

The author of the *Ad Herennium* exerted a considerable influence on the Renaissance conception of character.[6] An important task of the orator according to the *Ad Herennium* (4.51), is *notatio,* which is the depicting of natural characteristics in various persons. These persons must be presented as "haughty, envious, arrogant, miserly, ambitious, amorous, luxurious, thievish, treacherous." *Notatio* here was interpreted in the sixteenth century as about the same thing as *ethopoeia* and *mimesis,* and referred to Quintilian's explanation.[7]

Hermogenes discussed *ethopoeia* in Chapter 9 of his *Progymnasmata.* Priscian translated the Greek term as *allocutio,* but the general sense of his translation is pretty faithful to the original. Hermogenes recommended the following procedure:

> Ethopoeia is imitation of the character of a person assigned, e.g., what words Andromache might say to Hector; *prosopopoeia* when we put the person into the scene, as Elenchus in Menander, and as in Aristides the sea is imagined to be addressing the Athenians. The difference is plain; for in the one case we invent words for a person really there, and in the other, we invent also a person who was not there. They call it image-

---

[5]Cf. Erasmus, *De Copia Verborum,* edited by Weltkirchius (Cologne, 1551), pp. 303-06.

[6]See Erasmus *De rerum copia* in *Opera Omnia* 1.80; Trapezuntius *Rhetoric* 157v.

[7]See *M. T. Ciceronis rhetoricorum ad C. Herennium libri* (Venice, 1542), p. CXXIXv.

making (εἰδωλοποιία) when we suit words to the dead, as Aristides in the speech against Plato in behalf of the Four; for he suited words to the companions of Themistocles.

Characterizations are of definite persons and of indefinite; of indefinite, e.g., what words a man might say to his family when he was about to go away; of definite, e.g., what words Achilles might say to Deidamia when he was about to go forth to war. Characterizations are single when a man is supposed to be making a speech by himself, double when he has an interlocutor; by himself, e.g., what a general might say on returning from a victory; to others, e.g., what a general might say to his army after a victory.

Always keep the distinctive traits proper to the assigned persons and occasions; for the speech of youth is not that of age, nor the speech of joy that of grief. Some characterizations are of the habit of mind, others of the mood, others a combination of the two: (1) of the habit, in which the dominant throughout is this habit, e.g., what a farmer would say on first seeing a ship; (2) of the mood, in which the dominant throughout is the feeling, e.g., what Andromache might say to Hector; (3) combined, in which character and emotion meet, e.g., what Achilles might say to Patroclus—emotion at the slaughter of Patroclus, character in his plan for the war.[8]

Hermogenes, like both Horace and Aristotle, emphasized the typical traits of human character.

Aphthonius, in Chapter 11 of his *Progymnasmata Rhetorica*, presented a similar discussion of *ethopoeia*. Richard Rainolde, whose *Foundacion of Rhetorike* was based upon Aphthonius, combined Aphthonius, Priscian (i.e., Hermogenes), and Quintilian in his definition:

Ethopoeia is a certaine Oracion made by voice, and lamentable imitacion, upon the state of any one.

This imitacion is in iii sortes, either is it Eidolopoeia, Prosopopoeia, Ethopoeia.

That parte which is called Ethopoeia is that whiche hath the persone knowne: but onely it dooth faigne the maners of the same, and imitate in a Oracion the same.

Ethopoeia is called of Priscianus, a certain talkyng to of any one, or a imitacion of talke referred to the maners, aptly of any certaine knowen persone.

Quintilianus saith that Ethopoeia is a imitacion of other meane maners: whom the Grekes dooe calle, not onelie Ethopoeia, but mimesis, and this is in the maners, and the fact.

---

[8]Translation by C. S. Baldwin, in *Medieval Rhetoric and Poetic* (New York, 1928), pp. 34-35.

This parte is as it were a lively expression of the manner and affeccion of any thyng, whereupon it hath his name.[9]

Ethos necessarily overlaps with *decorum*, and much of what follows in the next section is ethical.

DECORUM

Cicero, in the *Orator* (21.70-72), defined the Latin term *decorum*, and his definition expresses the philosophical background as well:

In an oration, as in life, nothing is harder than to determine what is appropriate. The Greeks call it πρέπον; let us call it *decorum*. Much brilliant work has been done in laying down rules about this; the subject is in fact worth mastering. From ignorance of this mistakes are made not only in life but very frequently in writing, both in poetry and in prose. Moreover the orator must have an eye to propriety not only in thought but in language. For the same style and the same thoughts must not be used in portraying every condition in life, or every rank, position, or age, and in fact a similar distinction must be made in respect of place, time, and audience. The universal rule, in oratory as in life, is to consider propriety. This depends on the subject under discussion, and on the character of both the speaker and the audience. The philosophers are accustomed to consider this extensive subject under the head of duties (*officia*)—not when they discuss absolute perfection, for that is one and unchanging; the literary critics consider it in connection with poetry; orators in dealing with every kind of speech, and in every part thereof.

In his own *De Officiis* (1.34), which was well known to every educated man in the sixteenth century, Cicero discussed the decorum of youth and old age. Young men, according to Cicero, should avoid all loose behavior, endure both toil and fatigue, reverence old age, accept wise counsel, stay within the bounds of temperance and modesty. Old men, on the other hand, should pursue the labors of the mind rather than those of the body; they should serve as prudent guides and directors of others; above all they should avoid lust and wantonness, which are unbecoming to any age but doubly scandalous in old age. Cicero's conception of decorum in youthful and elderly character is rather severe; certainly it is less realistic than the frank appraisals of youth and old age in Horace and Aristotle. The *De Officiis* enjoyed great prestige, however, and time and time again formed the basis of sixteenth-century interpretations of comic character in Terence. Horace, in his *Art of Poetry*, without ever actually using the term, described the ways in which decorum should govern poetic composition, including the depicting of characters. The six-

---

[9]Rainolde, p. xlixr.

teenth-century critics drew their conception of decorum from Cicero and Horace, and from the Ciceronian and Horatian commentators. By the middle of the century, Aristotle's pronouncements on what is appropriate in both rhetoric and poetry came to share authority with Cicero and Horace.[10] As Landinus judiciously observed, "Decorum, in a word, should be preserved in all matters."[11] "To speak properly," said Melanchthon, "is to observe decorum."[12] Nowhere was the preservation of decorum more important than in characterization.

Iodocus Badius Ascensius, an influential early Renaissance commentator on Cicero, Horace, and Terence, may be taken as representative of Renaissance literary criticism just before the revival of Aristotelian criticism. In Chapter 20 of his *Prenotamenta* on Terence, Badius examined the decorum of characters. "Decorum," he stated, "what the Greeks call *prepon*, is decency, the seemly observance of propriety in persons, events, words, and the whole work of art." For the decorum of persons, he maintained, "it is necessary to consider their age, sex, fortune, country, and dispositions." Badius was following a recommendation of Horace in the *Art of Poetry* 114-18:

Vast difference will it make, whether a god[13] be speaking or a hero, a ripe old man or one still in the flower and fervor of youth, a dame of rank or a bustling nurse, a roaming trader or the tiller of a verdant field, a Colchian or an Assyrian, one bred at Thebes or at Argos.

For the decorum of age, Badius followed the famous four ages of man in the *Art of Poetry*—childhood, youth, manhood, old age. He pointed to an apt parallel in the *Andrian* (1.1.56-57), where Simo remarks that his young son has been devoting himself to horses and hounds. "The beardless youth," said Horace (161-65), "freed at last from his tutor, finds joy in horses and hounds and the grass of the sunny Campus, soft as wax for molding to evil, peevish with his counselors, slow to make needful provision, lavish of money, spirited, of strong desires, but swift to change his fancies." For the decorum of sex, Badius offered the general observation that manly deeds and manly speech should never be confused with womanish behavior and speech.

Women, according to this learned commentator, are fickle; now affable, now too surly, now very facetious, now too melancholy, now agreeable, now unfriendly. But, he wisely added, these attributes do

[10]Herrick, *op. cit.*, pp. 48-57.

[11]Landinus on *Ars Poetica* 86.

[12]*Elementorum rhetorices* (1533), p. 77.

[13]The sixteenth-century texts commonly read *Davus* rather than *divus*. Thus the opening line of this passage would mean: "Vast difference will it make, whether Davus (i.e., a slave) be speaking or a hero."

not fit all women; the honest matron, it is true, may be exemplary in her modesty, probity, amity, cheerfulness, peaceableness, and in her regard for husband and family. "In nothing," Badius admitted, "is there more diversity than in the minds of women; therefore various writings sometimes praise women and sometimes teach us to beware of them." Consequently the poet is more or less free to make his characters fit his matter. Terence, for example, could show a courtesan actually reconciling a lover with his wife. (Bacchis does so in the *Mother-in-law*.) The male sex, according to Badius, is more constant and more serious than the female. The decorum of fortune demanded that social ranks be preserved; thus a slave should not speak like a hero.[14]

Moral distinctions must also be preserved; the honest woman should speak differently from a wanton hussy. Mental states must be distinguished; a wise man should speak differently from an ignoramus. According to Badius, and he was merely repeating commonplaces, there was a decorum of nationality: Africans were crafty but timid, Germans bold, Frenchmen subtle, Colchians wily, Cretans untruthful, Jews stiff-necked. (This fixing of national traits of character has always been popular; the patterns may change but the principle of selecting a prominent characteristic remains. Thus the Elizabethans held that Frenchmen were reckless, Spaniards boastful, Dutchmen drunken, Welshmen proud, and Englishmen mad.)[15] Badius also described a decorum of dispositions; it was necessary to distinguish between various states of mind, even between various states of the same mind.

He cited Terence as authority:

As Terence says in his last comedy [*Mother-in-law* 3.3.379-80], "Surely, I think, we are all great and humble according to our circumstances."

Therefore angry speech should be assigned to angry persons, and mild speech assigned to mild persons.

Erasmus, who exerted a considerable influence upon the Terentian commentators of the sixteenth century, had something to say about decorum, and many of his remarks pointed to the comic characterizations in Terence. Perhaps his most influential statement—certainly it was repeatedly quoted throughout the century—is on the "description of characters" in *De Rerum Copia*.[16] Here Erasmus called attention to the distinctions among people of nationality, sex, fortune, in-

---

[14]See preceding footnote.
[15]See Marston *The Malcontent* 3.1.105 ff.
[16]*Opera Omnia* 1.79-81.

clinations, and emotions.[17] This description of persons, said Erasmus, is called *prosopopoeia*, and excellent examples are found in comedy, for the comic poets exhibit a variety of persons. What could be more dissimilar than Demea and Micio in Terence's *Brothers;* what more diverse than the calm, polite Chremes and the violent, mistrustful Simo, the discreet Pamphilus and the thoughtless Charinus, in the *Andrian?* If a person already created or described by earlier writers is treated, decorum must be preserved; that is, the traditional characteristics must be retained. Achilles, for example, must be kept as Homer made him, quick, wrathful, ruthless, fierce, and lawless; Ulysses crafty, lying, dissembling, and enduring; Agamemnon milder in spirit but greedy for rule, fearing the people, more eager for pleasure than for war; Hector lofty in spirit, heedless of death and omens, heedful only of his country. "In sum, whatever character Homer has formed, the tragic poets should represent him as such." Erasmus was doing little more here than paraphrase a well-known passage in Horace's *Art of Poetry* (119-27), a passage that greatly contributed to the conventionalized characters in drama:

Either follow tradition or invent what is self-consistent. If haply, when you write, you bring back to the stage the honoring of Achilles, let him be impatient, passionate, ruthless, fierce; let him claim that laws are not made for him, let him ever make appeal to the sword. Let Medea be fierce and unyielding, Ino tearful, Ixion forsworn, Io a wanderer, Orestes sorrowful. If it is an untried theme you entrust to the stage, and if you boldly fashion a fresh character, have it kept to the end even as it came forth at the first, and have it self-consistent.

Tragic poets, of course, would make use of historical personages like Achilles; the comic poets would create fictitious characters.

The most pertinent remarks in Erasmus on comic decorum appear in his *De Ratione Studii.* Here he presented a somewhat detailed account with illustrations from Terence:

In comedy, first of all decorum must be preserved, and the imitation of common life; the emotions milder, pleasant rather than sharp. Not only

---

[17]The attributes of character in both ancient and Renaissance classifications varied in number. Erasmus, Melanchthon, Minturno, and others sometimes offered a dozen or more—nationality, sex, fortune, age, education, learning, native talent, deeds, etc. Trissino, who was following a suggestion in the *Rhetoric* of Dionysius of Halicarnassus, presented a somewhat different interpretation in his *Poetica* (2.33 ff.). According to Trissino, characters fall into two classes, the general and the particular. The generalized character is philosophical and invites the reader to virtue or deters him from vice. The best examples of generalized characters are found in Homer. The particularized character is rhetorical and is in agreement with nature; he is presented in accord with nationality, age, fortune, disposition, and education.

must a general decorum be regarded, namely that young people fall in love, panders swear falsely, the courtesan flatter, the old man chide, the servant cheat, the soldier brag, but also that other particular kind of decorum which the poet uses at his own judgment to distinguish a certain character from others. Just so, in the *Andria* he introduces two old men of widely different natures: Simo violent, somewhat peevish, yet in no wise silly or dishonest; Chremes, on the contrary, polite and always calm, everywhere prompt, quieting everything as much as he can, gentle yet not at all stupid. Likewise, the two young men are of dissimilar nature: Pamphilus wise, considering his age, and discreet, but sharper so that you can recognize the son of Simo; Charinus, on the other hand, puerile, inept, and wanting in judgment. Yet again, the two servants have dissimilar manners: Davus cunning and abounding in plans, and the most persevering optimist; over aganist him Byrria of no counsel, a constant source of despair to his master. In the same way, in the *Brothers*, Micio is mild in the face of chiding, and merry; Demea spiteful even towards flattery. Again, Aeschinus, since he is used to city life and trusted by Micio, dares everything, but so that you perceive in him an honest character, dutiful to his brother, faithful to the girl. On the contrary, Ctesipho is somewhat clownish and timid because of the strangeness of these events. Syrus is clever and bold, so feigning and dissembling that only drunkenness uncovers his trick; Dromo stupid and dull.[18]

As Erasmus indicated, there were two kinds of decorum of character in the sixteenth century: (1) decorum in the philosophical or social sense, i.e., proper, conventional behavior according to established social custom—the "mirror of custom"; (2) artistic decorum, i.e., proper and natural behavior according to the dramatic art of the poet, according to what the particular dramatic situation calls for. From the aesthetic point of view the second kind is certainly more important, and it often appeared in sixteenth-century interpretations of Terentian comedy. The commentators, however, like many playgoers and critics of the twentieth century, often confused the two kinds of decorum. Willichius, for example, pointed out that Davus' impertinent behavior to his master Simo (*Andrian* 3.2.492) is indecorous in a servant, who should never mock his master. But it is certainly natural for the clever Davus to deceive his old master when he is serving his young master Pamphilus, and Willichius was ready to acknowledge that craftiness is proper in a clever servant. In other words, while Davus' behavior to Simo is indecorous in the philosophical sense, in this particular instance his impudence is natural and not a violation of dramatic decorum. In the *Eunuch* 2.1.222, Phaedria, who realizes his infatuation for Thais, exclaims, "I must shake off this weakness of mind; I am too self-indulgent." According to Willi-

---

[18]*Opera Omnia* 1.528.

chius, Phaedria was speaking "out of the decorum of a man, whose mind is strong and constant, not too self-indulgent." According to the precepts of moral philosophy, according to Cicero, for example, the decorum of sex demands strength and self-control from a man. Willichius was again imposing a philosophical standard upon a dramatic speech. Dramatically considered, however, Phaedria's self-confessed weakness for the beautiful courtesan is the most natural attribute in his character, and Terence by no means violated dramatic decorum when he put such a speech in his mouth. Willichius, to be sure, realized the difference between philosophical standards and a realistic "imitation of life," but the prestige of the philosophical decorum was so great that critics sometimes forgot or obscured the distinction. Virtually all the commentators, from Donatus to Erasmus and Willichius, agreed that the comic poet, who uses fictitious events and persons, may treat his characters as though they were individuals and therefore not always subject to the general rules of conduct. Consequently the sixteenth-century reader could condemn Davus' impertinence in general and yet admire Terence's portrait of a crafty, witty servant. And he could forgive Phaedria's weakness since the young man was in love with a beautiful woman.

Probably the main reason for emphasizing this general, philosophical decorum in comic characters lay in the twofold aim of the commentators, many of whom were schoolmasters. They wished first to point out examples of moral conduct that could be followed or avoided and only secondly to analyze the dramatic art of Terence. Many commentators were more anxious to find observances or violations of the accepted moral code than to find illustrations of lifelike characterizations. For example, in the *Self-Tormentor* (3.3.562 ff.), Chremes rebukes his son Clitipho for his familiarity with Bacchis, who is supposedly the mistress of young Clinia, the friend and guest of Clitipho. When Clitipho expresses surprise at his father's rebuke, Chremes cries, "I saw it myself; don't deny it. You do a shocking wrong to your friend in not keeping your hands off. A gross outrage to receive your friend under your roof and then tamper with his mistress. Last night at wine, how unmannerly you were." Petrus Marsus seized upon this episode as a good lesson in social decorum:

In the first part of the scene youthful incontinence is rebuked and the decorum of the host is preserved, who by the rule of hospitality ought to treat his guests civilly.

But the scene is far more than a lesson in deportment; it is rich in the subtle irony of good comic drama. Although Chremes does not know it, and Marsus wrote as though he had forgotten it, Bacchis is not the mistress of Clinia but the mistress of Clitipho, who was behaving naturally, if unwisely, in making love to her. In the eyes of Chremes, and Marsus, Clitipho violates social decorum; in the eyes of the audience he behaves as any spirited, thoughtless young man would, and Terence has certainly observed the dramatic decorum of the young lover.

This emphasis upon a general decorum of correct moral behavior tended to oversimplify the interpretation of character and to obscure the artistic decorum observed by the poet. Too often the sixteenth-century critics sought an absolute standard of decorum in character which was divorced from dramatic reality. One result was an abstract didacticism which encouraged conventionalized characterization. Marsus, who was ever vigilant to extract moral lessons from every scene in Terence, is perhaps an extreme example, but he was not alone. Even Donatus, who well understood the artistic use of decorum in characterization, sometimes used decorum in the general, philosophical sense. In the *Andrian* (2.1), Pamphilus comes to an understanding with Charinus. Pamphilus is in love with Glycerium but engaged by his father to marry Philumena. Charinus tells Pamphilus that there has never been any intimacy between him and Philumena. "Would there had been," says Pamphilus, who naturally would like to see Charinus matched with Philumena so that he might be freed from her. Donatus (on the *Andrian* 2.1.325) remarked that Terence has here preserved the "decorum of the maiden (τὸ πρέπον *uirgini*)." Petrus Marsus (*ibid*. 2.1.301) interpreted the scene as a lesson in the evils of amorous desire; a young man is corrupted by pleasure and loses sight of decorum. Rivius found a similar lesson:

The folly of lovers, their madness, blindness of soul, puerile tenderness, lack of judgment, immoderate desires, together with something indecorous and ridiculous in word, inept in deed, are exhibited in this scene.

Rivius' criticism upholds the established moral code but loses sight of the very natural behavior of two young men like Pamphilus and Charinus. Rivius, Marsus, and even Donatus, were here considering decorum as an abstract standard of human behavior outside the comic drama, which all of them would nevertheless have agreed should be an "imitation of life, a mirror of custom, an image of truth."

There are almost innumerable illustrations of this non-dramatic interpretation of decorum in the commentaries. In fairness, however, it should be said that even the most didactic of commentators did recognize that decorum can also mean dramatic appropriateness of character. Surprisingly enough, it may seem, Petrus Marsus acknowledged the decorum of characterization in young Chaerea in the *Eunuch*, the rowdiest, most harebrained character in Terence. Chaerea is the younger brother who, disguised as a eunuch, steals into the house of Thais and violates Pamphila. He gives a vivid account of his exploit (*Eunuch* 3.5.549 ff.). Marsus remarked that this scene "preserves the decorum of Chaerea who, because of age, weakness of judgment, the vehemence of a sensitive appetite, longs for nothing more than the enjoyment of carnal desire." Marsus obviously disapproved of Chaerea's conduct, but he evidently recognized the lifelike qualities of Terence's portrait. Willichius, who could be almost as didactic as Marsus when he chose, also appreciated youthful decorum in the dramatic sense. In the *Self-Tormentor* 1.2, Chremes delivers a lecture to his son Clitipho on the necessity of curbing youthful appetites, on how fathers should control their sons. Clitipho dutifully listens and agrees, but in the next scene (2.1.213 ff.), when he is left alone on the stage, he bursts out in a bitter lament:

What unfair judges fathers are to all young men! They think it right that we should be born graybeards straight away and have no touch of the tastes which youth suggests. They hold the reins to suit their own desires, the desires they have now, not those which they had years ago.

Apparently Willichius was willing to grant the reasonableness of Clitipho's complaint; at least he indicated that Clitipho's argument is based on the "neglected decorum of age." The neglect, to be sure, was on the part of old Chremes. It is proper for young men to fall in love, and Chremes had forgotten this. The Elizabethan dramatist George Chapman furnishes a good parallel use of the decorum of youth in his *All Fools*, which was modeled upon the *Brothers* of Terence. In Act 5, Scene 1, Gostanzo discovers what most fathers in classical comedy discover, that the young people have gulled him and married as they pleased. Accepting the inevitable with a good grace, Gostanzo says, "Good tricks of youth; i' faith, no indecorum."

So far as I have found, decorum in the sense of niceness, of avoiding any deed or word that is scurrilous or vulgar, is not prominent among the commentators of the sixteenth century. The affectedly fastidious distaste for anything that is "low" seems to be a later development that flourished in the seventeenth and eighteenth centuries despite the protests of sensible men like Molière, Dennis, Fielding, and Goldsmith. Nevertheless, there is some evidence of moral squeamishness among the Terentian commentators. Willichius furnishes an example. In the *Eunuch* 4.3.647-48, the maidservant Pythias rails at the ravisher of Pamphila: "If I could get at him, how I would fly at the sorcerer (*veneficus*) with my nails in his eyes." Willichius was gratified by the decorous choice of words here. Instead of calling the false eunuch a ravisher (*stuprator*), as he was, Pythias politely chose a euphemism. "Decorum (τὸ πρέπον)," said Willichius, "is here preserved, though he allows *sorcerer* for *ravisher*, which is incorrect phraseology."

THE INFLUENCE OF ARISTOTLE ON CHARACTERIZATION

Aristotle's *Ethics* was known to sixteenth-century scholars before the *Poetics* became familiar, and it exerted some influence on the discussions of characterization in the Terentian commentaries. Petrus Marsus, for example, whose annotations first appeared in 1503, repeatedly referred to the *Ethics*, and many of his references, though almost invariably didactic, are appropriate enough. Some of these sixteenth-century commentators knew Aristotle's *Rhetoric*, but neither the *Rhetoric* nor *Poetics* exerted any real influence on theories of characterization until near the middle of the century. So far as I can judge, Robortellus was the first critic to make extensive use of the remarks on character in the *Poetics*; in his essay *On Comedy* he systematically applied Aristotle's analysis of the ideal tragic character to comedy. In 1587, Antonius Riccobonus did virtually the same thing in his essay on comic art. Chytraeus, in 1576, used Aristotle in his *Propositions* on comedy, but followed the *Rhetoric* rather than the *Poetics*. All these scholars, of course, combined Horatian prescriptions with the Aristotelian. The comic poet, said Robortellus, "must note the characters of all ages and classes, just as Horace learnedly teaches in his *Art of Poetry*, and Aristotle in the second book of his *Rhetoric*."

Robortellus,[19] virtually paraphrasing Chapter 15 of the *Poetics*, recommended four qualities in the comic character. First, goodness and badness should be presented in several kinds of people. What is good in one person may not be good in another. Weaving and spinning are commendable accomplishments in a woman but not in a man. Praiseworthy traits and accomplishments in people of low birth are not praiseworthy in gentle folks. The character of even a good servant is a blemish in a gentleman; in fact, the highest virtue in a servant may be a vice in his master. Refraining from theft, for example, may be high merit in a servant, but not in a man of honor. Second, the comic character requires appropriateness (τὸ ἁρμόττον), which is about the same thing as decorum of sex. Strength, for example, is inappropriate in a woman. Third, the comic character must

---

[19]See p. 234.

be "like the reality (τὸ ὅμοιον), that is, true to his traditional reputation. Thus Achilles and Ulysses must be preserved as Homer left them. By implication, I take it, a comic character such as the braggart-soldier should be preserved as Terence left Thraso. Robortellus, however, did not say so; he merely said that the poet should introduce a certain person acting and speaking as people knew he has been accustomed to act and speak. Actually, of course, comic theorists of the Renaissance recommended the use of typical young men, old men, matrons, servants, and soldiers, the characters inherited from classical comedy. Fourth, the comic character should be consistent. If the poet introduces a person as cowardly, greedy, proud, he should keep him the same throughout the play.

This insistence upon self-consistency in tragic and comic characters, which had the authority of both Horace and Aristotle, led to highly conventionalized characterizations in both tragedy and comedy and is one of the distinguishing features of most neoclassical drama. According to Renaissance theory, tragic characters were historical, comic characters fictitious. Both sets tended to become fixed once and for all; the tragic characters because they were actual men and women such as the wrathful Achilles and the child-slaying Medea, the comic characters because as fictitious creations they were typical specimens of mankind, formed according to the precepts of moral philosophy. Robortellus, in his commentary on the *Poetics* (p. 290), neatly expressed the distinction and the trend:

Achilles was actually wrathful; he is portrayed as such by Homer. Chremes, a fictitious character in Terence, is portrayed as niggardly; not that he actually was such, but such old men are often wont to be.

In the *Poetics* 9.51^b11-15, Aristotle observed of contemporary Greek drama:

In Comedy this [universal quality] has become clear by this time; it is only when their plot is already made up of probable incidents that they give it a basis of proper names, choosing for the purpose any names that may occur to them, instead of writing like the old iambic poets about particular persons.

As a result, the New Comedy tended to use universal types as characters. Whenever, as rarely happens, a character in Terence does change his nature during the course of the play, this inconsistency offered a problem to the sixteenth-century critics. Both Micio and Demea in the *Brothers* do a rightabout-face; Micio learns to temper his easy-going ways with some firmness, Demea learns to soften his harsh, niggardly nature. Riccobonus (p. 154) tried to justify this seeming violation of an established rule in characterization. Ordinarily, argued

Riccobonus, a character must be of a constant nature from beginning to end, just as Horace advises. Some departure from this rule is allowable, however, when the alteration of character is like the change in Demea and Micio:

Demea, certainly, is harsh at the beginning, mild at the end; he appears stingy at first, afterwards prodigal. Micio, indeed, reverses his nature at the end. I say that change of character ought not to be admitted unless some very good reason is expressed, which is strong enough to bring it about; just as Demea expresses the reason for his change at some length, and offers this excellent sentiment: "Experience has taught me that there is nothing better in a man than affability and mercy."[20]

While some sixteenth-century classicists may have questioned the appropriateness of Roman characters for sixteenth-century comedy, the tendency was to accept the classical types and to judge contemporary drama by its degree of conformation to the classical. Thus Sidney, who measured English tragedy of his time by the yardstick of Senecan example and neoclassical theory, evidently expected good English comedy to conform pretty closely to classical standards. In objecting to the English practice of exhibiting deformed beggars and clowns on the comic stage he recommended characters that fit the classical types, with some important modifications. The amorous youth of Terence for example, has become the English courtier, and the schoolmaster has been added.

But rather a busy loving courtier, a heartless threatening Thraso, a self-wise-seeming schoolmaster, a wry transformed traveler—these if we saw walk in stage names, which we play naturally, therein were delightful laughter and teaching delightfulness.[21]

In general, the English comic playwrights of both the sixteenth and seventeenth centuries were more independent than the French. Dryden was right, as usual, when he called attention to the limitations of comic characterization inherited from the classical drama:

In their New Comedy which succeeded [Old Comedy], the poets sought indeed to express the ἦθος, as in their tragedies the πάθος of mankind. But this ἦθος contained only the general characters of men and manners; as old men, lovers, serving-men, courtesans, parasites, and such other persons as we see in their comedies; all which they made alike; that is, one old man or father, one lover, one courtesan, so like another, as if the first of them had begot the rest of every sort; *ex homine hunc natum dicas.*[22]

---

[20]See the *Brothers* 5.4.855 ff.

[21]*Elizabethan Critical Essays* 1.200-01.

[22]*Essays* 1.85. The quotation is from Terence's *Eunuch* 3.2.460: "You call this one his son."

Chytraeus, in his Propositions on comedy, presented a good summary of the sixteenth-century theory of comic characterization; he followed Horace and Aristotle, he took account of *ethos* and *decorum*, and he always had Terence in mind:

XIV. "Character" (ἦθη), or *mores*, is a seemly representation (*decora effictio*) of natures, dispositions, inclinations, emotions, and endeavors according to the diversity of persons.

XV. Character, moreover, is in a four-fold diversity of persons, who vary in regard to emotions, habits, age, and fortune. Aristotle has accurately explained this in the second book of his *Rhetoric*.[23]

XVI. Characters are also fittingly distinguished by means of sex, condition, or country, as one character is masculine, another feminine, another Greek, another Trojan, another Roman, another Carthaginian—what Aristotle, in the third book of his *Rhetoric*, has added to his previous remarks.[24]

XVII. Now by means of emotions: one character is angry, another mild, another hopeful, another fearful.

XVIII. By means of habits: one character is miserly, another prodigal; one a brave man, another timid; one Micio, another Demea; one Gnatho, another Thraso.

XIX. By means of age: one character is a boy, another a youth, another a man, another an old man.

XX. By means of fortune: one character is wretched, another happy; one plebeian, another powerful and wealthy; one rich, another poor; one the master, another the servant.

TYPES OF CHARACTER IN TERENTIAN COMEDY

In the Prologue to the *Self-Tormentor*, Terence mentioned several comic characters common in lively comedy (*motoria*): (1) slave on the run, (2) irate old man, (3) greedy parasite, (4) shameless in-

---

[23]*Rhetoric* 2.12.1-2: "Let us now describe the nature of the characters of men according to their emotions, habits, ages, and fortunes. By the emotions I mean anger, desire, and the like, of which we have already spoken; by habits, virtues, and vices, of which also we have previously spoken, as well as the kind of things men individually and deliberately choose and practice. The ages are youth, the prime of life, and old age. By fortune I mean noble birth, wealth, power, and their contraries, and, in general, good or bad fortune."

Then Aristotle proceeded to describe the characteristics of youth, old age, and the prime of life. There is an inevitable comparison here with Horace's *Art of Poetry* 156-78.

[24]*Rhetoric* 3.7.6: "Character also may be expressed by the proof from signs, because to each class and habit there is an appropriate style. I mean class in reference to age—child, man, or old man; to sex—man or woman; to country—Lacedaemonian or Thessalian."

former, (5) covetous pander. Calphurnius, the fifteenth-century commentator, added several more types: (6) forsworn pander, (7) burning lover, (8) cunning slave, (9) mocking lady-love, (10) forbidding wife, (11) indulgent matron, (12) scolding uncle, (13) helpful crony, (14) man of war, (15) stiff-necked parents, (16) courtesans. All of these are familiar figures in Roman comedy, and in many modern comedies as well. Notably missing, so far as modern comedy goes, are the professional and business men, the priests, lawyers, doctors, schoolteachers, shopkeepers, and merchants. And, to be sure, there is no mention of young women for the very good reason that respectable young women were not exhibited on the Roman stage. Other lists compiled by critics in the sixteenth century are similar.

Dryden remarked that the generalized characters in the New Comedy are all alike, and so they seem by comparison with the richer variety and larger numbers in English comedy. But there was some variety in Terence, and even more in Plautus. Terence, in fact, was repeatedly praised for the variety and contrast exhibited by his characters. Erasmus[25] emphasized the contrasts between the various old men, young men, and servants in Terentian comedy, and many commentators echoed him. Long before Erasmus, Donatus had praised Terence for his variety and contrast in characterization. Commenting on the *Eunuch* (3.2.454), Donatus remarked, "Here is shown a multiplex, dissimilar concourse of persons who are yet kept separate by the force and design of the poet so that no confusion of speech occurs." Latomus repeated this criticism: "Here are introduced various persons but so distinctly that they are easily discerned one from another." Willichius, also following the lead of Donatus, found a variety of speeches in this scene; he termed the speech of Thais "friendly," that of Thraso "censorious," that of Gnatho "sycophantic," that of Parmeno "panegyrical" when talking about his master's gifts and "jeering" when talking about the captain. The commentators recognized and valued diversity of *mores;* they even praised Terence for his occasional violation of the conventional *ethos.* Thus Georgius Fabricius, in his castigations on the Prologue of the *Self-Tormentor,* pointed out that Terence in presenting good courtesans changed the conventional *ethos* of comedy. The character of the courtesan was traditionally selfish and hard-hearted. In other words, Terence was not strictly bound by the conventional *mores,* but showed a certain amount of independence for the sake of variety, and the commentators recognized the right of the comic poet to depart from the "common manner" (*vulgata mos*) in particular individuals.

---

[25]See p. 139.

While the Terentian commentators admired the variety of characters in Terence and the contrasts between his various old men, young men, and servants, they were not prepared to accept much variety and contrast within a single character. The prescription of Horace, and of Aristotle, that a character must remain self-consistent from beginning to end was too strong and the illustrations of variety of *mores* within a single character too few to allow any large departure from the rule. I have already called attention to the difficulties raised by the rightabout-face of both Micio and Demea in the *Brothers*. Aristotle, to be sure, left a loophole in his prescription of self-consistency; he recognized the possibility of a naturally inconsistent character: "Even if inconsistency be part of the man before one for imitation as presenting that form of character, he should still be consistently inconsistent."[26] The commentators, however, even when they knew the *Poetics* seemed content to follow the clear-cut prescription of Horace. Consequently there was very little recognition of what later critics called "character development" or "growth of character," of contrasting virtues and vices, contrasting moods existing within the one character.

Some sixteenth-century critics did recognize mixed feelings within a character, and they recognized an inner conflict, but the strictest interpretation of the Horatian prescription of self-consistency hardly allowed any departure from custom. Jason Denores, for example, said of the *Art of Poetry* 126-27: "This means always angry like Achilles in Homer, or always sad like Orestes in Euripides; this means 'let it at least be simple and uniform'; for he plainly declares, 'have it self-consistent.' " But Terence's irascible characters are not always irascible, nor his gloomy characters always gloomy, as the Terentian commentators well knew. Furthermore, Terence occasionally broke the traditional pattern of comic character. Although the mother-in-law in comedy was supposed to be shrewish, Sostrata in the *Mother-in-law* is patient, kindly, and considerate. Donatus remarked that Sostrata in the fourth act (4.2.596) is not shown as angry but rather as moved by a mixture of indignation and grief, and that the poet does this "in order to portray manners and represent persons." Sometimes one of Terence's characters finds himself in a dilemma, torn between desire and duty. Such a state of mind is usually associated with tragedy, but it may, and does, appear in comedy as well. Aeschinus in the *Brothers* (4.4.610 ff.), for example, expresses such an inner conflict; he realizes that he must either bear the whole blame for kidnapping the music-girl or betray his brother Ctesipho. The sixteenth-

---

[26] *Poetics* 15.54a26-28.

century commentators labeled this scene a "tragic complaint," and Marsus, for one, pointed out that it portrays a struggle between mind and heart.

A more detailed examination of some common types of comic characters may help to clarify the general observations above.

YOUNG MAN

According to the brief sketch by Horace in the *Art of Poetry* (161-65), young men are fond of dogs and horses and sunshine. The young man easily yields to evil, disdains counsel, is improvident, prodigal, haughty, eager, but fickle in his loves. According to the more detailed analysis by Aristotle in the *Rhetoric* (2.12), young men have ardent desires, especially for sensual pleasure, but soon cool, for their will is sharp rather than strong. Passionate, hot-tempered, impulsive, they are unable to control their passions. They do everything in excess. They are ambitious for honor, but not for money. They are good-natured, confiding, hopeful, brave, sociable, and fond of laughter. In their actions they prefer the noble to the useful, and the wrongs they commit may be attributed to insolence, not villainy.

Horace, of course, was well known to all the Terentian commentators from Donatus on. Aristotle's *Rhetoric* and *Ethics* (which complements it) were familiar to many commentators in the first half of the sixteenth century. Therefore a good share of the critical comments on characterization consisted of attempts to square the general observations of Horace and Aristotle, plus those of Cicero, with the specific illustrations in Terence. The commentators found this method highly satisfactory, and it is true that Terence's young men do fit the philosophical pattern of youthful character pretty well. A few examples selected from dozens will show how his particular young men embody these general characteristics.

The leading characteristic of the youth in Roman comedy is his amorous quality, for he is always in love. The liveliest of all the young lovers in Terence is Chaerea in the *Eunuch*. Chaerea overflows with uncontrollable amorous desire. When successful he exults in unrestrained joy:

O good people, is there a living man happier than I? No one, by Jove! In me heaven has displayed all its power, heaping every blessing all at once. (5.8.1031-33.)

He loves to excess; he does everything to excess, and everything he does is aimed at fulfillment of his desire. Marsus, who quoted from Horace and referred to Aristotle here, gravely observed that this scene shows how the fulfillment of amorous desire is the *summum bonum* of youth. Of course Marsus did not approve of such youthful excess though he apparently appreciated the skill of the poet's characterization, and he did not condemn Chaerea outright. Donatus regarded the portrait of Chaerea as a masterpiece; though he preserved a sedate attitude throughout his comments on the character, he obviously relished the fine contrast between the vacillations of Phaedria, in his affair with Thais, and the lusty, unwavering frontal attack of Chaerea on Pamphila. According to Donatus (on the *Eunuch* 2.3.301), Terence does not portray Chaerea as incredibly lustful, but rather as precocious in love—*ante annos amator*. Donatus (*ibid*. 2.3.336), in a manner worthy of a twentieth-century "metaphysical" critic, called attention to a subtlety of characterization here. Chaerea tells Parmeno how he lost track of the beautiful slave girl in the streets because he was detained by an old friend of the family. Chaerea describes this shaky, wheezing, slack-jawed old neighbor with masterly strokes. And, argued Donatus, this description is appropriate and illuminating, for the sight of this old man accentuated, in the boy's mind, the youthful charms of the girl he was pursuing. Subtlety of characterization, however, is not the same as complexity. Chaerea remains a simple character; the contrast in youthful lovers in the *Eunuch* lies in the difference between Chaerea and his brother Phaedria.

Probably young Clitipho in the *Self-Tormentor* most nearly approaches Chaerea as a lover, though he never reaches the madcap exuberance of Phaedria's younger brother. Clitipho nevertheless provided the commentators with another good illustration of youthful excess. Calphurnius (on the *Self-Tormentor* 4.6.805 ff.) observed that this young man is heedless, inconsiderate of others, wholly preoccupied with his amorous desire. Marsus (*ibid*. 2.1.213) was also severe in his comments on Clitipho, who lives by emotions and is deaf to reason. Marsus referred to a famous passage in the *Nicomachean Ethics* (1.1), wherein Aristotle argues that the young, because of their emotional nature, are not proper students of political science and ethics. The conclusion of this passage, in Welldon's translation, runs as follows:

Knowledge is as useless to such a person as it is to an intemperate person. But where the desires and actions of people are regulated by reason the knowledge of these subjects will be extremely valuable.

The youth in Roman comedy is usually sociable, generous, frank, and honorable. In the *Eunuch* 3.4.539 ff., Antipho speaks to Chaerea of a dinner party that is being planned by the young sparks of the neighborhood. This speech provided Marsus with another opportunity to bring in Aristotle, who did observe in the *Ethics* (8.7) and *Rhetoric* (2.12) that young men are fond of company and pleasure. Good food, wine, and song, however, are not prominent in Terentian comedy, nothing like so prominent as they become in Elizabethan and Restoration drama. The young men of Terence are not singers, and they are not drinkers.

A good illustration of the heedless generosity of youth is provided by Aeschinus in the *Brothers*. Micio has discovered the secret love affair between Aeschinus and an obscure girl, and tries to draw his nephew out. Aeschinus tries to save the girl from harsh treatment. "Was a girl of that age," he cries, "to sit at home and wait for a kinsman to turn up? That's what in justice you should have said, my dear father, and stuck to it." The young man, with characteristic generosity, but heedless of consequences, had himself rescued the girl from her poor state. Donatus (on the *Brothers* 4.5.675) remarked, "He could not speak more like a lover or more like a boy." Frankness, or rather the inability to dissemble, is characteristic of Terence's young men. Pamphilus, in the *Andrian*, for example, is totally unable to conceal his feelings; when he is worried he appears worried. His father remarks to Davus that the boy is looking somewhat sad. Donatus (on the *Andrian* 2.6.447) regarded this incident as a masterly bit of characterization:

Decorum ($\tau\grave{o}$ $\pi\rho\acute{e}\pi o\nu$) is wonderfully preserved in the young gentleman, and plausibility ($\tau\grave{o}$ $\pi\iota\theta\alpha\nu\acute{o}\nu$) in the lover, for a crafty countenance does not fit an honest youth, and it would be absurd for a lover to conceal a sad disposition.

Donatus' praise may be excessive, but this characteristic of youth is certainly prominent and has often been used by dramatists. Beaumont and Fletcher, for example, made admirable use of the trait in their Amintor, the guileless young man in the *Maid's Tragedy*. Amintor is beside himself with shame and despair, but tries to appear gay and carefree. He fails miserably. His wife Evadne says to him, "You do it scurvily; 't will be perceived."[27]

Pamphilus, in the *Andrian*, is perhaps the most appealing of all the young men in Terence, for he exhibits other qualities than a strong appetite for amorous pleasure. Even more generous and openhearted than most young men, he has a high sense of duty and honor. He would not disobey his father, yet he cannot desert Glycerium. In 4.2.693-97, he assures Glycerium's servant that he will not desert his mistress:

[27] The *Maid's Tragedy* 3.1.119.

Mysis, I swear to you by all that's sacred that I will never forsake her, not if I knew I should have all men as my enemies. I wooed her, won her; our tempers agree; away with those that would part us; no one shall part us save death.

Marsus found this scene a good illustration of the Platonic lesson that love is a madness which distorts the senses. But Rivius, who was as staunch a moralist as Marsus, found evidence here of a fine character:

The integrity of Pamphilus is plainly shown in this scene; he resolves to preserve inviolate his plighted troth to his mistress, even if he knows that he will make all men his enemies.

By comparison with the lovers in Elizabethan and Restoration comedy, the young men in Roman comedy are callow and rather tame. The Roman youths are boys, endowed with no wit, possessing no resourcefulness. Davus or Parmeno do their thinking for them and plan their intrigues. The Roman youths are still sons within the family; none of them is a mature, self-reliant man. The gay, witty, reckless lovers in the comedies of Shakespeare, Fletcher, Wycherley, and Congreve are for the most part sophisticated men of the world. Naturally they have much more positive personalities, for they are older, more independent, and more experienced. Yet the advantages are not altogether on the side of the modern characters. If Pamphilus and Chaerea are callow, they are also fresh, boyish, innocent. Even Marsus and Rivius felt inclined to temporize their indictments of Chaerea's excesses, for they recognized that he was following the natural course of youthful desire, that for the moment he was both blind and deaf to reason. It is not hard to imagine how Marsus and Rivius would have judged the seventeenth-century descendant of Chaerea—Horner in Wycherley's *Country Wife*. Doubtless they would have out-fulminated Jeremy Collier, who drew sharp contrasts between the modest youths of Terence and what he considered the unprincipled libertines in Dryden, Congreve, and Vanbrugh. Wycherley's Horner is certainly no callow stripling; in him youthful desire has not driven out all reason. On the contrary, Horner is a mature, sophisticated man who knows well enough what he is doing and who needs no help from any Parmeno. Horner's assumed role of eunuch is his own deliberately calculated scheme, which he pursues with the intelligence and resourcefulness of an experienced rake. Chaerea's role is suggested to him in the first place by Parmeno, and the Roman youth pursues it with the reckless enthusiasm of thoughtless youth. While many readers have admired the skill of Wycherley in fashioning his character, few can like Horner. Most readers, including the moralists, have admired the skill of Terence's portrait and at the same time felt obliged to like the boyish Chaerea. As Jeremy Collier suggested, and as I have tried to demonstrate, there was a close connection between the comic characters of classical comedy and the precepts of moral philosophy:

> [Horace] advises a poet to form his work upon the precepts of Socrates and Plato, and the models of moral philosophy. This was the way to preserve decency, and to assign a proper fate and behavior to every character.[28]

Characterization of the young lover in Terence is too narrow, too thin, too generalized for modern tastes, but, as the sixteenth-century commentators recognized, it is right so far as it goes, and it is always wholesome.

SENEX

The old man in the New Comedy shares importance with the young lover, and provides a good foil to youth. As Aristotle observed in the *Rhetoric* (2.13), "Older men and those who have passed their prime have in most cases characters (ἤθη) opposite to those of the young." Cicero, in *De Officiis* 1.34, argued that decorum for the young man is different from the decorum of old age. According to Willichius, "The decorum of the old man is that he not indulge in misdemeanors, that he act altogether prudently."[29] Certainly the old man's behavior should be different from that of the young lover. "Nothing, indeed," said Marsus, "is more extravagant or more unseasonable than an old lover."[30] According to Horace, in the *Art of Poetry* 169-74, old men are utilitarian, miserly, cold, cowardly, timid, pessimistic, peevish, surly, censorious, and given to praising the days of their youth. Horace's analysis agrees substantially with that of Aristotle, who called old men hesitant, cautious, calculating, mistrustful, cold, malicious, petty, stingy, cowardly, selfish, shameless, pessimistic, garrulous, irascible in violent but feeble outbursts. "And they live not for the noble, but for the useful."

Neither Horace nor Aristotle offered a flattering picture of old age. The old men in Terence, however, more often than not conform pretty closely to the philosophical pattern. There are some important exceptions to these philosophical models, for the old men in the New Comedy had to serve as manly specimens of wisdom as well as comic specimens of senility. Since Terence did not portray men in the prime

---

[28] *A Short View of the Immorality and Profaneness of the English Stage,* Fourth Edition (London, 1699) p. 151.

[29] On the *Mother-in-law* 5.1.

[30] On the *Brothers* 5.8.924.

of life, save perhaps the slaves, panders, parasites, and soldiers, what-- ever virtues of mature manhood he depicted had to be supplied by the fathers and uncles. Some of the slaves are highly intelligent and worldly wise, but their sagacity is hardly the high-minded prudence demanded of the gentleman. Consequently the *senex* in Terence sometimes acts and speaks in a manner worthy of a man in the prime of life; that is, Terence's old man is not always senile. A little later on, I shall offer some specific examples of old men who do not fit the philosophic descriptions of Horace and Aristotle.

Quintilian[31] identified the Greek ἦθος, inadequately translated into Latin by *mores*, with comedy since *ethos* generally designates the mild and gentle emotions. *Mores*, therefore, were considered spe- cially appropriate to old age. *Pathos*, which designates the more vio- lent emotions proper to tragedy was appropriate to people in the prime of life, though comic characters, both young and old, might sometimes express strong emotions. "Yet at times even Comedy raises her voice, and an angry Chremes storms in swelling tones."[32] Donatus, for example, in a comment on the *Mother-in-law* 4.1.578, remarked: "*Mores* are properly ascribed to old people; from whence 'peevish old age' (*senectus morosa*) and 'peevish men' (*morosi hom- ines*), who are of such a temper." One is reminded at once of Jon- son's old gentleman, Morose, in the *Silent Woman*. In the eyes of the sixteenth-century commentators, Demea in the *Brothers*, and Simo, in the *Andrian*, were the most typical representatives of old age. Both are *morosi homines;* Demea, in the words of Willichius,[33] is a *pater morosus*. In more modern terminology, Demea is the "heavy father," an ancestor of the family tyrant in modern comedies and novels, who rules his children with an iron hand. Irascible as well as peevish, Demea embodies many traditional characteristics of old age. Willichius (on the *Brothers* 3.3.432) observed that his gruffness is that of old men, whose outbursts of anger, as Aristotle says, "are sharp but feeble." The anger of old men is feeble because their desires are actually weak and because they have become cautious and timid. Willichius considered Demea an example of timidity and coldness, a character corresponding to Aristotle's description in the *Rhetoric* (2.13): "They are timid . . . old age paves the way for timidity, for fear is a kind of chill."[34] Simo, in the *Andrian*, is another heavy father, peevish and irascible, of "sharp anger but feeble desires."[35]

---

[31]See p. 132.
[32]Horace *Art of Poetry* 93-94.
[33]On the *Brothers* 5.4. Cf. Marsus on *ibid*. 5.3.792.
[34]Willichius on the *Brothers* 4.2.
[35]Marsus on the *Andrian* 5.4.904.

According to Marsus, Simo embodies several traits of old age as enumerated by Aristotle. Marsus was following a Latin version of the *Rhetoric* (2.13.5-6):

Old men are mean-spirited because humbled by nature, and desire only the necessary things of life. Moreover, they are miserly, for they know by experience how hard it is to get and how easy to lose property. They are also cowardly, afraid of everything; wherefore one says, "Old age has prepared the way for fear." They do not crave sensual pleasure, but money.[36]

Avarice has always been considered the vice of old age. Willichius observed that old men are generally like Chremes in the *Self-Tormentor* (4.7.829 ff.), "that is, miserly." Marsus, commenting on the same passage, said, "The old man is naturally miserly, and those who love money argue over expenses." Then he bolstered his statement with a quotation from the *Nicomachean Ethics* (4.3):

Illiberality on the other hand is incurable; for it seems that old age and impotence of any kind makes men illiberal. Also it runs in human nature more than prodigality; for most people are fonder of money than of giving money away.

Demea is also miserly; his own brother says as much (*Brothers* 5.3.831-34):

Oh my dear Demea, in all other respects we grow wiser as we grow older; there is only this one flaw that old age brings on men—we all become more mindful of money.

In commenting on this scene, Willichius quoted two pertinent passages from Aristotle: (1) "Old men live more than they ought for the useful, not for the noble"; (2) "Young men have not the least desire for money because they have never yet experienced want."[37]

Avarice is apparently a natural outgrowth of the caution and cowardice that come upon men with bitter experience. The young man rushes ahead, heedless of counsel; the old man, said Willichius of Menedemus in the *Self-Tormentor* (4.8.873), "is unwilling to do anything without the counsel and prescience of his neighbor." Menedemus, indeed, is more cautious and pessimistic than most; he can scarcely believe the news that his son Clinia has actually returned home from foreign service.

> *Menedemus:* My son?
> *Chremes:* That's so.
> *Menedemus:* Come back?
> *Chremes:* Sure enough.
> *Menedemus:* My Clinia come back?

---

[36]*Ibid.* 2.6.432.   [37]*Rhetoric* 2.13.9; 2.12.6.

Calphurnius regarded this dialogue (*Self-Tormentor* 3.1.431) as a just expression of the old man's character, and so it is. Demea provides even more striking illustrations of the gloomy outlook of old age, for he always imagines the worst; he is sure that his city-bred son is going to the dogs. Yet Willichius found Demea typical of old age:

Moreover one may see in this old man as if in a mirror that old men, as in Aristotle, are wrangling, doubtful. In truth, they say and stand to nothing soundly and firmly. . . . Malicious, of a perverse nature, they interpret everything in a bad light.[38]

Later, Willichius added:

Old men are most apt to imagine future evils. According to Aristotle, they are little given to hope owing to their experience; for very many events are useless and most of them turn out for the worse. Yet they are rapacious from cowardice, since they are strong in memory rather than in hope.[39]

This senile pessimism takes a more ridiculous turn in Laches of the *Mother-in-law*, and a turn that has long furnished stock humor in comedy. When Laches' wife expresses the hope that they may both be spared to live out their lives together, he exclaims, "God avert misfortune!" Donatus (on the *Mother-in-law* 2.1.207) remarked that an old man detests the wife he desired in his youth.

According to Aristotle, the hopeless attitude of old men is responsible for their garrulity, since they live in recollection and are incessantly talking of the past. Certainly many old men in comedy, and the old men in Terence are no exceptions, are garrulous. Willichius found Demea typical; in him one may observe a fine example of the poet's use of decorum:

Old men for the most part are garrulous, and given to praising their own deeds, as Horace says. Even so, the poet, for the sake of decorum, has taken good heed of garrulity. "This is the reason," says Aristotle, "for their loquacity; for they are incessantly talking of the past, because they take pleasure in recollection." Therefore, because they are loquacious they delight in recalling to mind past deeds, and in recounting these they most stubbornly and tediously persevere.[40]

Demea is not a cheerful character; his garrulity is sour and tedious. Sometimes, however, an old man may combine great good humor with his garrulity. Laches in the *Eunuch* (5.5.973) is a pretty cheerful old man who says that he never grows tired of either country or

---

[38]On the *Brothers* 3.3.360. Cf. Aristotle *Rhetoric* 2.13.2-3.

[39]*Ibid.* 3.3.383. Cf. *Rhetoric* 2.13.11-12.

[40]Willichius on the *Brothers* 3.3.419.

town: "When I feel fed up with either of them I change the scene." Donatus called attention to the vividness (ἐνάργεια) of Laches' speech here, which is both garrulous and droll. Every student of the drama can readily call to mind many descendants of both Demea and Laches, that is, many old men who are either tediously garrulous or amusingly talkative. Simon Eyre in Dekker's *Shoemaker's Holiday* is one of the finest examples in all modern comedy of cheerful loquacity. Few old men are more loquacious than Eyre; none is merrier.

This last characteristic, namely facetious loquacity, would have been considered exceptional by Aristotle, who maintained that old men are neither witty nor fond of laughter.[41] Nevertheless, many old men, and women, too, are merry, and merry old people abound in comedy. As I have indicated above, the *senex* in Terence sometimes displays *mores* that are at variance with Horatian and Aristotelian ethics. The commentators accepted these Terentian variations from type, but they usually felt obliged to offer some explanation for the variance. In the *Mother-in-law* (5.1.727 ff.), for example, old Laches holds a polite, amiable conversation with Bacchis the courtesan. Donatus considered this scene remarkable:

> A rare color of life is blended in this discourse; for a courtesan and an old man converse, and, what is more astonishing, a good courtesan and a mild old man. So you may perceive that Terence has slipped and departed from the law of comic poets, yet retained custom in the action.

By "custom" Donatus obviously meant reality, action that is true to life, though not strictly in accord with theatrical tradition. Latomus remarked of the same scene, "But take heed of what is otherwise rare, a good courtesan and a mild old man." Willichius, who apparently believed that Aristotle and Horace were infallible guides to truth and nature, said, "A good courtesan and a discreet old man, contrary to nature." But Laches, in the *Mother-in-law*, is not always polite and mild; his behavior towards his good wife is usually harsh and peevish. Terence, as his commentators recognized, was not a slave to the "law of comic poets"; he could portray an old man as usually peevish and irascible yet amiable upon occasion.

The only consistently mild, good-humored old men in Terence are Chremes, the father of Philumena in the *Andrian*, and Hegio, the friend and protector of the widow Sostrata in the *Brothers*. Chremes, as Donatus (on the *Andrian* 3.3.533) observed, is a "gentle, good-natured friend throughout the whole play." Chremes is an old man who can still understand and sympathize with youth. Marsus (*ibid.*)

---

[41]*Rhetoric* 2.13.15.

said of him, "Chremes is introduced as a wise man who well knows the ways of young people." Rivius (*ibid.*) also admired Chremes, and not the less so because Erasmus had praised his character. Hegio is not so friendly as Chremes, but is nevertheless a kindly old man, a staunch friend and a wise counselor.[42] Certainly neither Chremes nor Hegio fits the philosophical picture of old age that Horace and Aristotle drew. They do, however, fulfill the demands of Cicero, in *De Officiis* 1.34, who said that old men should make it their business, by wise counsels, to do what they can for young people, for friends and dependents, and for their country. Therefore the commentators, even the most didactic ones, could readily accept Chremes and Hegio as worthy comic characters.

There is more variety of characterization among the old men of Terence than among his young men. The young men are all pretty much alike, though some are duller than others. In fact, after repeated and careful readings of the six comedies I find it virtually impossible to distinguish between the characters of Clinia, Phaedria, Antipho, Aeschinus, and Pamphilus (of the *Mother-in-law*). Pamphilus (of the *Andrian*), perhaps because he undergoes more vicissitudes than do the other young men, retains some individuality. Chaerea, to be sure, is a masterpiece of characterization in miniature. Several of the old men in Terence, however, are not difficult to distinguish one from the other. Demea and Simo are both peevish, irascible, tyrannical fathers, but the reader does not confuse the two. Micio and Chremes (in the *Andrian*) are both easy-going, mild old gentlemen, yet they are readily distinguishable. Chremes (in the *Self-Tormentor*) and Menedemus, though typical, possess some individuality; Menedemus, in particular, the old man who punishes himself for his harsh treatment of his son, goes somewhat beyond the type. In general, however, Dryden's criticism of the *ethos* in the New Comedy is justified. Certainly there are no old men in Terence so memorable as Dekker's Simon Eyre and Friscobaldi, Jonson's Morose, Farquhar's Boniface, Goldsmith's Hardcastle, Sheridan's Sir Anthony Absolute, Shaw's Captain Shotover.

MATRON

If the characterization of old men in Terence will not bear comparison with the best characterizations in modern English comedy, the old women can scarcely be expected to rival the sparkling matrons and dowagers of Jonson, Congreve, Sheridan, Wilde, and Shaw; for the position of women on the Roman stage was distinctly subordinate.

---

[42]See Donatus on the *Brothers* 3.4.447, 449.

According to ancient and Renaissance critics, the *mores* of old age applied to women as well as to men though the decorum of sex demanded certain modifications; the women, of course, had to behave like women. The Terentian matron never displays that aggressive masculinity that English dowagers often acquire, on the stage at least, after they have reached a certain age. The sixteenth-century commentators were alert to detect any breach of decorum, and eager to praise any notable display of decorum. Willichius called attention to a good example of feminine decorum (*decorum mulierculae*) in the *Andrian* (4.3.721). Mysis, a maidservant, sees Davus hurrying along the street with a baby. Alarmed at the sight, she cries, "My man, what is going on; where are you carrying the child?" As Willichius pointed out, Mysis as a woman is very properly concerned over the child.

First of all, the Roman wife should be obedient to her husband, even when her husband is peevish and unreasonable. In the *Mother-in-law* (4.1.524 ff.), for example, Phidippus berates his wife Myrrina for concealing from him their daughter's pregnancy:

Phidippus: Am I your husband? Do you account me your husband or even a fellow human being? If you had ever thought me either, woman, you would never have made game of me with these doings.
Myrrina: What doings?
Phidippus: You ask? My daughter has been brought to bed. What, not a word? Who is the father?

The confirmation of Phidippus' argument here, said Willichius, is "from decorum and circumstance; for it is not seemly that a wife make game of her husband." A little later, Willichius pronounced:

It is fitting, indeed, that wives obey their husbands, not rule them, and so Euripides means when he says that wise women manage affairs by means of their husbands' counsel.[43]

In the *Self-Tormentor*, Sostrata has also deceived her husband; years ago she had disobeyed Chremes' order to do away with an infant daughter. Now, having discovered that this daughter, Antiphila, may still be alive, she confesses her disobedience and tries to mollify her indignant husband. Willichius commented on this scene (4.1): "It is fitting that wives appease angry husbands by soft words and by asking pardon for their guilt." Again Willichius remarked (*ibid.* 4.1.623), citing St. Paul as authority: "This is the duty of wives, that they obey their husbands in everything." Although Myrrina and Sostrata thought they were acting for the best interests of their husbands

---

[43]On the *Mother-in-law* 4.1.561. See Euripides *Suppliants* 40-41.

and families, they nevertheless violated decorum. The commentators could hardly blame Terence, however, since the disobedience of Myrrina and Sostrata not only provided all-important elements in the plot but enlivened the comic characterization. Willichius was again confusing philosophical decorum with dramatic decorum.

According to both Horace and Aristotle, old men are peevish and malicious. So are old women. Laches, in the *Mother-in-law* (2.1.198-204), rails at women in general and at his wife in particular:

> *Laches:* Heaven and earth, what a tribe they are, what a conspiracy between them! What a thing it is that all women are set on the same thing and set against the same thing, and not one of them can you find an inch different from the bent of the rest! Mothers-in-law and daughters-in-law they are all of one mind in hating each other. Their keenness in opposing their husbands is all of a match, their obstinacy in it all of a pattern, and it seems to me they've all been at the same school taking lessons in mischief. If there is such a school, I am quite sure this wife of mine is headmistress.

The commentators found this masterly little oration very gratifying although Laches' attack here is unjustified. Willichius approved the sentiments:

> This same maliciousness is the nature of women in general. And so Menander considered: "Wherever women are, there all is bad." And Sophocles said the same: "Among all the calamities that befall mortal men, nothing is worse, or ever will be worse, than woman."[44]

Sostrata, however, successfully defends herself in a later scene (2.3.274-80), where she argues that husbands are unfair in blaming all wives because of a few bad ones; she maintains that all mothers-in-law are not unkind, that she, for one, has always treated Philumena as her own daughter. Willichius was willing to concede the justice of Sostrata's complaint, and to admit that in her we may see an example of a quiet, agreeable old woman. Dropping into his native German, Willichius admitted that Sostrata is not "wie ein alter teufel." Donatus explained that Terence was careful to clear her from blame since it is the duty of the poet never to wrong any kind of person.[45] Sostrata, however, was evidently considered exceptional among mothers-in-law. Latomus, for example, remarked, "Notice, moreover, how the poet endeavors by every means in this play to introduce a good mother-in-law, just as later on he tries to introduce a good courtesan.[46] But Sostrata is hardly exceptional among Terence's matrons,

---

[44]See Menander *Sentences* 694; Sophocles *Fragment* 187.2-3.

[45]On the *Mother-in-law* 2.3.274.

[46]On the *Mother-in-law* 4.2.593. Cf. Donatus on *ibid.* 3.2.337; Willichius on *ibid.* 3.2.336.

for all his wives are moderate, well-behaved women. Plautus provides better prototypes of the nagging females that appear as wives and mothers-in-law on the modern comic stage. Nevertheless, dutiful wives were considered desirable on the stage, and old women in general were more restrained than the old men of the New Comedy. The sixteenth-century commentators obviously preferred the good-natured old women in Terence to the livelier ones in Plautus, and Terence was readily forgiven for his departure from the strict philosophical decorum of old age.

COURTESAN

Since representations of respectable young women were virtually barred from the Roman comic stage, the courtesans provided all the feminine charm of the New Comedy. The typical courtesan was supposed to be a selfish gold-digger, faithless, fickle, and unprincipled. Terence himself recognized the type in the Prologue to the *Eunuch* when he listed among the stock characters of comedy "good matrons" (*bonas matronas*) and "naughty courtesans" (*meretrices malas*). Actually three kinds of courtesans may be distinguished in Terence: (1) the conventional gold-digger, such as Bacchis in the *Self-Tormentor;* (2) the exceptional good courtesan, such as Bacchis in the *Mother-in-law;* (3) the in-between type, the gold-digger with amiable qualities, such as Thais in the *Eunuch.*

The commentators regarded Bacchis in the *Self-Tormentor* as the typical courtesan, largely because she is the most avaricious of all her kind in Terence. Bacchis threatens to leave Clitipho for a soldier if he cannot gull his father of fifty pounds. Calphurnius, the premier commentator on the play, remarked, "Here is expressed the complaint of the courtesan, whose anger rises altogether from the failure to surrender money."[47] Then he added, "For this sort of women mind nothing else, care for nothing else, than somehow to extort something from their lovers."[48] The other commentators followed the interpretation of Calphurnius. Marsus (on *ibid.*, 4.4.723) expressed as vigorous an opinion as any:

Day and night, without fail, the courtesan lies in wait for wealthy and lecherous young men. . . . And accordingly, because of her power over men, the clever courtesan inflames young men, when for the most part she loves nothing but money and the torture of her lovers.

With a promise of ready cash, Syrus manages to persuade Bacchis not to leave Clitipho for the time being. Barlandus (on *ibid.* 4.4.743) remarked:

[47]On the *Self-Tormentor* 4.4.723.   [48]*Ibid.* 4.4.732.

Inasmuch as Bacchis is suddenly persuaded, the poet preserves the decorum of character of the courtesan. It is customary, indeed, for this breed to be wheedled by a very small gain.

Bacchis in the *Mother-in-law*, on the other hand, is an amiable courtesan of some moral principle. She voluntarily gives up her lover Pamphilus after he is married and, what is more remarkable, actually tells the truth to his family, thereby bringing about the happy reunion of Pamphilus and his estranged wife Philumena. When old Laches asks her to go to Philumena and her mother (Myrrina) and explain matters, Bacchis consents without any protest. She is conscious, however, that her generous behavior is exceptional among her kind: "I will do what I know no other woman of my profession would do, show herself before a married woman for such a purpose."[49] The commentators remarked this unusual behavior in a courtesan and carefully explained that Terence, while justified in his particular portrait of Bacchis, was proceeding contrary to the usual practice in comedy, which was to portray courtesans as bad. Evanthius, in *De Fabula*, praised Terence for boldly introducing courtesans who are not bad —"contrary to comic precepts" (*contra praescripta comica*). Earlier I called attention to Donatus' explanation of the amiable conversation between Bacchis and Laches, which seemed remarkable because the courtesan is kindly and the old man gentle.[50] In commenting on another passage in the *Mother-in-law* (5.2.774) Donatus said:

Trusting to art, Terence has been very bold, for, contrary to common usage, he exhibits gentle mothers-in-law and courtesans eager to be honest. But he subjoins so much attention to causes and so much weight of reason that the whole action seems lawful on its merit alone.

Willichius (on *ibid*. 5.1.750) remarked that Terence's creation of a good courtesan who repairs a broken marriage is "rather by means of art than according to the law of comedies."

Nevertheless, the commentators were careful to show that Terence has managed to preserve decorum even though the portrait of Bacchis is exceptional. In the *Mother-in-law* 5.3, for example, Bacchis explains at length, and with great self-satisfaction, how she has been able to help Pamphilus and his family. Marsus remarked:

This scene portrays the bragging courtesan exulting in her good turns. For whatever is improper for men who live a decorous life to do may be rightly assigned to a courtesan.

Gentlemen, to be sure, do not boast about the benefits they confer upon others. Donatus found other evidence of the fundamentally

---

[49] *Mother-in-law* 5.1.756-57.
[50] See p. 158.

meretricious character of Bacchis. In the *Mother-in-law* 5.2.797, Laches says that if Bacchis has actually given up Pamphilus her action will "redound to her renown and to her good name." According to Donatus, it is proper to speak of "renown" (*nobilitas*) in connection with gladiators and courtesans. Barlandus remarked that "good name" (*gloria*), however, is rare in this breed. Donatus called attention to another subtlety of characterization in the dialogue between Laches and Bacchis. Laches, delighted by the amiability of the young woman, says, "You are charming (*lepida*)." According to Donatus (on *ibid.* 5.1.753), *lepida* is an epithet that may be applied to courtesans but hardly to a *mater familias*.

Bacchis, in the *Mother-in-law*, remains true to the traditional character of the courtesan even when she behaves in an exceptional manner. Bacchis is that paradox, an "honest whore." Bellafront in Dekker's celebrated play is a true descendant of Bacchis; she, too, for all her amiable and heroic qualities, exhibits, in Part I at least, the speech and manners of the courtesan.

Thais in the *Eunuch* is the most particularized of all the courtesans in Terence, and probably the most convincing human portrait of the lot. There is never any doubt about her behaving like a courtesan, for throughout the play one may witness in her the "decorum of courtesans."[51] Thais always keeps her eye steadily on money matters. She is very fond of young Phaedria and would like to be faithful to him, but she cannot pass up the opportunity that the wealthy Thraso throws in her way. Furthermore, when provoked, she drops her polite manners and reverts to a more primitive female. When she learns that Thraso has threatened to carry Pamphila away, she cries, "If he lays a single finger on her he'll have his eyes snatched out on the spot." Willichius (on the *Eunuch* 4.6.740) regarded this speech as characteristic of the courtesan: "The threat is very proper (*decora*) for courtesans, and here are their weapons, namely tongue and fingernails." Nevertheless, although she always makes sure of her reward, Thais is not solely a gold-digger. Terence has humanized her so that she is much more than just a courtesan. Willichius, by implication, acknowledged the humane touch in her portrait. In the *Eunuch* 3.2.504-06, for example, Thais, as she prepares to leave her house for a while, says to her maidservant: "What is it? What else did I wish to say? Oh yes, take good care of the girl and mind you all stay indoors." Willichius, as though he had forgotten for the moment that Thais is a courtesan, interpreted this speech as the words of a prudent

---

[51]See Willichius on the *Eunuch* 1.2.

housewife: "Here is preserved the decorum of one leaving in haste and of anxious care for household matters."

Thais is the kind of courtesan who often makes the reader forget her profession and regard her merely as a lively, attractive, good-natured young woman. Terence was too astute an artist ever to describe her person; he lets the reader perceive her charm as it strikes Phaedria, Thraso, and other characters in the play. The naive young Chaerea gives us one of the best pictures of Thais when he discusses her with Parmeno (*Eunuch* 2.3.359-61):

Chaerea: But I didn't know that Thais lived close to us.
Parmeno: She hasn't been here long.
Chaerea: Confound it, why have I never seen her? I say now, tell me, is she the beauty she is said to be?
Parmeno: Indeed she is.

Later on, Chaerea meets Thais and is won over at once. Thais has been chiding the youth for his attack on Pamphila. Then comes the following dialogue (*ibid*. 5.2.877-83):

Chaerea: Of one thing you may be sure; insult was not my motive, but love.
Thais: I know, and for that reason I am rather inclined to forgive you. I am human enough and experienced enough, Chaerea, to know the power of love.
Chaerea: As I hope to be saved, Thais, I now love you as well.
Pythias: Then I swear, Ma'am, you must be on your guard against him.

MANSERVANT

The manservant, or slave, is a prominent and important character in the New Comedy. It is he, in fact, who engineers all the comic intrigues. While Erasmus and others have praised Terence for his contrasts between the resourcefulness of Davus and Syrus and the dull stupidity of Byrria and Dromo, there is relatively little attempt at individual characterization among the slaves. The Terentian manservant is either a clever fellow who deceives his old master while helping the young master or a dull, faithful family retainer who does what his old master orders. And the clever rogues are all alike. I confess that I can see very little difference between Davus of the *Andrian* and Parmeno of the *Eunuch*, who in turn are very like Syrus of the *Self-Tormentor*, Geta of *Phormio*, Syrus of the *Brothers*, and Parmeno of the *Mother-in-law*. The clever slave in Terence is more of a fixed type, I believe, than is the young lover, the old man, the matron, or the courtesan. The sixteenth century did not object to these typical features of the comic servant. What did trouble them was how to reconcile the social decorum demanded of the servant by classical authorities with the impudent behavior of some servants in the New Comedy. Terence himself, in the Prologue to the *Self-Tormentor* (31), which is a quiet play, of course, scoffed at the stock comic figure of the "slave on the run." Calphurnius commented as follows:

In this phrase his adversary is rebuked, who did not preserve the decorum of character. What, indeed, is more contrary to decorum than that people should have to give way to a slave in the street and to take heed of a madman?

In his livelier plays, Terence did introduce slaves who bustle to and fro. Donatus, for one, praised the portrait of Geta in the *Brothers* (3.2.299 ff.), who runs about the stage lamenting the sorry state of affairs his mistress and her daughter are now in. Donatus remarked, "This passage expresses, according to comic art, the servant on the run reporting bad news." Social decorum, however, demanded that a servant be respectful. Simo in the *Andrian* (3.2.492) rebukes Davus for trying to deceive him, and Davus mocks the old man. Willichius found such behavior very reprehensible: "Servile indecorum. It is not proper that a servant mock his master and aggravate his anger by questions and repetitions." But Willichius was again confusing social decorum with dramatic appropriateness. This scene between the irate old Simo and the sly Davus is one of the most diverting in the play, and Davus' behavior here is characteristic of the clever servant in comedy. In an earlier scene (*ibid*. 1.1.34), Simo praises Sosia, another servant, for his fidelity and taciturnity. According to Barlandus, fidelity is the primary virtue in a servant; but Sosia is a very dull dog and fortunately for the audience makes only a brief appearance. Donatus, with his usual insight, made a more pertinent observation on the loquacious Davus in *Phormio* (1.1.41): "Comedy fancies babbling and sententious servants; tragedy, sad and closemouthed ones."

Of course comedy has loquacious servants, and Terence created his share of them. Parmeno in the *Mother-in-law* (1.2) is perhaps the most talkative of the lot. Willichius, though he considered Parmeno here more swaggering than is proper and decent in a servant, recognized the scene as a good "example of servile garrulity." Petrus Marsus must have been more distressed than most by the impudent behavior of comic servants, though he, too, recognized the skill of Terence in these characterizations. At least Marsus was highly gratified by a scene in the *Andrian* (5.2), wherein Davus has his comeuppance. Simo has now discovered how Davus has been gulling him, and angrily orders him put in chains. Marsus observed:

This scene teaches that servants who riot about with too much cunning and malicious intent, who take too much upon themselves, or who are deceitful, ought to be punished. Indeed, with license they become worse, and, bold in their deceits, confound the discipline of the home.

Neither Marsus nor Willichius would ever have denied the comic value of these cunning, talkative rogues, but they sometimes had difficulty in squaring their behavior with the all-important didactic function of comedy.

The fact that most of the slaves in Terence are smarter than their masters presented another problem to the commentators. Social decorum would hardly allow this distinct superiority among such a humble class, yet Parmeno, Syrus, Geta, and Davus are unquestionably quicker witted, more resourceful than both young and old masters. Donatus judiciously resolved the problem by pointing out that while such mental superiority would not do in a drama of Roman life, (i.e., *togata*) it was permissible in the Grecian play (*palliata*). Commenting on Parmeno in the *Eunuch* (1.1.57), who delivers wise advice to his young master Phaedria, Donatus said, "Comic poets are allowed to portray household servants as wiser than their masters in a *palliata*, but the same treatment is not permissible in a *togata*." Willichius echoed Donatus: "Here also Terence follows the manner of Grecian comedy; for in this the servants are very knowing and sententious."

Although the manservant in the New Comedy is a more or less fixed type, he is often a very lively character. And he has bequeathed many characteristics to the household servants of modern comedy. Any one who has studied Terence will recognize the *mores* of Davus and Parmeno in both the male and female servants that have delighted audiences and readers from the time of Shakespeare to that of Bernard Shaw. To mention only a few modern characters who remind us of the clever, resourceful slave in Terence and Plautus, there are Brainworm in Jonson's *Every Man In His Humor*, Mosca in his *Volpone*, Face in his *Alchemist*, Waitwell in Congreve's *Way of the World*, Crichton in Barrie's *Admirable Crichton*. Among the numerous female descendants of the witty, loquacious slave of the New Comedy are the Nurse in *Romeo and Juliet*, the incomparable Dorine in Molière's *Tartuffe*, Cherry in Farquhar's *Beaux' Stratagem* and Louka in Shaw's *Arms and the Man*.

PARASITE

The conventional parasite of the New Comedy, as we find him in Plautus, for example, is a penniless loafer whose soul is in his belly, forever scheming for the next meal. Jonson's description of Carlo Buffone in *Every Man Out of His Humor* fits him admirably:

A good feast-hound or banquet-beagle, that will scent you out a supper some three miles off . . . a slave that hath an extraordinary gift in pleasing his palate, and will swill up more sack at a sitting than would make all the Guard a posset.

Terence's characterizations of Gnatho in the *Eunuch* and of Phormio in *Phormio* retain the essential quality of the conventional parasite and yet transform him into something more than a hungry feast-hound. As Terence humanized the conventional courtesan of the New Comedy, so he humanized the parasite. Both Gnatho and Phormio are individuals. Since Gnatho is the more celebrated, and since he furnished the basis for most of the sixteenth-century interpretations of the comic parasite, I shall confine my brief analysis to him.

The commentators called attention to a passage in the *Eunuch* (3.2.459) which portrays the traditional hungriness of the parasite. Gnatho interrupts Thraso's affectionate greeting to Thais with these words: "Then let's go to supper; why do you stay?" In the eyes of the commentators, this speech expresses the decorum of his character. "It befits a parasite, to hint at supper out of season," said Donatus. "He [Terence]," said Barlandus, "preserves the decorum of the character very well, since the parasite hints at supper out of season." Gnatho himself describes another prominent trait of the parasite, his servile flattery, in one of the most brilliant speeches in classical comedy (*ibid*. 2.2.232 ff.). This speech is a monologue or soliloquy, with Parmeno eavesdropping and interjecting asides. Gnatho enters declaiming to himself:

Good heavens! how much one man excels another! What a difference between a smart man and a fool!

He proceeds to explain how much smarter he is than the shabby, penniless wretch who has lost everything, including his native wit. Then he divulges the secret of his own success:

There is a class of men who wish to be first in everything, but aren't. It's them I dog. I don't provide them opportunities to laugh at me, but I willingly smile on them and marvel at their genius. Whatever they say I praise; if, on the other hand, they deny the same, I praise that too. If one says no, I say no. If one says yes, I say yes. Finally I have taken this order with myself, to agree with them in everything. It's the best way to get ahead nowadays.

The commentators generally regarded this scene as not only a superb portrait of parasitical *mores* but as a fine lesson in the evils of servile flattery. Marsus so regarded it, and he remarked that "nothing in public life is more pernicious than this breed of men." Ambrosius Berndt[52] called the scene a complete picture of the whole art of the parasite. He recommended that this notable description, together with the portrait of Thraso the braggart-soldier, be diligently studied and kept always in view, because here we may see, as in a mirror, the servile flatterer and the yes-man.

Marsus and Ambrosius Berndt were preoccupied with the ethical lesson to be learned from Gnatho. Other commentators perceived the social satire implied in the monologue. Donatus, for example, said, "He portrays the parasite and in his words shows the corrupt morals in flattering complaisance, as verily honest characters are also met with who are guilty of this fault." He very properly referred to a speech of Sosia in the *Andrian* (1.1.68-69). Sosia, who is also a yes-man, says to his master Simo, "Nowadays it's complaisance that makes friends, and it's truth that makes enemies." Then Donatus added:

This is a wonderfully satirical rebuke of the times by Terence, because the parasite calls him "fool" who is guileless and him "intelligent" who is "evil."

Barlandus remarked the oblique satire on morals implicit in the scene.

Finally, Terence showed Gnatho as a resourceful rascal, an opportunist who has the wit to wring profit out of loss. When his patron Thraso is outwitted and exposed as a coward, Gnatho does not sneak away in disgrace. On the contrary, he produces a masterpiece of persuasion, which not only reinstates him in favor but reconciles all the quarreling principals. Dropping the conventional parasitical pose of servile flatterer, Gnatho does not beg Phaedria and Chaerea to make up with the captain; he cooly offers them a proposition, that the two young men allow Thraso to continue as a rival for Thais so that everyone concerned may continue to enjoy the benefits of the soldier's fat purse. Why, argues Gnatho, should sensible people let a good thing like Thraso get away; why not use him?

Gnatho, and Phormio as well, have left a rich heritage to modern comedy. Although the hungry feast-hound is not so prominent in modern comedy as in the classical, he, too, often appears. I have already mentioned Carlo Buffone in *Every Man Out of His Humor*. A more notable descendant is Justice Greedy in Massinger's *New Way to Pay Old Debts*. Partridge in Fielding's *Tom Jones*, to go outside the drama, is often reminiscent of the hungry parasite though he has many other comic qualities as well. More important for modern comedy, I think, are the artful flattery, the brazen impudence,

---

[52]Riccius' edition of Terence 1.274v; cf. 1.218v-20r.

and the cool resourcefulness of Gnatho and Phormio. The student of Elizabethan and Restoration comedy will readily call to mind many persons whose whole stock of character is based upon these qualities.

Soldier

Plautus' Pyrgopolinices in the *Braggart-Soldier* is a caricature of the military braggart who always has to eat his own boasts. Pyrgopolinices is all brag, and the audience feels little or no sympathy for him. When he has his inevitable come-uppance, when he is beaten and humiliated, when he is made utterly ridiculous and contemptible, everyone feels that he receives no more than his just deserts. While Plautus' characterization is most entertaining, and while it has been imitated innumerable times, the characterization of Thraso in Terence's *Eunuch* has probably been equally, if not more, influential. And Thraso is something more than a vainglorious coward. Again Terence has humanized a stock character of the New Comedy.

Partly owing to the celebrated model of the *miles gloriosus* in Plautus and partly owing to their anxious care for moral instruction, the Terentian commentators, beginning with Donatus, were pretty harsh in their judgments on the comic soldier, sometimes, indeed, harsher than the evidence warranted. The stock comic soldier, according to the commentators, is a man who has no redeeming qualities; he is silly, ignorant, noisy, boastful, and, worst of all, inhumane. The commentators found evidence to support their analysis in Plautus and in Terence as well. In the *Mother-in-law* (1.2.86), the courtesan Philotis says to Parmeno: "Very little pleasure I've had, going away to Corinth with a most unkind (*inhumanissimus*) captain." Donatus had the following comment:

How can one speak of a soldier without superlatives? For every soldier is inhuman, this one, indeed, most inhuman.

Barlandus agreed with Donatus, adding a few graphic touches to the earlier comment: "This breed of men is devoid of all humanity, he of the glittering eye, pale face, mad gait, raging voice, and outrageous clamor."

For the most part, the commentators regarded Thraso in the *Eunuch* as fairly typical; they found him silly, childish, cowardly, garrulous, arrogant, and ignorant. His silliness and garrulity were merely ridiculous, not harmful. Thus Parmeno's mocking use of military terms when in the presence of the captain, and Thraso's unwitting complacency as he accepts these terms, was considered harmless and highly entertaining. For example, Parmeno, turning politely to Thraso, and with all the air of one general addressing another, says (*Eunuch* 3.2.466-67):

I beg, Sir, I do indeed, that we may be allowed, with your good leave, Sir, to give the lady the presents we wish to give her, to treat and parley with her.

Thraso himself naturally delights in military language and in big talk about war. His vainglorious sham is best exhibited in the scene (*ibid.* 4.7.771 ff.) wherein he rallies his household troops for the assault on the stronghold of Thais:

Thraso: What? *I* put up with a gross insult like this, Gnatho? I'd rather die. Simalio, Donax, little Syrus, come with me. First I'll storm the house.

Gnatho: Right!

Thraso: Then I'll carry off the girl—

Gnatho: Excellent!

Thraso: —and pay off my lady Thais.

Gnatho: Splendid!

Thraso: You to the center here, Donax, with the crowbar, you Simalio, to the left wing, you, Syrus, to the right. Bring up the rest: where's Lieutenant Sanga with his detachment of thieves?

Sanga: Here, Sir.

Thraso: What, you good-for-nothing, is it with a sponge you think to do battle, bringing one here like that?

Sanga: O Sir, I knew the commandant's valor and the strength of the troops. An affair of bloodshed, says I; how am I to wipe the wounds? says I.

Thraso: Where are the rest?

Sanga: Rest? What the devil? There's only Sannio left at home to keep guard.

Thraso: (to Gnatho) You draw up these troops; I'll post myself behind the van; from there I shall give the signal to all.

Gnatho: He's wise; his arrangement secures his own safety.

Thraso: My tactics are just the same as those of Pyrrhus.

Donatus and other commentators greatly relished this fine scene. So did Marsus, who also saw in it a valuable lesson in ethics:

This scene portrays the silly ostentation of the vainglorious captain, his great, vaunting words, his boldness before the danger, his cowardice during the event itself. . . . Thus Aristotle, in the *Ethics* 3.[7], says: "The rash are confident and eager for danger beforehand, but then hang back; the brave who actually seek danger are calm beforehand."

Marsus was not the only critic who found an important moral lesson in the portrait of Thraso. Ambrosius Berndt and other commentators who contributed to Riccius' edition of Terence admired the characterization here, but regarded the Roman captain as a man destitute of virtue; in fact, they saw in Thraso a most dangerous type of citizen, the noisy, ignorant busybody who too often attains high position and high honor in the state. As Ambrosius said, "There are, moreover, innumerable such Thrasos, whose arrogance is tolerable and very ridiculous in private affairs, but quite dangerous in public affairs."[53] But Ambrosius was carrying his interpretation of character beyond the limits of comedy that were recognized in the sixteenth century. There is no hint in Terence that Thraso would ever become an important public figure, that he would ever be taken seriously by any one outside his own household.

Terence's braggart-soldier has another quality which tempers and humanizes the vainglorious man of war. The poet has endowed Thraso with some sense, with at least a glimmering of perception. Stupid and vain as he is, Thraso yet knows that he is not actually loved by Thais. He says so in a somewhat plaintive speech that momentarily arouses some sympathy in the reader. Gnatho has been urging his patron to win Thais by making her jealous.

Thraso: Why?
Gnatho: Why? Don't you know that whenever she mentions Phaedria or praises him it burns you up?
Thraso: I feel it.
Gnatho: This is the only way to get rid of it. She mentions Phaedria, you counter with Pamphila. She says, "Let's have Phaedria for supper," we call on Pamphila for a song. If she praises the beauty of Phaedria, you counter with the beauty of Pamphila. In fact, give her tit for tat to gall her.
Thraso: That might do some good, Gnatho, if she loved me.

Donatus, always alert to detect subtle shades of characterization, observed that for the moment the captain spoke like a wise man, that is, not like a soldier. Then (on the *Eunuch* 3.1.446) he added the following significant statement:

Therefore it is well to remember that comic poets do not represent characters as altogether stupid and foolish, for there is no delight where the person hoodwinked has no sense at all.

The modern reader will doubtless call to mind Bobadill in *Every Man In His Humor*. Jonson's braggart-soldier also has his pathetic side, for he, too, is not altogether fool. Furthermore, Jonson made Bobadill even more human than Thraso by adding poverty to his other qualities. Donatus' criticism here is very penetrating, and he applied this interpretation to other characters than the soldier. He pointed out,

---

[53]Riccius' edition of Terence 1.219r. Cf. 1.315v-16r.

for example, that the gulling of Demea in the *Brothers* is the more delightful because Demea fancies himself as a pretty wily fellow.[54]

There are other minor types among the characters in Terence, such as the pander or slave-dealer, the maidservant, nurse, midwife; but these make infrequent appearances and have little to say. The commentators paid some attention to the slave dealer, but must have found Plautus far richer in this type than was Terence. The bawds and pimps that thronged the English comic stage during the sixteenth and seventeenth centuries certainly owe more to Plautus than to Terence. The main characters in Terence are limited to a half-dozen or so types, and his art of characterization is relatively narrow in range and shallow in depth. So far as they go, however, the Terentian characters are admirably done, as Donatus and his fellow commentators well knew, and they provided principal and indispensable models for modern comedy. Wherever readers were sensitive to subtle and economical strokes of characterization there Terence was esteemed and imitated.

The sixteenth-century commentators did not quarrel with the generalized characters in Terence. Far from objecting to them, they welcomed any agreement they could find between the Terentian characters and the philosophical patterns of human character described by Horace, Aristotle, and Cicero. With the exception of Latomus, who was primarily interested in dramatic structure, these commentators were actually more concerned with characterization than with plot. Emphasis upon characterization was the natural result of the traditional emphasis upon the didactic function of comedy; for comedy was supposed to present a mirror of everyday life which showed the spectator what he might follow and what he should avoid. In other words, the lesson of comedy came largely from the characterization, from the *ethos* and decorum exhibited. Even Robortellus, who upheld the Aristotelian primacy of plot in poetry, apparently concluded that characterization is of the first importance in comedy. In his essay *On Comedy*, he summed up his discussion of character with this statement:

> Let this be enough about Character, upon which almost the whole art of the comic poet depends.[55]

The emphasis upon characterization in modern theories of comedy has been explained as the natural result of an increased use of humor, which depends more on characterization than on plot. John Dennis, one of the ablest English critics of comedy, presented such an explanation in the early part of the eighteenth century. Dennis, who be-

[54]Donatus on the *Brothers* 4.2.560, 578.   [55]See p. 236.

lieved with Aristotle that the "Fable alone" makes the poet, neverthe-less found it necessary to modify this principle when he examined the theory and practice of comedy. He even found fault with Terence for introducing too much action in his adaptations from Menander:

As the chief force of Tragedy must proceed from the moving com-passion and terror strongly, and the chief force of epic poetry from the exciting admiration powerfully, so the chief force of comedy must con-sist in exciting laughter. By this *vis comica*, then, can never be meant the bare vivacity of the action, and the tying and solving the knot of intrigue, which is common to both kinds of dramatic poetry, as has been observed above, but the lively ridicule of the incidents, and especially of the catas-trophe, which yet is but a part of the *vis comica*, for there is likewise the ridicule of the characters proceeding from their several humors and the pleasantry of the sentiments and of the dialogue. When Caesar therefore says that Terence is but a demi-Menander, what does he say but that Terence had turned four or five of Menander's comedies into Latin and lost half the ridicule and the pleasantry of that Athenian poet in trans-lating him.[56]

Dennis, like Marsus and Rivius, put a high value upon characteriza-tion because it is the characters that chiefly instruct. He remarked of Etherege's *Man of Mode:*

To give a true character of this charming comedy, it must be acknowl-edged that there is no great mastership in the design of it. Sir George had but little of the artful and just designs of Ben Jonson. But as tragedy in-structs chiefly by its design, comedy instructs by its characters; which not only ought to be drawn truly in nature, but to be resembling pictures of our contemporaries, both in court and town. Tragedy answers to history-painting, but comedy to drawing of portraits.[57]

Further, Dennis attributed the instruction of right comedy to the philosophical or ethical content in the characterization. "Every legiti-mate dramatic poem," he said, "either of the comic or tragic kind, is not a mere diversion . . . but a philosophical and moral lecture, in which the poet is teacher and the spectators are his disciples."[58] Den-nis also welcomed the universal or typical quality of comic charac-ters since this universality bespoke a philosophical basis: "The char-

---

[56]*Critical Works* 2.160.

It must not be supposed, however, that Dennis did not admire Terence. Later in the same paragraph he added: " 'Tis my humble opinion that there is no dialogue extant in any language which has half the charms of the Terentian dialogue; what comes nearest to it is that of Etherege in Sir Fopling Flutter. I, who have been acquainted with Terence above forty years, am now more delighted with him than ever."

[57]*Ibid.* 2.245.

[58]*Ibid.* 2.308.

acters in every comedy are always at the bottom universal and allegorical, or else the instruction could not be universal."⁵⁹ Finally, Dennis, like his sixteenth-century predecessors, bolstered his theory of comic characterization by quotations from Horace's *Art of Poetry* and Aristotle's *Rhetoric*. In praising the lifelike characters in Etherege's *Man of Mode*, Dennis observed that pleasing and instructive characters "must be drawn with those qualities that are proper to each respective season of life." Then he proceeded as follows:

This is the chief precept given for the forming the characters by the two great masters of the rules which Nature herself dictated, and which have been received in every age for the standards of writing successfully and of judging surely, unless it were with poetasters and their foolish admirers.⁶⁰

The first of these two great masters is Horace, who, in the estimation of Dennis, "is but an epitomizer of Aristotle in giving rules for the characters." Dennis referred, of course, to the familiar passages in the *Art of Poetry* and in the *Rhetoric* that were usually quoted when Renaissance critics discussed characterization.

The comic theory of Dennis was the soundest in his generation. While English comedy, under the domination of Richard Steele and his followers, was dissolving in tearful sentimentality, Dennis upheld the traditional *vis comica* of laughter. It is apparent, I think, that Dennis' theory was essentially the same as that evolved by the Terentian commentators and critics of the first half of the sixteenth century.

---

⁵⁹*Ibid.* 1.187.
⁶⁰*Ibid.* 2.245.

Chapter VI: The Terentian Commentators on Comic Sentiment and Diction

THE THIRD qualitative element of dramatic poetry in the Aristotelian scheme is Thought (διάνοια), usually translated into Latin as *sententia*. Before the *Poetics* became generally known in western Europe the Latin term for sentiment was *oratio*. Thus Georgius Fabricius (on the *Andrian* 11-12) paired μῦθος (plot) with *argumentum*, διάνοια (thought) with *oratio*, and λέξις (diction) with *stilus*. Fabricius knew something about Aristotle's *Poetics*, but here he was following the terminology of Terence and Donatus. In the Prologue to the *Andrian* Terence himself remarked that his play was similar to two of Menander's in plot (*argumentum*), but different in sentiment (*oratio*) and style (*stilus*). Donatus helped to fix the terms for the early sixteenth-century commentators: "They say that *oratio* is in the sentiments, *stilus* in the words, and *argumentum* in the events."[1] After Paccius' Latin translation of the *Poetics* became widely known the usual term was *sententia*, the *Sentiment* of English literary criticism between Ben Jonson and Samuel Johnson.

According to Aristotle (*Poetics* 6), Sentiment is primarily rhetorical:

Third comes the element of Thought (διάνοια), i.e., the power of saying whatever can be said, or what is appropriate to the occasion. This is what, in the speeches in Tragedy, falls under the arts of Politics and Rhetoric; for the older poets make their personages discourse like statesmen, and the moderns like rhetoricians. One must not confuse it with Character (ἦθος). Character in a play is that which reveals the moral purpose of the agents, i.e., the sort of thing they seek or avoid. . . . Thought, on the other hand, is shown in all they say when proving or disproving some particular point, or enunciating some universal proposition.

In *Poetics* 19, Aristotle made clearer his assignment of sentiment to the art of rhetoric:

As for the Thought, we may assume what is said of it in our Art of Rhetoric, as it belongs more properly to that department of inquiry. The

---

[1]Donatus on the *Andrian* 12.

Thought of the personages is shown in everything to be effected by their language—in every effort to prove or disprove, to arouse emotion (pity, fear, anger, and the like), or to maximize or minimize things.

Rhetoric, in the Aristotelian sense, was closely allied to Dialectic; it was considered, in fact, a branch of Dialectic. Consequently reasoning was a necessary basis for all true rhetoric and *dianoia* was primarily a rational element. Robortellus, in his commentary (p. 225) on the *Poetics*, stated:

For a syllogism is nothing else but *dianoia* or something from *dianoias*, by which indeed we reason, and that which we gather together by means of reason can truly be called a *sententia*.

A century later, Alexander Richardson, an English disciple of Ramus, wrote (p. 333): "In truth I hold *dianoia* and *syllogismus* to be all one." In his essay *On Comedy*,[2] Robortellus followed Aristotle's remarks on Thought in the *Poetics*, merely adding that comic thoughts are relatively simple, humble, and not concerned with weighty issues or with searching inquiry. Riccobonus, in his essay on comedy (pp. 154-55), illustrated Aristotle's theory from Terence:

The third qualitative part [of comedy] is sentiment, to which every invention of demonstration, stirring the mind, and amplification is said to belong, as in the *Brothers* [60-67]:

[*Micio*] [My brother] comes to me perpetually, crying, "What are you about, Micio? Why are you bringing the boy to ruin on our hands? Why this license? Why these drinking parties? Why supply him with money for these things, and let him spend so much for clothes? You are very foolish." He himself is extremely hard, past right and sense, and in my opinion it's a great mistake to suppose that the authority which is founded on force has more weight and stability than that which hangs by the link of friendliness.

This speech, according to Riccobonus, illustrates the full range of sentiment: it demonstrates that Demea's harsh attitude toward his son is wrong; it stirs the mind because Demea's want of foresight has roused a sense of shame in Micio; it is a sentiment of amplification because the mischief and injury are amplified by Micio's own affability.

When Aristotle's theory of sentiment in the drama became known to the sixteenth-century critics it was easily reconciled with Quintilian's discussion of *sententia* (8.5), which was doubtless familiar to all students of rhetoric in the Renaissance. In his emphasis upon the reflective quality of *sententiae*, Quintilian said in different words

---

[2]See p. 236.

about what Aristotle said of *dianoia*. The oldest type of *sententiae*, according to Quintilian, is the aphorism or maxim, the *gnome* of the Greeks.[3] Often a *sententia* is part of an *enthymeme* or *epichireme* (a kind of syllogism). One of Quintilian's illustrations here is from the *Andrian* (68): "Complaisance wins us friends, the truth enmity." Quintilian (8.5.9), in fact, maintained that the enthymeme, which is all-important in rhetorical arguments, enjoys a pre-eminence among *sententiae* like that of Homer among poets and of Rome among cities; he said that *sententia* is shown in enthymemes and aphorisms. Aristotle, it may be recalled, said that *dianoia* is shown in proofs and disproofs or in "enunciating some universal proposition." In other words, both Aristotle and Quintilian led the Terentian commentators who wished to consider thought in comedy back to argumentation, to proofs, to syllogisms and enthymemes, to figures of thought—to logic and rhetoric, from which, to be sure, the commentators seldom strayed very far anyway.

Castelvetro, who had somewhat broader literary interests than did many of the Terentian commentators, expressed the typical sixteenth-century attitude when he said that character belongs to philosophy and sentiment to rhetoric. He (p. 127) called *sententia* the "substance and soul of rhetoric." He referred aptly enough to Quintilian's famous estimate of Lucan: "Lucan is fiery and vehement and renowned for his sentiments, but, to speak frankly, should be imitated by orators rather than by poets." (10.1.90.) He also referred, no less aptly, to Quintilian's comparison of Euripides with Sophocles. The speech of Euripides, said Quintilian (10.1.68), while less dignified than Sophocles, "has a closer affinity to that of oratory, and is full of sentiments in which he rivals the philosopher, and for affirming and replying he is comparable to the masters of forensic oratory."

Reduced to its simplest terms, sentiment is largely expressed in proofs and disproofs, specifically in enthymemes and maxims. And maxims, according to Aristotle,[4] are actually the premises or con-

---

[3]Victorius, in his commentary (p. 76) on the *Poetics*, remarked that what the Greeks called γνώμη and the Latins *sententia* is Aristotle's διάνοια.

[4]"Now a maxim is a statement, not however concerning particulars, as, for instance, what sort of man Iphicrates was, but general; it does not even deal with all general things, as for instance that the straight is the opposite of the crooked, but with the objects of human actions, and with what should be chosen or avoided with reference to them. And as the enthymeme is, we may say, the syllogism dealing with such things, maxims are the premises or conclusions of enthymemes without the syllogism. For example:

No man who is sensible ought to have his children taught to be excessively clever,

is a maxim; but when the why and the wherefore are added, the whole makes an enthymeme." (*Rhetoric* 2.21.2.)

clusions of proofs. The syllogism is the formal, logical proof in reasoning; the enthymeme is a rhetorical syllogism which cannot be demonstratively proved; the maxim is an incomplete enthymeme. Syllogism, enthymeme, and maxim were often treated during the Renaissance as figures, and I shall consider the maxim under *paroemia* in my discussion of rhetorical figures. Since the syllogism and enthymeme, as principal elements of logical and rhetorical proof, are much broader than most figures, I shall discuss them separately under proofs.

PROOFS

The quest of rhetorical proofs in Terence did not arise from the study of Aristotle's *Rhetoric* and *Poetics*. As I have repeatedly stated in earlier chapters, criticism of Terence was rhetorical from the beginning, from the time of Cicero, and from the time of Donatus. The drama, comedy in particular, has always been a form of debate; the Attic comedy of Aristophanes, the Roman comedy of Plautus and Terence, the medieval morality play, the Elizabethan comedy of Shakespeare and Jonson, the Restoration comedy of Dryden, Wycherley, and Congreve, the contemporary "play of ideas" or "thesis-drama" of Zola, Ibsen, Galsworthy, and Shaw, all have emphasized disputation. Aristotle's *Rhetoric* and his references to the art of rhetoric in the *Poetics* merely added important authority to the long established rhetorical procedure in dramatic criticism. In a 1570 edition of Terence, for example, Vincentius Cordatus (p. 206r) analyzed the *Andrian* as a disputation between young men and old. The subject of the controversy is: "Ought the young man to marry; specifically should one young man marry Glycerium, the other Philumena?" The affirmative side, the *confirmatio*, is taken by young Pamphilus and Charinus. The negative side, the *confutatio*, which denies the right of any young person to marry without the father's consent, is taken by old Simo and Chremes. The stand of the servants in this controversy, according to Cordatus, is "mixed."

The analysis of Cordatus is certainly correct from one point of view, and while the sixteenth-century commentators seldom reduced the argument of a Terentian comedy to so bald a rhetorical basis, they all thought of comedy as fundamentally controversial and therefore necessarily made up of proofs and disproofs. Melanchthon, it may be recalled, remarked of the *Andrian:* "The whole play is like the persuasive type of oration, for old men, youths, and servants deliberate (*consuliant*) on the whole matter in various ways."[5]

---

[5]See page 73.

According to both Aristotle and Quintilian, there are two classes of proof, the *inartificial* and the *artificial*. Inartificial proofs are decisions of previous courts, documents, witnesses, oaths, and sometimes signs. The speaker who makes use of inartificial proofs has them at hand and merely adduces them in his argument. Artificial proofs, on the other hand, are superior, since they depend upon the artistic effort and judgment of the speaker. "Every artificial proof," said Quintilian (5.9.1), "consists either of signs or arguments or examples." Arguments in artificial proof, according to Quintilian (5.10.1), comprise the "enthymemes, epichiremes, and ἀποδείξεις of the Greeks, terms which, in spite of their difference, have much the same meaning." According to Aristotle,[6] the two kinds of artificial proof common to all branches of rhetoric are *example* and *enthymeme* (including the *maxim*). Aristotle considered examples best suited to deliberative oratory; for examples from the past throw light on the future. In forensic oratory, which deals with the existence or non-existence of facts, enthymemes are more suitable. In demonstrative oratory, where the facts are generally taken for granted, amplification is generally employed to show that something is honorable or useful.[7]

The New Comedy used all modes of arguments, all kinds of proof and disproof. The historian's task is not to find illustrations of inartificial and artificial proof in the plays of Terence, for Donatus, Willichius, and others were always pointing them out; the principal task is to select illustrations that best reflect the dramatic as well as the rhetorical art of Terence. I shall follow Quintilian's scheme, since most, if not all, of the Terentian commentators followed him, and illustrate inartificial and artificial proofs as found by the commentators. The inartificial proofs consist of witnesses, oaths, and signs; the artificial proofs of signs, arguments (i.e., syllogisms and enthymemes), and examples. This division of proofs into inartificial and artificial is not altogether satisfactory, for it is sometimes difficult to distinguish between ready-made matter and matter assembled or created by the speaker. Consequently there is bound to be some overlapping of classifications in my illustrations.

INARTIFICIAL PROOFS

WITNESSES

Donatus, who was familiar with the traditional classification of proofs, found a good example of inartificial proof in the *Brothers* 478-79. Here Hegio is explaining to Demea that Aeschinus had rav-

---

[6]*Rhetoric* 2.20.1; cf. 1.2.8.
[7]*Ibid.* 1.9.40-41; 3.17.3-6. See p. 190 for a discussion of *amplificatio*.

ished Pamphila, who is now in childbed, but that the young man has evidently deserted her for another woman. Demea asks Hegio if he is sure of his facts. Hegio replies: "The girl's mother is at hand, the girl herself, the fact itself, and here's Geta too." As Donatus observed, the argument here is manifest and hence inartificial; that is, the proofs consist of witnesses, not of arguments built up by the art of the speaker.

Witnesses are often used in comedy to establish the identity of characters. Crito in the *Andrian* is a witness who appears in the nick of time and proves that Glycerium is actually the daughter of Chremes. In the *Self-Tormentor*, the Nurse is the witness who establishes the identity of Antiphila. Witnesses, of course, may be used to corroborate any truth or alleged truth. A good illustration of the comic use of a witness, that is, the use of the wrong witness to back the right cause, is in the *Andrian* 576-79. Here Simo is trying to persuade Chremes to match his daughter Philumena with Pamphilus. Chremes objects to the match; he has heard of Pamphilus' affair with Glycerium. Simo, however, tries to override this objection by assuring him that Pamphilus has now reformed and is eager to marry Philumena. (So far as Simo knows, indeed, Pamphilus is ready to obey his father.) To crown his argument, to prove his contention, Simo offers the testimony of Davus.

Simo: Davus himself, who is deepest in their counsels, told me so, and he's urging me to hasten the match as fast as I can. Do you think he would do this unless he were sure that my son desires the same? But you shall hear his own words. Here, bring out Davus.

And so Davus, who has cunningly done everything in his power to thwart Simo's plan to match Pamphilus with Philumena, is brought forward as Simo's chief witness.

OATHS

Oaths require no artifice and actually prove nothing, especially in comedy, but are often used as proof. Donatus called attention to the "inartificial persuasion" in the *Mother-in-law* 697. Laches has accused Pamphilus of various shady tricks. Pamphilus replies, "I'll take my oath it was none of these things." Needless to say, Laches needs more proof than this.

SIGNS

The dividing line between the inartificial and the artificial use of signs is seldom clear; sometimes an argument may be a mixture of inartificial and artificial signs, or rather a mixture of the inartificial and artificial employment of signs by the speaker. I shall also discuss the use of signs under artificial proofs.

The commonest and most obvious proof by signs is the recognition of persons or the establishment of evidence, true or false, by means of rings, jewels, clothing, scars, birthmarks, documents, tokens of various kinds. All drama abounds in such devices, and Terentian comedy is no exception. In the *Mother-in-law*, Pamphilus recognizes, by means of a ring, that his estranged wife is the same young woman he ravished before his marriage. Also by means of a ring, Antiphila, in the *Self-Tormentor*, is recognized as the long-lost daughter of Sostrata and Chremes. Any reader of plays will readily call to mind countless other illustrations in ancient and modern comedy.

A convincing argument by means of signs appears in a speech by the maidservant Dorias in the *Eunuch* (615-28). Dorias is alarmed over an impending crisis in the affairs of her mistress Thais; she is afraid that Thraso and young Chremes will be at loggerheads over the beautiful slave girl Pamphila. The conclusion of her speech is the inartificial use of signs.

Dorias: Meanwhile my mistress secretly took off her jewels and gave them to me to carry home. This is a sign, I know, that the first chance she gets she'll retire from the party.

Artificial Proofs

SIGNS

One of the best illustrations from Terence of confirmation by means of signs, and here there is certainly some art displayed by the speaker, is Davus' attempt to persuade Pamphilus that Simo has now given up hope of marrying him to Philumena. Simo has declared that his son must be married today, but the facts, as Davus interprets them, do not point to a wedding. The *Andrian* 359-69 runs as follows:

Davus: On my way back all on a sudden the circumstances struck me with suspicion. Hollo, I thought, not much to eat, master dejected, the match a sudden affair; they don't hang together.
Pamphilus: What's it point to?
Davus: I went straight off to Chremes'; when I got there, not a soul about the door; now I was glad of that.
Charinus: You're right.
Pamphilus: Go on.
Davus: I waited a bit. All the time I saw nobody go in, nobody come out; no brideslady in the house, no preparation, nothing stirring. I went up and peeped in at the door.
Pamphilus: I know: an important sign.
Davus: Is all this in tune with a wedding?
Pamphilus. No, Davus, I think not.
Davus: "Think" say you? You don't rightly understand. The thing's a

certainty. What's more, as I came away I met a servant of Chremes; he was bringing a pennyworth of greens and sprats for the old man's supper.

According to Willichius, there are six signs employed in this *confirmatio:*

(1) There was very little food in the house.
(2) Simo was sullen.
(3) There was no one stirring about the door of Chremes' house.
(4) There were no bridal matrons coming in and out.
(5) There was no decoration, no bustle.
(6) Chremes' servant was bringing in an old man's supper of greens and sprats.

EXAMPLES

All arguments using examples must be "from things like or unlike or contrary." So said Quintilian (5.11.5), who went on to discuss various kinds of examples, including historical parallels, quotations from poets, similes, and analogy. In the Terentian comedy of everyday life there is little use of historical parallels or of quotations from poets. In fact, the use of examples in Terence is not prominent; at least the commentators did not cite many uses. Willichius called attention to two illustrations which will serve pretty well.

In the *Andrian* 716-20, the maidservant Mysis, in despair at the bad turn of events that has befallen her mistress, complains that nothing in life is sure. Then she confirms this hypothesis by the example of her mistress' lover, Pamphilus·

Nothing's really our own. Heavens! I thought that Pamphilus was the chief blessing to my mistress, friend, lover, husband, ready to help in any circumstances; and now, poor soul, what distress he causes her!

Willichius admired Gnatho's brilliant soliloquy in the *Eunuch* (232 ff.), and partly because of the artful use of example. The whole speech, in fact, is a confirmation by example of Gnatho's initial statement, "What a difference there is between a fool and a man with brains!" Gnatho illustrates, and proves, his point by first describing a shiftless colleague and then by describing his own parasitical success. His conclusion runs as follows:

Mine is a new craft, and I am the inventor of it. There is a class of men who wish to be first in everything, but aren't. It's them I dog. I don't provide them opportunities to laugh at me, but I willingly smile on them and marvel at their genius. Whatever they say I praise; if, on the other hand, they deny the same, I praise that too. If one says no, I say no. If one says yes, I say yes. Finally, I have taken this order with myself, to agree with them in everything. It's the best way to get ahead nowadays.

Another good illustration of proof by examples will be presented later on under the rhetorical figure *epagoge*.

SYLLOGISM

The syllogism is the special tool of the logician and does not fit the ordinary purpose of the orator or dramatist, who must address the mob. And the mob can hardly comprehend formal syllogisms. Both orator and poet must understand syllogisms, but they seldom use them, depending rather upon enthymemes and maxims. Nevertheless, dramatists occasionally use syllogisms in both tragedy and comedy. Aristotle, who betrayed his fondness for logic in both the *Rhetoric* and *Poetics*, recommended as one of the better types of Discovery or Recognition, "Discovery through reasoning" (ἐκ συλλογισμοῦ). In Aeschylus' *Libation-Pourers*, Electra, upon finding a lock of hair that seems familiar, argues syllogistically:

> One like me is here.
> There is no one like me but my brother Orestes.
> Therefore Orestes is here.[8]

Aristotle was thinking of this syllogism as part of the plot, but he would certainly have acknowledged that it overlaps Thought since Thought is shown in "every effort to prove or disprove."

Actually there are fewer syllogisms in Terence than in Shakespeare or in other Elizabethan dramatists. The Terentian characters seldom indulge in intellectual fencing; they do not chop logic though they often argue logically. Donatus found a "negative syllogism" in the *Andrian* 546 ff. Here Chremes, who is unwilling to match his daughter Philumena with Simo's son Pamphilus, argues as follows:

If the match is for the good of both let her be fetched; but, if it involves more misfortune than blessing for both of them, pray think of it in a mutual spirit as though the girl were yours and I were the father of Pamphilus.

Donatus commented:

In the second syllogism he proposed wrongly so that he might reply rightly. This syllogism is called negative, for in the second proposition he denies what he first said, "but if it involves more misfortune than blessing."

Chremes' speech is not a conventional syllogism. It looks more like a dilemma, and Willichius so named it. Nevertheless, Donatus called it a "negative syllogism," and the great Paris edition of 1552 so labeled it. If I understand Donatus, who may have been more familiar with

---

[8]*Poetics* 16.55ª4-6.

the Stoic type of syllogism than with the Aristotelian kind, he meant that there are two implied syllogisms in this speech. Rearranged in more conventional form, the two syllogisms might be stated as follows:

(1) If a match promises well, then the girl should be fetched and betrothed to the youth.
   This match promises to be for the good of both.
   Therefore let the girl be fetched.

(2) If a match does not promise well, then the girl should not be fetched and betrothed to the youth.
   This match involves more misfortune than blessing for both.
   Therefore the girl should not be fetched.

Willichius found a syllogism in the opening lines of the first act of the *Mother-in-law* (58-64). Philotis, a courtesan, is talking with an old crone, Syra.

Philotis: On my word, Syra, women of my class find very few faithful lovers. This Pamphilus here, how many times he swore to Bacchis, so solemnly that any one might readily believe him, that he would never take a wife in her lifetime. See, he has taken one.

Syra: Therefore I earnestly advise and urge you to have no pity on any man.

Rearranged in accord with Willichius' suggestions, the syllogism would read:

Major: Few lovers are faithful to their oaths.
Minor: Even Pamphilus has broken his oath.
Conclusion: Therefore no man deserves pity from any courtesan.

Donatus merely remarked of this passage, "Rhetoricians call sentiments of this kind *dianoias*."

In the *Mother-in-law* 480-81, Pamphilus says that he must choose between his mother and his wife, who has refused to live with her mother-in-law:

I must part, Phidippus, either with my mother or with Philumena. Now filial respect urges me to prefer the happiness of my mother.

Willichius called this sentiment a "disjunctive syllogism." Rearranged, it would read:

Major: Pamphilus must desert either his mother or his wife.
Minor: Filial respect prevents his deserting his mother.
Conclusion: Therefore he must desert his wife.

ENTHYMEMES

By the common consent of most ancient and Renaissance authorities the enthymeme is a principal tool of the rhetorician, and the

Terentian commentators found dozens of enthymemes in the comedies. Willichius, in particular, was tireless in calling attention to passages employing this important device. I have selected a half dozen from the many illustrations at hand in the commentaries. If the reader will keep in mind that an enthymeme is a rhetorical syllogism, that it is drawn from probable premises and therefore is not a strictly demonstrative proof, the following illustrations ought to be clear enough.

(1) Donatus called Davus' retort to Charinus in the *Andrian* 372 an enthymeme. Charinus is rejoicing that Chremes has refused to match his daughter Philumena with Pamphilus. Davus replies: "You chucklehead, it doesn't follow from his not letting *him* marry her that *you'll* marry her."

(2) Syrus says to Clinia in the *Self-Tormentor* 402: "From what I've seen of your father's disposition, he'll deal roughly with you yet."

(3) In the *Brothers* 179, Sannio the pander complains to Aeschinus, who has stolen one of his girls: "What greater right have you to keep my girl, for whom I paid my money?"

(4) In the *Mother-in-law* 336-37, Sostrata argues, in Willichius' phrase, "enthymematically from a sign":

> Oh dear, for some time I've heard a disturbance going on there. I sorely fear that Philumena's illness is growing worse.

(5) There is a debate between Pamphilus and Parmeno in the *Mother-in-law* 281-92, Pamphilus arguing that it is better to be ignorant of coming evil, Parmeno that it is better to anticipate and so forestall evil. Both speakers employ enthymemes.

Pamphilus: Was ever a man that met with more bitterness from love than I have? Distraction! was this the life for which I was so careful to save myself? Was this the reason that made me so eager to return home? Bah! how much better to live in the worst hole in the world than to come back here and learn to my misery that things were like this! If our path ahead is blocked by any trouble, all the time before we find it out is always pure gain.
Parmeno: But this way you will quicker hit on a path out of these distresses. If you hadn't come back, these resentments would have grown immensely. As it is, you may be sure that both ladies will respect your arrival. You will learn the facts, clear away the resentments, make them friends again. They are really trifles, the things you've made yourself to imagine very serious.

(6) Perhaps the best comic use of the enthymeme in Terence is a remark of Parmeno in the *Eunuch* 960. The maidservant Pythias has informed Parmeno that Chaerea is going to be punished as an adulterer. (Chaerea is the youth who gained access to Pamphila in the

house of Thais by disguising himself as a eunuch.) Parmeno replies, "Who ever saw a man seized as an adulterer in a bawdy house?" According to Willichius, Parmeno's *confirmatio* is by means of the unusual situation, for a patron of such a house is "simply a fornicator, not an adulterer."

Closely allied to the last illustration, although the commentators did not call it an enthymeme, is an earlier speech in the *Eunuch* (654-55). Here Pythias is berating Phaedria, the older brother of Chaerea. Pythias says:

That eunuch you gave us, what an uproar he's caused! He has ravished the girl the Captain gave my mistress.

From Phaedria's point of view the accusation is ridiculous, and a false proof; Phaedria, of course, does not yet know that Chaerea took the place of the eunuch whom he (Phaedria) had presented to Thais, and he thinks that Pythias is talking about the wizened Dorus. Barlandus, apparently in all seriousness, analyzed the accusation as a false proof since it was based upon an impossibility. He summoned Trapezuntius as authority:

The impossible is when something is said that is contrary to the true nature of things, as if some one proclaims that Apollo lies or an infant is accused of adultery because he sleeps with another man's wife.[9]

So much for enthymemes in Terence. Needless to say, perhaps, the ancient writers had no monopoly on enthymemes; many modern writers have made more extensive use of them than did Terence. The reader may find hundreds of them in Shakespeare, Jonson, Dryden, and Congreve. More recent English playwrights like Shaw and Galsworthy, who wrote "thesis-dramas," will doubtless provide even more illustrations than do the Elizabethan and Restoration dramatists. Shaw's masterpiece, *Man and Superman*, is a storehouse of argumentative devices, particularly in the dream scenes, which present numerous debates between Don Juan and the Devil.

I shall conclude my brief discussion of enthymemes in comedy with a quotation from Sir John Vanbrugh, who has never been ranked among the leading intellectuals of English drama. Nevertheless, I know of no clearer illustration of the effective use of enthymemes in Shakespeare, Jonson, Dryden, Congreve, or Shaw than a speech by Lady Brute in the first scene of the *Provoked Wife*. Sir John has just made his customary surly exit, leaving his wife to soliloquize. The reader who cares to may find enthymemes and maxims here and at least one syllogism.

---

[9]Trapezuntius *Rhetoric* p. 18v.

Lady Brute: The devil's in the fellow I think—I was told before I married him, that thus 'twould be; but I thought I had charms enough to govern him; and that where there was an estate a woman must needs be happy; so my vanity has deceived me, and my ambition has made me uneasy. But some comfort still; if one would be revenged of him, these are good times; a woman may have a gallant, and a separate maintenance too—the surly puppy—yet he's a fool for't: for hitherto he has been no monster. But who knows how far he may provoke me? I never loved him, yet I have been ever true to him; and that in spite of all the attacks of art and nature upon a poor weak woman's heart, in favor of a tempting lover.

Methinks so noble a defense as I have made should be rewarded with a better usage—or who can tell. Perhaps a good part of what I suffer from my husband may be judgment upon me for my cruelty to my lover.—Lord, with what pleasure could I indulge that thought, were there but a possibility of finding arguments to make it good.—And how do I know but there may—Let me see—What opposes?—My matrimonial vow?—Why, what did I vow? I think I promised to be true to my husband.

Well, and he promised to be kind to me.

But he hasn't kept his word—

Why then I'm absolved from mine—ay, that seems clear to me. The argument's good between the king and the people, why not between the husband and the wife? O, but that condition was not expressed—No matter, 'twas understood.

Well, by all I see, if I argue the matter a little longer with myself I shan't find so many bug-bears in the way as I thought I should. Lord, what fine notions of virtue do we women take up upon the credit of old foolish philosophers. Virtue's its own reward, virtue's this, virtue's that—virtue's an ass, and a gallant's worth forty on't.

Refutation or disproof employs the same methods that proof does. One of the better illustrations is in the *Andrian* 567-71. Simo is trying to remove Chremes' objections to the proposed match between Philumena and Pamphilus.

Simo: Why, at the worst the inconvenience reduces itself to this, the possibility of a divorce, which heaven forbid. But, if the boy is reformed, think of all the advantages. To start with, you will have restored a son to your friend, you'll get a faithful son-in-law for yourself and husband for your daughter.

Donatus found here a negative syllogism "by means of contrary propositions." Willichius considered the speech a *confutatio* by means of diminishing the disadvantages and amplifying the advantages of the match. In other words, Simo's speech employs amplification, a major device in rhetoric and usually a kind of proof. According to Aristotle, amplification and depreciation are "enthymemes which serve to show that a thing is great or small, just as others serve to show that it is good or bad, just or unjust, or anything else."[10] In the *Poetics* (19), it may be recalled, Aristotle said that *dianoia* is shown in "every effort to prove or disprove, to arouse emotion (pity, fear, anger, and the like), or to maximize or minimize things." Maximizing (*amplificatio*) and minimizing (*meiosis*), then, are forms of proof or disproof. I shall discuss *amplificatio* and *meiosis* in the next section on rhetorical figures.

FIGURES

Every student of Renaissance literature is familiar with the emphasis that most grammarians and rhetoricians, and many critics, placed upon figures. Discussions of composition and style in the rhetorical and critical works of Erasmus, Melanchthon, Julius Caesar Scaliger, Joannes Susenbrotus, and English rhetoricians such as Thomas Wilson, Richard Sherry, Henry Peacham, and Puttenham, are devoted in large part to figures. This emphasis was not peculiar to the Renaissance, of course; it was an inheritance from medieval and classical times. Among the ancient authorities on rhetoric and poetics, Aristotle, Horace, and Aphthonius, it is true, did not emphasize figures; but Cicero, the author of the *Ad Herennium*, Quintilian, and Hermogenes discussed figures at some length. According to Quintilian (9.1), there was no uniformity among the ancients in their classifications of figures. *Tropes*,[11] for example, were often confused with figures (σχήματα) and figures of thought sometimes overlapped with figures of speech. While Quintilian was somewhat impatient of classifications, he adopted the division into figures of thought and figures of speech:

It is, however, to the best of my knowledge, generally agreed by the majority of authors that there are two classes of *figure*, namely *figures of thought* (διάνοια), that is of the mind, feeling, or conceptions, since all these terms are used, and *figures of speech* (λέξις), that is of words, diction, expression, language, or style.[12]

I shall use the same divisions, but call them Rhetorical and Grammatical figures.

[10]*Rhetoric* 2.26.2.

[11]A *trope*, according to Quintilian (9.1.4), is the "transference of expressions from their natural and principal signification to another, with a view to the embellishment of style." *Metaphor* and *metonomy*, for example, are tropes. *Figure* is the term used "when we give our language a conformation other than the obvious and ordinary." *Irony*, for example, may be either a trope or a figure.

[12]Quintilian 9.1.17. Cf. Cicero *De Oratore* 3.52.200-01; *Orator* 39.136.

So far as I know, no one handbook of rhetoric, ancient or modern, contains a complete list of figures, which would run to two hundred or more in number. The following lists do not pretend to be complete, but they represent the rhetorical and grammatical figures that Donatus and the sixteenth-century commentators found in Terence. Since the authorities, ancient and Renaissance, did not always agree on the classification or even on the meaning of particular figures, I have tried to ascertain what Donatus, Willichius, and Barlandus meant by the Terentian figures, regardless of whether or not their interpretations always square with those of the rhetoricians and figurists.

RHETORICAL FIGURES

ADMONITIO: Encouraging exhortation.

Geta says to his mistress Sostrata in the *Brothers* 335: "Dry your tears, Mistress; rather look to the future and see what must be done."

AETIOLOGIA: A brief statement of reasoning, giving a cause; similar to an enthymeme.

In the *Mother-in-law* 327-28, Parmeno says: "My going in after him is of no use now, for I know none of them can abide us."

AGNOMINATIO: See *Paronomasia*.

ALLEGORIA: An extended metaphor.

Willichius called *Phormio* 330-32 a "proverbial sententious allegory." Here Phormio the parasite explains why he has never been caught in the toils of the law: "A net isn't spread for a hawk or a kite, birds of prey; it's spread for harmless birds because these pay for the catching; the others are labor lost."

AMPLIFICATIO: Dilating an argument, and sometimes diminishing one, for some Renaissance authors used *amplificatio* and *meiosis* indifferently.

A very comprehensive figure, amplification was usually divided into various subheads such as *auxesis, congeries, incrementum*. Quintilian (8.4.3) spoke of four principal methods of amplification: augmentation (*incrementum*), comparison, reasoning, and accumulation (*congeries*). Cicero, in *De Oratore* 3.26.104, said: "The highest distinction of eloquence consists in amplification by means of ornament, which can be used to make one's speech not only increase the importance of a subject and raise it to a higher level, but also to diminish and disparage it." Aristotle, in the *Poetics* (19), mentioned "maximizing and minimizing" as important elements of Thought in the drama. In the *Rhetoric* (2.26.1) he remarked that amplification and depreciation are "enthymemes which serve to show that a thing is great or small." Quintilian, Cicero, and Aristotle clearly thought of amplification as something larger than a figure. Melanchthon, in his *Elementorum Rhetorices* (1533, p. 76), said: "The universal design of eloquence consists of three things: first in grammatical speech, next in figures, third in amplifications." Nevertheless, Donatus and the sixteenth-century commentators regarded amplification as a figure, and I shall select illustrations from their comments.

(1) In the *Brothers* 470-74, Hegio relates to Demea how Aeschinus fell in love with Pamphila and debauched her. His recital, according to Willichius, is a *congeries*.

Hegio: The night, passion, wine, young blood, these moved him; it's human nature. When he realized what he had done, he came of his own volition to the girl's mother, weeping, praying, begging, promising, swearing that he would marry her. The matter was forgiven, hushed up, his word taken.

(2) Chremes, in the *Self-Tormentor* 1033-34, employs a similar *congeries* in scolding his son Clitipho: "You are a trifler, an idler, a fraud, a glutton, a whoremaster, a spendthrift." One is reminded of the exchange of abusive names between Prince Hal and Falstaff in the first part of *Henry IV*.

(3) A *congeries* of injuries is recited by Sannio the pander in the *Brothers* 197-200:

God in heaven! I don't wonder that injustice drives men insane. He tore me out of my home, beat me, carried off my girl despite me, showered a thousand blows or more on me an unhappy man, and in requital for these injuries he demands to have the girl at cost.

(4) Latomus called Micio's rebuke of Aeschinus in the *Brothers* 691-92 an "amplification from time and consequences." It might also be called a *congeries*.

Micio: While you were hesitating ten months went by. So far as you could, you have undone yourself, this wretched woman, and the child.

(5) Donatus called the last part of Laches' tirade against women, in the *Mother-in-law* 201-04, an *auxesis*, a more general term than either *congeries* or *incrementum*.

Laches: Mothers-in-law and daughters-in-law they are all of one mind in hating each other. Their keenness in opposing their husbands is all of a match, their obstinacy in it all of a pattern, and it seems to me that they've all been at the same school taking lessons in mischief. If there is such a school, I am quite sure this wife of mine is head-mistress.

(6) A good illustration of *auxesis*, of the effective emotional build-up in address, appears in young Aeschinus' rebuke of his uncle Micio in the *Brothers* 662-64: "You people have acted harshly and bar-

barously, and what's more, father, if I must speak more openly, not like gentlemen."

(7) The authorities did not agree on distinctions between *congeries* and *incrementum*, though *incrementum* supposedly carries the notion of augmentation rather more than does *congeries*, which may be merely an accumulation without any emotional climax. Willichius labeled Hegio's speech to Demea in the *Brothers* 500-04 *incrementum*.

Hegio: Yes, Demea, but see that you take this thought to heart: the more easy your life and your brother's, the greater your influence, riches, prosperity, rank, the more you are bound in the spirit of justice to recognize what is just, if you wish to have a reputation for probity.

(8) The best comic use of amplification in Terence, to my mind, appears in the *Eunuch* 553 ff. Willichius called the passage *auxesis per incrementum*. The boy Chaerea is speaking:

To think of no busybody meeting me now to follow me all about and deafen and stifle me with questions, asking why I am frisking for joy or why I am cheerful, where I'm going, where I've been, where I found this dress, what I'm looking for, and whether I'm sane or crazy.

The comic force of the *auxesis* is fully brought out in the next moment by Antipho, who confronts his young comrade and asks:

Chaerea, why are you frisking for joy? What's the purpose of this dress? Why are you so cheerful? What do you mean? Are you in your senses? Why do you stare at me? What are you going to say?

ANADROME: A figure of repetition; specifically returning to a point, repeating an idea in different words.

Donatus called Demea's brief description of his brother Micio, in the *Brothers* 864, an *anadrome*. Demea says: "He's complaisant, easygoing, speaking ill of none, having a smile for everybody."

ANACLESIS: Another figure of repetition, closely allied to the grammatical figure of *anaclasis*.

Phormio 997-1000 will illustrate.

Phormio: The poor creature raves from fear.
Nausistrata (to Chremes): It's not for nought that you so fear.
Chremes: I fear?
Phormio: Very well. If you fear nothing, and what I say is nothing, tell your story.

Willichius called Phormio's last speech above an "ironical *anaclesis*."

ANAMNESIS: Recalling past matters.

In the *Andrian* 105-06, when Simo tells his servant Sosia that Chrysis is dead, Sosia cries: "O happy chance! You've made me glad; ah, I was afraid of Chrysis."

ANTEISAGOGE: See *Antithesis.*

ANTHYPOPHORA: See *Anticipatio.*

ANTICIPATIO: A very important figure; anticipating something before it happens, raising and answering objections that may arise.

Many terms were used, including *anthypophora, occupatio, praeoccupatio, praesumptio, praeteritio, procatalepsis, prodiorthosis, prolepsis.*

Anthypophora is the term most often used by the commentators on Terence. I have selected three illustrations from many.

(1) In the *Brothers* 687-88, Micio rebukes Aeschinus for having wronged a young woman, but anticipates his excuse: "Now that's a great fault, yet human enough; other men, and honest ones, have often done the same."

(2) In the *Brothers* 217-19, Syrus says to Sannio the pander: "You were afraid, you stupidest of stupid men, if you gave up a little of your rights and humored the young gentleman, that it wouldn't be repaid with interest."

(3) In the *Eunuch* 682-84, Phaedria argues with Pythias, trying to persuade her that the eunuch who entered Thais' house is the same eunuch he presented to the courtesan. But Pythias knows better, and tries to set Phaedria straight; she points out that the "eunuch" who outraged Pamphila was young and handsome while Phaedria's Dorus is old and withered. Phaedria stubbornly persists in his argument: "He looked so just now because he had gay clothes on. Now he seems ugly to you because he hasn't."

The commentators did not always agree on the terms for anticipation. Barlandus called *Eunuch* 926 an example of *occupatio;* Willichius called it *praeteritio.* Both commentators meant the figure which pretends to omit something and then mentions the matter—a very common device in rhetoric, of course, and about the same thing as *paralepsis* (*q.v.*). In *Eunuch* 926, Parmeno says, "I say nothing of a very difficult, very costly love affair," thereby calling attention to it.

Willichius used *praeoccupatio* and *procatalepsis* indifferently. Thus he called the *Brothers* 165-66 *praeoccupatio* in the margin and *procatalepsis* in his notes. In this passage, Sannio the pander says to Aeschinus: "I know what you'll say: 'I'm sorry; I'll take my oath that you did not deserve this injury.'" Another example of *praeoccupatio,* according to Willichius, is *Eunuch* 202-05, where Thais has been trying to appease her lover Phaedria: "All I have done in this has been for the girl's sake, for I have hopes that I have already all but discovered her brother, a young man of the highest rank, and he has arranged to pay me a visit this very day."

A good illustration of *praesumptio,* i.e., anticipating and refuting objections, is in the *Andrian* 386-91. This passage also employs *mimesis.* Davus is arguing with Pamphilus:

Davus: Not at all. For I think it is this way: your father will say, "I want you to marry today"; you'll say, "I'll marry." Pray how will he quarrel with you about that? All his plans, now quite fixed, you'll unfix, and with no risk.

Prodiorthosis is a setting right by anticipation. In the *Self-Tormentor* 1-3, the speaker of the Prologue says: "It may surprise you that the poet has given to an old man a task usually assigned to a younger actor; let me explain before delivering what I have come to deliver."

Prolepsis is applying a name to something before it has a name. In the *Brothers* 634-35, Aeschinus says: "Open the door at once, some of you. Somebody is coming out; I don't know who. I'll stand aside."

ANTIPHRASIS: A form of irony, specifically the use of a word or phrase to be taken in the opposite sense.

Donatus found an *antiphrasis* in the *Andrian* 782. Chremes has just overheard Davus telling Mysis that Pamphilus' lady-love, Glycerium, has had a baby. Chremes, who had let himself be persuaded to match his daughter with Pamphilus, now exclaims: "What a merry scrape I nearly tumbled into unawares." The use of "merry" (*iocularium*) here is ironical, of course.

ANTITHESIS or ANTITHETON: The use of contraries, opposites, the contrast of ideas.

A very important figure in ancient and Renaissance times as well as in the twentieth century, and apparently appreciated by the Terentian commentators, who did not, however, make so great a fuss over it as do some twentieth-century critics. This figure is appropriate for characters who are wily or who think that they are wily.

Old Simo makes use of *antitheton,* in the *Andrian* 167-68, when he explains to Sosia that he is going to find a "*true* reason from the *false* marriage" for reproving his son. Gnatho, in the *Eunuch* 1075, when he is trying to persuade Phaedria to stay friends with Thraso and with Thraso's purse, reminds the young man of how difficult it will be to keep the beautiful Thais: "You have little to give, and she must have much to receive." Willichius admired an *antitheton* in another speech of Gnatho (*Eunuch* 242-44): "What a complexion, what sleekness, what dress, what a handsome body! I have everything and yet have nothing, and though I have nothing, I lack nothing." Parmeno makes use of *antithesis* in the *Eunuch* 283-85; he says to Gnatho: "Let but two days pass, and though you, lucky fellow, now open this door with your little finger, I'll make you kick your heels against it again and again and nobody answer." Parmeno closes the *Mother-in-law* with an *antitheton*: "Truly, I've done more good to-day unknowingly than I ever did before knowingly." A more elaborate *antithesis* appears in a dialogue between Geta and Phormio in *Phormio* 337-45:

Geta: My master can never fully repay your services.
Phormio: No, it's the other way, a man can never fully repay his patron. Just think of it: you come contributing nothing, perfumed and comfortable after a bath, your mind at ease, while the patron is devoured by care and expense. While everything is done to please you, he's on the growl. You may smile, be helped to wine before him, take your place before him, a puzzling dinner is served you.
Geta: Puzzling? What does that mean?
Phormio: Where you'd be puzzled what dish to try first. When you start reckoning up how delightful and how costly it all is, wouldn't you count the man who gives it a very god before your eyes?

A special kind of antithesis, and one specially suitable for comedy, is *anteisagoge*, which might be called a compensatory antithesis. There are numerous examples in Terence as in all good comic writers. Geta says to Phormio the parasite, in *Phormio* 324-25: "O valiant man and a friend indeed. But, Phormio, I often fear that your valor will land you in jail." Parmeno says to the love-sick Phaedria, in *Eunuch* 61-63: "If you try to turn these uncertainties into certainties by reason, you'll do no more than if you tried to go mad by reason." Better, perhaps, is another quip of Parmeno to Phaedria, in *Eunuch* 210-11: "Would to God, Phaedria, you could find something as easily as you'll lose this."

All of the illustrations above are from the mouths of the Roman servants. But the Terentian servant is usually the wittiest man in the play, and it is no accident that the best uses of *anteisagoge* come from him. The witty servant in Elizabethan and Restoration comedy, a descendant of Geta and Parmeno, often makes use of *anteisagoge*. The most brilliant illustration of the figure, however, that I can recall is a speech by Mirabell in Congreve's *Way of the World*. Mirabell and Fainall are talking.

Fainall: For a passionate lover, methinks you are a man somewhat too discerning in the failings of your mistress.
Mirabell: And for a discerning man, somewhat too passionate a lover; for I like her with all her faults; nay, like her for her faults. Her follies are so natural, or so artful, that they become her; and those affectations which in another woman would be odious serve but to make her more agreeable. I'll tell, thee, Fainall, she once used me with that insolence

that in revenge I took her to pieces; sifted her and separated her failings; I studied 'em, and got 'em by rote. The catalogue was so large that I was not without hope, one day or other, to hate her heartily: to which end I so used myself to think of 'em that at length, contrary to my design and expectation, they gave me every hour less and less disturbance; 'till in a few days it became habitual to me, to remember 'em without being displeased. They are now grown as familiar to me as my own frailties, and in all probability in a little time longer I shall like 'em as well.

APHORISMUS: A pithy saying, similar to a *proverbium*.

There are many pithy sayings in Terence, but the commentators seldom used the term *aphorism*. Willichius called *Self-Tormentor* 325 an *aphorimus*: "It's scarcely wise of you to wish for something you can't have."

APODIOXIS: Rejection of an argument as false or absurd.

Willichius found a "comic apodioxis" in *Self-Tormentor* 550-55. Here Syrus has maneuvered Chremes into asking him to help Clinia with tricks and lies. Chremes gives the slave a free hand, and Syrus assures the old man that all will go well. Syrus rejects, with certain reservations, the notion that anything could go wrong.

Syrus: But mind, Sir, you remember what you told me if anything by chance should happen—human affairs *are* human—if your son should do something.

Chremes: Nothing will happen, I hope.

Syrus: By Jove, Sir, I hope so too, and I don't say I've noticed anything in him: still, if anything happens, don't be offended.

APODIXIS: Confirming a statement by the general experience of mankind.

In the *Self-Tormentor* 97, Menedemus explains to Chremes that his son Clinia had fallen in love with the daughter of a poor old woman from Corinth, thus providing explanation enough for his disapproval—daughter of a foreigner and poverty-stricken.

APODOSIS: Repetition or parallelism of words and ideas.

In the *Andrian* 277-80, Pamphilus says to Mysis: "Do you think me so unmanly, so unfeeling, so inhuman, so brutish, that neither intimacy nor love nor shame could stir me, could prompt me, to keep troth?"

APORIA: Deliberating with oneself.

There are several illustrations of *aporia* in Terence. As good as any is a speech by Charinus in the *Andrian* 639-40: "But what am I to do? go to Pamphilus and protest against this wrong? heap abuse on him?"

APOSIOPESIS: A sudden breaking off of speech, with the full meaning nevertheless well understood.

An effective figure in oratory and naturally very common in dramatic dialogue. Many illustrations were cited by the commentators in Terence, of which I have selected five.

(1) A good example of "if-you-don't-I'll" is in the *Andrian* 791, where the maidservant Mysis threatens Davus: "I vow, if I don't run to Glycerium with all this and. . . ."

(2) In the *Andrian* 872, Simo calls his son to account. Pamphilus is so confused that he can do little more than mutter. The old man cries, "What do you say? Of all the . . . ."

(3) In the *Brothers* 135, Demea expostulates with his brother Micio, who is spoiling Aeschinus: "Very well, if it pleases you, let him squander, ruin, and be ruined, it's no concern of mine. Now, if ever again one word. . . ."

(4) In the *Eunuch* 989-90, Laches threatens Parmeno: "If I live, you rogue, I'll. . . . But first explain whatever this matter is."

(5) In the *Self-Tormentor* 1041, Chremes protests against the behavior of his son Clitipho, who has brought his mistress into the family home. The old man's speech has a familiar ring even to modern ears. "Did you not by tricks introduce into my very presence . . . I'm ashamed to name the ugly word before your mother."

APOSTROPHE: Direct address of a real or imaginary person or of an abstraction personified.

This figure is commonly used in tragedy, and may appear in comedy. As Donatus pointed out, *apostrophe* may be used for ridiculous purposes, as in *Eunuch* 790-91. Thraso is planning to attack the house of Thais and carry off Pamphila. When he delays launching the attack he pompously explains to Gnatho the parasite that a wise general ought to try every method before arms. Thereupon Gnatho launches the following ironic apostrophe:

O good lord in heaven, what a great thing it is to be wise! I never come near you without going away a more learned man.

ARITHMUS: Enumeration.

In *Phormio* 129-31, Geta says: "Who her father was, who her mother, how she's kin to you, all these I'll make up."

ASTEISMUS: A jesting figure of reply, an urbane, witty saying.

Not very common in Terence, who did not try to write a comedy of wit. *Asteismus* is prominent in Shakespeare, Fletcher, Shirley, and the Restoration dramatists. Willichius labeled Sannio's reply to Syrus in the *Brothers* 211-13 ἀστεῖον in both situation and words. Sannio the pander has had a row with Aeschinus. He says to Syrus:

> I never saw a more unequal fray than that between us today. I with being drubbed, he with drubbing, we're both tired out.

AUXESIS: See *Amplificatio.*

AXIOSIS: A petition on the grounds of merit.

In the Prologue to the *Self-Tormentor* (26-27), the author appeals to the audience: "I must appeal to you then not to let the remarks of the slanderers have more weight than the remarks of the candid."

CATACHRESIS: Implied or mixed metaphor, the wrenching of a word out of its proper use.

The use of "damned" in the *Self-Tormentor* 629 is a *catachresis*. When Sostrata tells her husband that their long-lost daughter is still alive, Syrus, the slave, remarks in an aside: "Another mistress for me, and master damned with another expense."

CHARACTERISMUS: Description of the body or mind of a person.

In the *Mother-in-law* 352, Sostrata sees her son approaching and says: "How sorrowful he looks!"

CHARIENTISMUS: Mitigating or mollifying expression, with a connotation of wit.

Willichius cited the *Mother-in-law* 735, where Bacchis the courtesan speaks of her "livelihood" (*quaestus*).

CHLEUASMUS: Mocking sarcasm, a form of irony.

Willichius labeled Sanga's reply to Thraso in *Eunuch* 778-79 *chleuasmus.*

> *Thraso:* What, you good-for-nothing, is it with a sponge you think to do battle, bringing one here like that?
> *Sanga:* O Sir, I knew the commandant's valor and the strength of the troops. An affair of bloodshed, says I: how am I to wipe the wounds? says I.

COMMINATIO: A threat.

In the *Brothers* 181-82, Aeschinus says to Sannio the pander: "If you persist in annoying us you shall instantly be haled inside and whipped until you're half dead."

CONGERIES: See *Amplificatio.*

CORRECTIO: See *Epanorthosis.*

DEINOTES (δεινότης): A figure of forcefulness.

Donatus pointed to the *Brothers* 410, where Syrus remarks, "It's not money you're squandering, but your life."

DIALOGISMUS: See *Mimesis.*

DIAPORESIS: A figure expressing doubt as to what among several matters of importance the speaker should begin with.

Diaporesis is a common device in oratory and often appears at the close of a comedy. In the *Eunuch* 1044, Chaerea, now exulting in his match with Pamphila, says, "What shall I speak of first? Whom shall I praise most?"

DILEMMA: An argument presenting alternatives.

Willichius called Geta's speech in the *Brothers* 338-42 a "dilemma of deliberation." Geta is presenting the hard facts to his mistress Sostrata:

In the first place, the facts show that he is estranged from us: now, if we disclose the thing, he'll deny it, I'm sure of that; consequently your good name and your daughter's life will fall into hazard. What's more, even if he owned up to the full, as he's in love with some one else, it would be a bad thing for her to be married to him. So, take it as you will, we must hold our tongues.

DISTRIBUTIO: As a figure, dividing the argument into several parts.

Willichius labeled *Phormio* 352-54 *distributio*. Here Phormio, pretending not to see old Demipho in the background, talks with Geta.

Phormio: Does Demipho deny that Phanium is kin to him? Demipho denies that she is kin?
Geta: He denies it.
Phormio: And denies that he knows who her father was?
Geta: He denies it.

EMPHASIS: Selective stress.

Donatus called attention to an example of comic *emphasis* in the *Eunuch* 994. Old Laches has just heard the news that his youngest son, Chaerea, has been arrested as an adulterer. The old man is naturally flabbergasted. At this point Parmeno, in order to divert his master's wrath from Chaerea to Thais and her household, emphatically exclaims, "Look at the impudence of those strumpets." Technically, according to Donatus, the *emphasis* here is in making "strumpet" plural.

ENANTIOSIS: A form of irony.

Willichius called Phormio's rebuke of the old men in *Phormio* 948-51 *enantiosis*.

Phormio: What the devil do you mean by playing with me in this way, you fools, with your childish shilly-shallying? I won't, I will; I will, I won't again; take, give back; what was said unsaid, what was settled upset.

ENERGIA, or ENARGIA: Vivid, lifelike description, making the hearer or reader see and hear what is described.

A very important element in oratory and poetry. Perhaps the best illustration of *energia* in Terence, and there are many, is Chaerea's narrative in the *Eunuch* 574 ff. Donatus remarked that the shift from past tense to present tense by Chaerea is *enargia*. For example, in *Eunuch* 594, Chaerea says, "I stand waiting for what they might order me to do."

ENTHYMEME: See earlier discussion under Proofs.

EPAGOGE: Also called *inductio*. Proof by adducing similar examples. Micio's reply to Demea's accusation that he has been spoiling Aeschinus is an *epagoge*.

Micio: You gave me your son to adopt; he has been made mine; if he commits an offense, Demea, he offends me; the main share of it is mine. He feasts, he drinks, he reeks of perfume—at my cost. He has a love-affair; I shall give him money so long as I like. If he runs out of money, perhaps his mistress will put him outofdoors. He has forced a door; it will be repaired. He has torn somebody's coat; it will be mended. I have, thank God, the wherewithal to do these things, and as yet they are not grievous to me.

EPANGELIA (ἐπαγγελία): An oratorical figure, according to Donatus, in which the speaker promises to prove something in the future.

Donatus called Sostrata's speech in the *Mother-in-law* 208 *epangelia*: "Someday you'll find out that you have wrongfully accused me, I know."

EPANORTHOSIS: Also called *correctio*. A correction, often in the form of a question.

In the *Eunuch* 563, Chaerea sets his friend Antipho straight: "Do you know her whom my brother is in love with?" Antipho then knows that he means Thais. A better example, perhaps, is *Self-Tormentor* 94-96, where old Menedemus says to his friend Chremes:

I have an only son, and he a mere stripling. Ah, what did I say? Have one? No, I had a son, Chremes; now I doubt whether I have one or no.

EPEXEGESIS: The insertion of words to make clear the thought expressed.

In the *Mother-in-law* 446, Pamphilus says: "I don't know how in the world I can hush up what Myrrina begged me to do, that is, her daughter's childbirth."

EPIBOLE: A figure of repetition.

Willichius called the opening of Chaerea's speech in *Eunuch* 549 ff.

an *epibole*. Chaerea advances on stage, saying, "Anyone here? No one. Anyone following me from the house? Not a soul."

EPIMONE: Usually defined as a figure of repetition, dwelling on an expression.

Donatus, however, applied the term to interjections, to inserted matter not pertinent to the main statement. In *Eunuch* 127, Thais interrupts the story of her life to say to Phaedria: "You know how dear I've held you ever since."

EPIPHONEMA: A pithy summary at the close of a speech.

Barlandus cited *Eunuch* 41, a line near the end of the Prologue: "Now nothing is said that has not been said before."

EPIPLEXIS: Asking a question with no intention of receiving an answer, but in order to upbraid some one.

In the *Self-Tormentor* 563, Chremes says to his son Clitipho: "Didn't I see you just now thrust your hand into that strumpet's bosom?"

EPITHERAPEUSIS: Reiteration of a charge.

In the *Brothers* 500, Hegio says, "Yes, Demea, take this thought to heart."

EPITOME: An abridgment. Donatus called it *syntomia*.

Terence was celebrated for his concise expression, and there are many examples of *epitome*. Chaerea's narrative in *Eunuch* 593 is a good example: "She went, bathed, returned; then the maids settled her on a couch."

EPITROCHASMUS: A rapid flow of questions to harry an adversary.

In the *Eunuch* 804, Thraso says to Chremes: "Who may you be? what do you mean? what have you to do with her?" More elaborate is Micio's questioning of Aeschinus in the *Brothers* 670-72:

What reason have you to say so? Who betrothed her? Who gave her in marriage? Who's her husband? When was she married? Who is behind all this? Why did the fellow marry another man's wife?

EPITROPE: Ironical permission to do what is not desired.

In the *Brothers* 991, Demea says to his happy-go-lucky son Aeschinus: "Squander, spend, do what you like."

ETHOPOEIA: See *Mimesis*.

EUCHARISTIA: Giving thanks for benefits received.

Near the end of *Phormio* (894-95), Demipho says, "I am heartily and deeply thankful to heaven, brother, for this successful issue."

EUPHEMISMUS: The substitution of a mild expression for something harsh.

Davus' *bona verba* in the *Andrian* 204 is an ironical euphemism, meaning "Don't be angry." Pythias' use of "sorceror" (*veneficus*), in *Eunuch* 648, when she means "ravisher" is certainly a euphemism.

EXARITHMESIS: A reckoning up, according to Donatus.

In the *Mother-in-law* 818-20, Bacchis recounts the favors she has done to her former lover Pamphilus:

I gave him back his son, who was almost lost by his and the women's doings; I gave him back his wife with whom he never again expected to live; I have freed him from the suspicions of his father and Phidippus.

EXCLAMATIO: An emotional outcry, specially suitable to tragedy but allowable in comedy upon occasion.

The commentators called the *Brothers* 789-90 a *tragica exclamatio*. Here Demea cries:

Ah me, what shall I do? How shall I act? How shall I complain, how lament? O heaven, O earth, O seas of Neptune!

Donatus observed that this speech illustrates what Horace meant when he said, in *Ars Poetica* 93, "At times, nevertheless, Comedy raises her voice."

EXUTHENISMUS: An expression of belittlement or contempt.

In the *Mother-in-law* 320-21, Parmeno says to Pamphilus: "They said your wife had some kind of trembling fits. I don't know how that may be."

GNOME: See *Paroemia*.

HORISMUS: A brief definition.

Willichius said that Sostrata uses *horismus* in her speech of self-defense in the *Mother-in-law* 274 ff. Sostrata attacks the prejudice that all wives are bad and all daughters-in-law hostile. Her own use of *horismus*, however, is not altogether clear.

HYPERBOLE: Magnification beyond the bounds of truth. *Hyperbole* often overlaps *amplificatio*.

There are numerous examples of *hyperbole* in Terence, as there are in every comic writer. The Terentian character often uses the expression "to perish" (*perire*) when he means merely that he is embarrassed, just as nowadays we might say "I died" or "I nearly died." Equally familiar to the modern man is Clitipho's *hyperbole* in the *Self-Tormentor* 239-40. Clitipho is trying to soothe the impatience of his young friend Clinia, who is waiting for his mistress:

Don't you consider that she lives a long way off? And you know how women are: preparing and getting ready to leave takes them a year.

HYPOCORISMA: A diminutive for endearing or comic effect.

In the *Andrian* 710, Davus uses the word *diecula* (little day). In the *Brothers* 763, Syrus addresses himself as *Syrisce* (little Syrus).

HYPOLEPSIS: Picking up a cue.

This figure is naturally very prominent in the drama although it was seldom mentioned by the commentators. Willichius called the opening lines of the *Brothers* 2.2 (210-11) *hypolepsis*. Here Syrus addresses the pander: "What's this I hear, Sannio, about your having a row with my master?"

HYPOPHORA: Asking a question and then answering it. An effective figure, much used in both oratory and the drama.

Probably the most celebrated illustration from the English drama is Falstaff's "What is honor?" Among several examples in Terence, a soliloquy by Geta in *Phormio* 779-82 will serve as well as any for illustration:

What about the future? What will be done? You're still stuck in the mud; you'll gain nothing by this, Geta; the present evil is but put off for a day; the blows increase unless you look out.

HYPOTYPOSIS: A vivid description or sketch.

This figure is sometimes called *energia* (or *enargia*), i.e., the power to express reality in vivid terms. I have selected three illustrations from the many in Terence.

(1) Willichius called *Eunuch* 727-28 a "hypotyposis of drunkenness." Young Chremes enters drunk, saying:

Ah ha, by God, I've been imposed upon; the wine I've drunk has got the better of me. It's true I seemed sober enough while I sat at table. Since I got up neither my feet nor my wits serve me very well.

Chremes reminds one of Cassio in *Othello*.

(2) A good domestic *hypotyposis* is Menedemus' account of how badly he felt after his only son ran away from home (*Self-Tormentor* 124-27):

I sink into a chair; up run my servants; they pull off my shoes. I see others hurrying about to arrange the cushions, to prepare supper, every one doing his best to ease me of my unhappiness.

(3) My own favorite Terentian *hypotyposis* is the reply of Clitipho to his father's recommendation of a bride (*Self-Tormentor* 1061-62):

What, that redheaded, cat-eyed, sparrow-mouthed, crooked-nosed wench? Impossible, father!

ICON: Describing a person by imagery. Similar to *hypotyposis*.

In the *Eunuch* 688-89, Pythias describes Dorus, the eunuch that Phaedria bought for Thais: "This is an ancient, withered, spiritless old man, tawny-colored as a weasel." In the *Mother-in-law* 439-41, Pamphilus describes an acquaintance: "I'll describe him so you'll know him: tall, ruddy, curly-headed, fleshy, cat-eyed, with a face like a corpse."

IMITATIO: See *Mimesis*.

INCREMENTUM: See *Amplificatio*.

INDUCTIO: See *Epagoge*.

IRONIA: Irony, as Quintilian remarked, is difficult to classify as a figure. There is no question, however, about the importance of irony in the drama, in both tragedy and comedy, and the Terentian commentators were alert to point out innumerable examples of ironical expression in the comedies. I have selected several illustrations which exhibit some variety.

(1) In the *Andrian* 847, Simo addresses the scheming Davus: "Greetings, O honest man!"

(2) Similar to the above is Gnatho's mocking salutation to Parmeno in the *Eunuch* 270: "Gnatho greets his great friend Parmeno with many salutations."

(3) In the *Andrian* 869, Simo complains to Chremes about his undutiful son Pamphilus: "O Chremes, the dutifulness of my son!"

(4) In the *Brothers* 721-22, Demea brings his brother Micio news about Aeschinus: "I bring you news of other villainies, monstrous villainies, of that honest young man."

(5) In the *Eunuch* 907-08, Pythias indulges in some irony as she talks to Chaerea, who refuses to be seen on the street in the clothes of a eunuch.

Pythias: Why, pray? Because you are ashamed?
Chaerea: That's just it.
Pythias: Just it? Just a virgin!

(6) The conclusion of Chaerea's speech in the *Eunuch* 313-17 is a good example of boyish irony. He is talking about the girl (Pamphila) he spied on the street:

She's a girl unlike the maidens of our set, whose mothers try to fit 'em with slack shoulders and tight-laced bosoms to make 'em slim. If one of them is a little plumper than the others, they call her a boxer and dock her rations. Our maiden is naturally lusty, but dieting turns her into a bulrush. And therefore she has suitors.

(7) Barlandus called special attention to a fine bit of irony from Demea in the *Brothers* 967-69. Demea is speaking of the clever rogue Syrus, who has aided Aeschinus in his escapades:

Finally, he helped today in the purchase of the music-girl; he managed it. It's right to reward him; it will encourage the other servants. Besides, the boy desires it.

(8) An ironical reply of the servant Byrria, in the *Andrian* 315-16, is in the spirit of English Restoration comedy. Charinus, who is in love with Philumena, asks Byrria if he should go to Pamphilus and ask him to postpone his marriage with Philumena. Byrria replies: "Yes, why not? If you obtain nothing, he will at least know that you are ready to make him cuckold after he is married."

(9) The conclusion of the *Eunuch* strikes a fine ironical note. In this closing scene, the discomfited braggart-soldier, Thraso, is lurking in the background. Gnatho, the parasite, has persuaded Phaedria and Chaerea to remain friends with the wealthy soldier. Now Gnatho turns to Thraso (*Eunuch* 1088 ff.):

Gnatho: Thraso, come forward when you like.
Thraso: I pray, how are we doing?
Gnatho: How? These gentlemen didn't know what a fellow you were; but after I displayed your character to them and praised you according to your deeds and virtues, I won them over.
Thraso: You have done well. I am extremely grateful. I was never yet anywhere but everybody loved me exceedingly.
Gnatho: (*to Phaedria and Chaerea*) Didn't I tell you that you would find Attic elegance in this man?
Phaedria: He comes up to your promise.

LIPTOTES or LITOTES: A form of understatement, familiar enough to all of Anglo-Saxon blood, but not specially prominent in Terence.

Old Laches obviously uses *litotes* in the *Mother-in-law* 482 when he hears his son utter a dutiful sentiment. "Pamphilus," he says, "your words are not unwelcome to my ears." *Litotes* is also expressed when a speaker affirms something by denying its contrary. Thus Parmeno, in the *Eunuch* 936, expresses his distaste for courtesans by saying that nothing looks more orderly or elegant than these courtesans "when they toy over a dinner with a lover."

MEIOSIS: Extenuation, minimizing, belittling.

Actually Donatus and other commentators treated *meiosis* as a kind of *auxesis* (amplification). And it is often difficult to tell in some instances, since the very act of belittling may build up the emotional effect. Willichius found a *meiosis* in the following speech of Micio, in the *Brothers* 147-51; Donatus called the first line *litotes*.

Not but what Aeschinus has done us some injury in this matter. What courtesan here has he not been in love with? To whom has he not given something? At last, only the other day—I believe he's now tired of them all—he said that he wished to marry.

Willichius found *meiosis* in a speech of Parmeno, in the *Eunuch* 67; but Donatus called it *auxesis*. Parmeno is talking to Phaedria about Thais:

She will quench these words, by Jove, with one little counterfeit tear, which she will hardly squeeze out by vehemently rubbing the eyes, and she'll turn the accusation against you and make you suffer instead.

METADIORTHOSIS: Correcting oneself.

Donatus used the term several times. In *Phormio* 231-33, Demipho says:

So Antipho has taken a wife without my leave? What, no regard for my authority—I won't mention authority—not even for my displeasure!

METALEMPSIS: (Donatus wrote μετάλημψις, but the Paris edition of 1552 puts *metalepsis* in the margin). A figure which puts the consequent for that which precedes.

In the *Andrian* (502), Davus is being questioned by Simo, who suspects that the clever slave is at the bottom of his son's love affair with Glycerium. Davus says, "That's as if you say it was done by my advice." But Simo has not actually said so, though he obviously believes so and will say so.

METALEPSIS: See *Metalempsis*.

METANOIA: Change of heart or repentance.

In the *Brothers* 681-83, Aeschinus says to his uncle Micio: "May I never deserve your love in all your life, my father, if my offense doesn't cause me grievous pain and make me ashamed to look you in the face."

METASTASIS: Turning back objections.

In the *Eunuch* 1069-71, Gnatho says to Phaedria and Chaerea: "First I should very much like both of you to believe that whatever I do here is done mostly for my own sake; but if it is also for your profit, it would be foolish for you not to do it."

METONYMIA: Letting one word stand for another word or for an idea.

In the *Eunuch* 733, Chremes quotes an old saying: "Without Ceres and Bacchus Venus is a-cold." Richard Bernard's school translation explains the metonymy here: "Without fine feeding and drunkenness, lecherous lust is out of courage." Micio says of his nephew Aeschinus, in the *Brothers* 152, "I hoped his youth had cooled down," thus expressing a metonymy the opposite of the first illustration.

MIMESIS: *Mimesis* is the broad term and includes *ethopoeia, prosopopoeia, prosographia, dialogismus, sermocinatio,* etc.

Whenever a character mimics the action or speech of another character he is expressing *mimesis.* There are innumerable examples in Terence, many of which I have already called attention to in earlier chapters. Two illustrations must suffice here, one a pathetic *mimesis,* the other in the spirit of comedy.

(1) In the *Andrian* 282 ff., Pamphilus relates the scene at the death-bed of Chrysis, who left Pamphila in his charge:

"Dear Pamphilus," she began, "you see the girl's beauty and youth, and you know how weak a shield all that is to chastity and to property."

(2) In the *Andrian* 386 ff., Davus gives realistic advice to Pamphilus:

Not at all. For I think it is this way: your father will say, "I want you to marry today"; you'll say, "I'll marry."

MYCTERISMUS: Mockery or sarcasm, a scornful expression.

In the *Eunuch* 679-80, when Phaedria, who is unaware that his brother Chaerea has been posing as a eunuch, shows the real eunuch Dorus to the maidservant of Thais, Pythias scornfully retorts, "Do you believe, pray, that this was the fellow that was brought to us?"

OBTESTATIO: Supplication.

This figure is common in tragedy and may be used in the pathetic parts of comedy. Donatus called the *Mother-in-law* 387 an *obtestatio*: "By that chance we both beseech you."

OCCUPATIO: See *Anticipatio.*

ONOMATOPOEIA: Fitting the sound to the sense.

Donatus pointed to the use of *vagire* (to squall) in the *Mother-in-law* 517.

OXYMORON: A combination of contradictory ideas.

In the *Eunuch* 243, Gnatho says, "I have nothing, yet I lack nothing."

PARADOXON: A statement of contraries.

Donatus called the *Andrian* 68—"Complaisance makes friends, truth enemies"—a paradoxical sentiment.

PARAENESIS: A warning or admonishment.

In the *Mother-in-law* 766-67, Laches says to Bacchis, "My one piece of advice to you is that you make trial of me as a friend rather than as an enemy."

PARALEPSIS: Pretending to pass over something but actually emphasizing it.

In *Phormio* 168, Phormio says "I do not add"—and then proceeds to add in detail. In the *Self-Tormentor* 901, Menedemus says, "I say nothing about kissing and embracing."

PARASCEUE: Sometimes called *prupergasia* or *praemunitio*. Preparation for what is to come. Similar to *anticipatio* and allied figures. As I have indicated in the chapter on plot, however, *parasceue* is often part of the economy of action.[13]

Examples of *parasceue* are everywhere in Terence. One obvious example is *Self-Tormentor* 561, where Syrus says, "Who's that coming out at our door?" This speech prepares the way for a new scene. Another example is Micio's remark in the *Brothers* 78: "But isn't that the man I was talking about? It certainly is."

PARENTHESIS: Insertion of an aside, an interrupting thought.

In the *Mother-in-law* 385, Pamphilus interrupts his narrative with —"When I remember her words I cannot refrain from tears."

PAROEMIA: *Paroemia* is a proverbial saying or aphorism. It was also called *proverbium*, *gnome*, and sometimes *sententia*.

There was no uniformity of terminology, but the figure is readily recognized and very prominent in Terence. Proverbial sentiments are common, indeed, in most comedy, for middle-class and lower-middle-class characters delight in such saws. Notice, for example, the large number of proverbial expressions in the tales of Chaucer's Miller, Reve, and Cook. Old men in particular delight in proverbs, and the majority of the proverbs in Terence come from the old men. The *Self-Tormentor*, for example, is especially rich. The servants, however, also use them, and occasionally one of the young men will become sententious, if he is feeling out of sorts.

The following list of saws does not begin to be complete; it merely offers some typical specimens of what Donatus and his followers termed *paroemia*, *proverbium*, *gnome*, or *sententia* γνωμική.

"Lover's quarrels are love's renewal." (*Andrian* 555.)
"Fortune favors the brave." (*Phormio* 203.)
"Without Ceres and Bacchus Venus is a-cold." (*Eunuch* 733.)
"Make trial by others of what is profitable for yourself." (*Self-Tormentor* 210.)
"A great and memorable exploit is always dangerous." (*Ibid.* 314.)
"Time removes men's grief." (*Ibid.* 422.)
"We all are the worse for too much liberty." (*Ibid.* 483.)

---

[13]See p. 102.

"All of us see and judge other men's affairs better than our own."
(*Ibid.* 504.)

"Nothing is so hard but it can be found out by diligent search."
(*Ibid.* 675.)

"Nothing is so easy but it is hard when you do it unwillingly."
(*Ibid.* 805.)

PAROMOEON: See *Paronomasia.*

PAROMOLOGIA: An admission of something unfavorable in order to
strengthen the argument.

Byrria, the servant of Charinus, uses the figure in the *Andrian*
426-30:

It's a true saying you hear everywhere, that every one sets his own
good before his neighbor's. I have seen Philumena. I remember the girl
seemed a beauty. Therefore I don't blame Pamphilus so much if he would
embrace her himself rather than leave her to Charinus.

PARONOMASIA: Playing on the sound and meaning of words.

The sixteenth century used *paronomasia* for nouns, *paromoeon* for
verbs. *Syllepsis*, a grammatical figure, might also be a pun. There are
puns enough in Terence, but he was not so fond of them as many
modern writers have been. It is virtually impossible to illustrate Latin
puns in English.

PERIPHRASIS: Circumlocution.

Periphrasis is not common in Terence, whose expression is usually
very crisp and succinct. Donatus called attention to *nostrae industriae*
(our zeal) in the Prologue to the *Mother-in-law* (32); Willichius to
Bacchis' phrase (*ibid.* 756), "another one of my profession."

PERISTASIS: Amplifying by giving circumstantial details.

In the Prologue to *Phormio* (6-8), the author remarks that a rival
playwright found fault with his play because he never wrote about
a "mad stripling seeing a doe in flight and dogs giving chase and the
beast begging for help." Donatus explained that this *peristasis* is tragic
and therefore bad when introduced into comedy.

PRAEMUNITIO: See *Parasceue.*

PRAEOCCUPATIO: See *Anticipatio.*

PRAESUMPTIO: See *Anticipatio.*

PRAETERITIO: See *Anticipatio.*

PROCATALEPSIS: See *Anticipatio.*

PRODIORTHOSIS: See *Anticipatio.*

PROLEPSIS: See *Anticipatio.*

PROSOPOPOEIA: See *Mimesis.*

PROSOGRAPHIA: See *Mimesis.*

PROVERBIUM: See *Paroemia*.

PRUPERGASIA: See *Parasceue*.

PYSMA: Questions requiring various answers.

In the *Eunuch* 706-07, Phaedria asks Dorus the eunuch: "Come a little this way, do you hear? a little closer: that'll do. Now tell me again: did Chaerea take your clothes?"

SARCASMUS: A figure that is about the same as *chleuasmus*.

Willichius called Phormio's taunt of Chremes in *Phormio* 1026 *sarcasmus*. Phormio says, "It's time now to go to Chremes' funeral."

SERMOCINATIO: See *Mimesis*.

SYLLOGISMUS: See the discussion of syllogisms in the preceding section on proofs.

SYNATHROISMUS: A collection or union of separate things. This figure is very similar to *congeries*.

In the *Self-Tormentor* 194, Chremes argues that young Clinia ought not to be miserable since he has all those things which are accounted blessings: "parents, a prosperous country, friends, family, relatives, riches." Geta's speech in the *Brothers* 303-04 is a *synthroismus*:

Violence, poverty, injustice, hopelessness, disgrace! What a world! O the sins, O the impious breeds, O the abandoned fellow!

SYNCHORESIS: A deliberate concession, made in order to strengthen the retort.

In the *Brothers* 188-89, Sannio the pander says to Aeschinus: "I am a slave-dealer, I confess, the common bane of young men, a liar and a plague; yet I have done you no wrong."

SYNECDOCHE: Stating the part for the whole or the whole for the part, the species for the genus or the genus for the species. *Synecdoche* is like a metaphor.

In the *Andrian* 371, Davus calls Charinus "chucklehead" (*ridiculum caput*), putting the part for the whole. In similar fashion, in the *Brothers* 261, Ctesipho calls Syrus "merryhead" (*festivom caput*).

SYNGNOME: A figure of forgiveness.

Phaedria, speaking in behalf of his cousin Antipho and seeking forgiveness for him, argues that wicked people "set a trap for our youthfulness." (*Phormio* 274.)

SYNONYMIA: Repeating the idea in different words. A kind of amplification.

Willichius called the *Andrian* 886-89 an amplification by means of *synonymia*. Here Simo laments the undutifulness of his son Pamphilus:

Why torture myself? Why vex my mind? Why trouble my old age with this fellow's senselessness? Am I to be punished because he has sinned? No, let him keep her and have done with me, let him live with her.

SYNTOMIA: See *Epitome*.

GRAMMATICAL FIGURES

Since Latin grammatical figures are usually meaningless when translated into English, for the most part I merely list the figures that the commentators found in Terence and supply convenient references.

ACYROLOGIA: Impropriety of speech, the use of wrong terms. This figure is a stock device in comedy, especially in broad comedy, and there is some use of it in Terence. Willichius found *acyrologia* in the *Eunuch* 85, where Parmeno speaks of Thais as a "flame." Phaedria complains that the sight of Thais gives him a chill. "Take courage," says Parmeno; "go near this flame and you'll soon be hot enough."

AMPHIBOLIA: Grammatical ambiguity. Very common in Elizabethan comedy, but not common in Terence, whose characters all speak pretty well (*Andrian* 261).

ANACLASIS: A play on words, specifically returning to a word but giving it a different meaning. Donatus cited *incerta certum* in the *Mother-in-law* 17.

ANACOLUTHON: Abandonment of regular grammatical sequence; naturally very common in comic dialogue. There are many examples of *anacoluthon* in Terence (*Andrian* 837).

ANADIPLOSIS: Repetition of a prominent word in a clause at the beginning of the following clause. Cf. *epanalepsis*. *Phormio* 352-53: "That Phanium is kin to him is denied by Demipho? Demipho denies that she is kin?"

ANAPHORA: Repetition of the beginning word in a series of clauses. Also termed *epanaphora*, it is a very effective device. Demea, in the *Brothers* 546-47, says: "I'm the first to sense our troubles, the first to find out everything, the first also to report it."

ANASTROPHE: Unusual word order. *Andrian* 211 has *primum iam* instead of *iam primum*.

ANTAPODOSIS: Correlation or parallelism of words or phrases. See Donatus on the *Mother-in-law* 43.

ANTIMERIA: Substitution of one part of speech for another. As Rivius remarked, it is freely used by comic poets. See the *Andrian* 522.

ANTIPTOSIS: Putting one case for another. See the *Eunuch* 653.

ASYNDETON: Omission of conjunctions between clauses. See the *Brothers* 266-67. *Asyndeton* is sometimes called *brachylogia*. *Dialyton* is also similar.

CACOZELON: Affected or faulty diction. Naturally common in comedy, though not prominent·in Terence. In the *Eunuch* 722, Dorias speaks in characteristic maidservant style: "If you're wise, what you know you don't know, either about the eunuch or the violation of the girl."

CLIMAX: A series of words or phrases rising in emphasis. *Climax* is similar to *anadiplosis* though usually more extended. Gnatho's sketch of his patron Thraso, in the *Eunuch* 1078-79, was called a *climax:*

To start with, he has the means to give, and none gives more bountifully. He is a witless, tasteless sluggard who snores day and night.

DIAERESIS: Dividing a word and re-forming it in abnormal order. See Donatus on the *Andrian* 486.

DIALYTON: See *Asyndeton*.

ECLIPSIS: Omission of a word easily supplied by the listener. As Donatus (on the *Andrian* 57) pointed out, *eclipsis* was a favorite device of Terence. It would naturally appear often in any conversational style.

ENALLAGE: The substitution of one part of speech, or of one gender, case, tense, etc., for another. See *Phormio* 447.

EPANALEPSIS: Repetition of word or clause. About the same figure as *anadiplosis* (*q·v.*).

EPANAPHORA: See *Anaphora*.

EPENTHESIS: Inserting a letter in the middle of a word, often to fill out the meter. See Donatus on *Phormio* 225.

HOMOEOTELEUTON: Like ending in words, similar to rhyme. See Donatus on *Eunuch* 236.

HYPALLAGE: Changing the normal order of words or the grammatical construction. See Donatus on *Mother-in-law* 307.

HYPERBATON: Inverted word order. See Donatus on *Eunuch* 785.

HYPOZEUGMA: Joining several subjects with one verb; similar to *zeugma*. See the *Mother-in-law* 263.

HYPOZEUXIS: Parallel clauses, each with its own subject and verb. See *Phormio* 162.

HYSTEROLOGIA: Changing the normal order of verbs, putting the first verb last, the last first. Barlandus used *hysterologia* as a synonym for *hysteron proteron*. In the *Self-Tormentor* 430, Chremes tells Menedemus that his son "is well and lives" (*valet atque vivit*).

HYSTERON PROTERON: See *Hysterologia*.

METABASIS. Transition from one subject to another. In the *Andrian* 487, Lesbia, speaking of the child that has just been born to Glycerium and Pamphilus, says: "I beseech the gods that it live, since he [Pamphilus] is a man of parts."

PARELCON: Addition of a superfluous word. There are many examples in Terence, as there must be in any conversational style. See Donatus on the *Andrian* 29.

PARENTHESIS: Insertion of an aside. "Heaven forbid" in the *Andrian* 568. *Parenthesis* is a figure that may be classified as either grammatical or rhetorical.

PLEONASMUS: Redundancy. See *Phormio* 340.

PLOCE: Emphatic repetition of a word. See Donatus on the *Andrian* 41 and on *Phormio* 108.

POLYPTOTON: Repetition of a word in different inflections. In the *Brothers* 455-58, Geta pleads with old Hegio as follows:

Hegio, all our hope rests on you; we have only you: you are her patron, you her father: our old master on his death bed entrusted us to you: if you desert us, we are lost.

POLYSYNDETON: Repetition of conjunctions. See Donatus on *Brothers* 301.

SYLLEPSIS: The use of a verb, or adjective, to govern two or more words without agreeing grammatically with more than one word. This figure is very prominent in Terence. In the *Brothers* 103, Micio says to Demea: "If neither I nor you did (*fecimus*) these things. . . ."

SYNCOPE: Omission of a letter or syllable from the middle of a word. *Circumspexti* for *circumspexisti* in the *Brothers* 689.

TAPINOSIS: Degradation by the use of debasing terms, calling people bad names. This figure is very common in low comedy and in some high comedies; but it is seldom used by Terence, whose diction was much prized because it never stooped to foul or obscene words. A very mild example, cited by Donatus, is *Eunuch* 274, where Gnatho rudely speaks of Pamphila as a "slave" (*mancupium*).

TAUTOLOGIA: Vain repetition. Willichius found an example in the *Brothers* 916.

TMESIS: Breaking up compound words with insertions. See Donatus on *Eunuch* 721.

ZEUGMA: The use of one verb to serve several clauses. See Donatus on *Eunuch* 611.

Even a cursory analysis of Terentian figures of speech and figures of thought will contribute something to an understanding of this comic writer's art. Many of the grammatical figures listed above, for example, are figures of repetition, and repetition is, of course, a fundamental principle in all the arts. Many of the rhetorical figures are unifying structural devices of repetition, parallelism, anticipation, and emphasis. It is hardly necessary to labor the importance of poetic analysis by means of figures, for nowadays scholars are coming more and more to recognize that the sixteenth-century figures were not mere decorations, but rather logical and persuasive elements of composition.[14] Twentieth-century "metaphysical" critics have been telling us for some time that figure and image in John Donne and Andrew Marvell, in William Butler Yeats and T. S. Eliot, are often the very structure of the poem. Donatus and the sixteenth-century commentators on Terence were also aware of poetic structure and of its logical and rhetorical elements, conveniently represented for them by these figures of speech and figures of thought.

DICTION

Diction (λέξις) and Thought (διάνοια) overlap in many instances. The figures of speech, or grammatical figures, which I have placed immediately following the rhetorical figures, actually belong under diction, which is primarily grammatical. Grammatical criticism of Terence, as one might expect, was a prominent feature of the commentaries, for the commentators were much concerned with the vocabulary, syntax, and usage that constituted a principal basis for teaching schoolboys how to read, write, and talk. Unfortunately it is almost impossible to discuss Latin diction in terms that will be illuminating or useful to most modern readers. Consequently I shall have to confine my brief discussion of comic diction to more or less general observations on Terentian style.

Comedy, as has been mentioned earlier,[15] was traditionally coupled with the humble, everyday style. As Robortellus[16] said, "Diction in comic discourse ought to be simple, easy, open, clear, familiar, and, finally, taken from common usage." Terence pre-eminently fulfilled the traditional demands for a pure, simple style, with Plautus a doubtful second. "Amongst Roman writers, in prose and verse," said Erasmus, "Terence, for pure, terse Latinity has no rival, and his plays are

---

[14]See, for example, Sister Miriam Joseph's *Shakespeare's Use of the Arts of Language* (New York, 1947) and Rosemond Tuve's *Metaphysical Imagery and Renaissance Poetic* (Chicago, 1947).

[15]See p. 36.

[16]See p. 237.

never dull."[17] Then he added, "I see no objection to adding carefully chosen comedies of Plautus." Melanchthon, who made much of the three styles of speaking and writing, said of the humble style:

The humble species does not rise above everyday conversation, very carefully preserves propriety of speech, and tries distinctly to express the subject matter in the most proper words. It does not love numerous figures; it makes free use of metaphors, but not far-fetched ones, rather those drawn from everyday speech. It does not amplify very much, but the species as a whole is modest, designed to dissemble, and, as it were, carefully eschewing the ornate. It discourses of the matter discreetly and in due order. It generally sticks to the proposition, and deceives its auditor by a kind of plain dealing. It has very few periods (*circumductiones*); it reproduces the carelessness of everyday speech in its word order. The master artist of this style is Terence.[18]

Wagnerus, with the needs of the schoolboy in mind, wrote in 1550:

This poet [Terence] is profitable for the polishing of language, for the unlearning of rudeness, for the wealth and abundance of words and sentiments, for the invention of arguments for every kind of cause, for providing the knack of both speaking and writing. His speech is delightful and fitted above all to the understanding of boys—plain, simple, clear, never having anything obscure or ostentatiously affected.[19]

While Terence was particularly esteemed for the purity of his language and for the conciseness of his expression, his variety of style was also praised. Erasmus said that his plays are never dull. Long before Erasmus, Cicero had set the fashion for admiring the variety of Terentian style. In *De Oratore* 2.80.327, Cicero cited Simo's account of his son's life, in the *Andrian* 51 ff., as a model of *narratio:* "the character of the young man, the slave's inquiry, the death of Chrysis, the face, the figure, and the wailing of her sister, and the rest, all narrated delightfully and in a great variety of style." Terentian diction, for all its simplicity, is never flat or monotonous. Nor is it exclusively humble, for that matter, since the comic poet exercised his license to depart now and then from the familiar style. For one thing, Terence varied his easy, conversational diction by judicious mixtures of serious, even tragic, words and phrases. Yet Terence, as Evanthius noted, "never swelled to tragic heights."

Georgius Fabricius, in an epistle to the Duke of Saxony, dated 1546, presented an analysis of two great models of the Latin language,

---

[17]Quoted by T. W. Baldwin, *William Shakspere's Small Latine and Lesse Greeke* 1.80.

[18]*Elementorum Rhetorices* (1533), pp. 148-49.

[19]Willichius' edition of Terence, p. 10.

Terence and Cicero. Terence, according to Fabricius, addressed his speech to banquets and theater, Cicero to senate and court. While Terence imitated the lower classes, such as slaves, parasites, pimps, and soldiers, Cicero dealt with the superior sort in the affairs of state. Terence presented an image of ordinary, daily life, yet his speech, though drawn from common usage, contains a considerable variety of expression: "Since the speech of comic poets deals with times, persons, and events, many old, very many poetic, not a few super-fluous, and now and then outlandish words are used, derived from the nature and feeling of the writer but intermingled with common usage."[20] This variety of speech, said Fabricius, must be handled with decorum lest the illumination that comes from everyday, customary speech and proper terms be obscured by obsolete, alien, long-sought terms. Fabricius knew well enough that the language of the comic drama is not a mere transcript of common speech. For one thing, the language of comedy must answer the demands of verse. For an-other, the Latin comic poets, e.g., Terence, deliberately sought to avoid vulgar expressions since they aimed to please the discriminat-ing, learned gentlemen of the audience. Fabricius, in fact, found the rhythms of the comic poet and the course of comic diction more tortuous, less natural than the easy and plain diction of some orators.

Fabricius was merely pointing out what every intelligent commen-tator and critic of the sixteenth century knew, that the simple and humble diction of comedy has a relative simplicity and humility, that it can, and should, rise upon occasion to a loftier plane. From the time of Donatus in the fourth century to that of Congreve[21] in the late seventeenth, the advice of Horace, in the *Art of Poetry* 93-94, was always in mind:

At times, nevertheless, Comedy raises her voice, and angry Chremes rants with swelling speech.

In the *Brothers* 789-90, Demea, fretted by the loose behavior of his brother and son, loses patience:

Ah me, what shall I do? How shall I act? How shall I complain, how lament? O heaven, O earth, O seas of Neptune!

This speech, said Donatus, is what Horace meant by his statement.[22]

Another instance of elevated diction to indicate a serious mood is in the *Brothers* 638. Here Micio tests his nephew Aeschinus with a

---

[20]Bergius' edition of Terence, p. 9.

[21]Horace's *Art of Poetry* 93 appears on the title page of Congreve's *Double-Dealer*, together with a quotation from Terence's *Self-Tormentor*.

[22]Cf. Barlandus, Latomus, and Willichius on the same passage in the *Brothers*.

false account of Pamphila's betrothal to a stranger. While Micio is testing and teasing the youth, Aeschinus is suffering real pangs. Donatus called attention to the elevated diction of Micio when he asks his nephew, "Was it you beating on the door?" The poet's verb here is *pepulisti*, a strong term and one not ordinarily used for such an everyday experience. Donatus commented: "Notice the elevated word *pepulisti*, adapted to the tragic cothurnus rather than to comic discourse." Similar is the use of an archaic reduplicated verb form, *tetulit*, in the *Andrian* 832. Donatus remarked of this usage: "*Tetulit* is put in place of the simple form, and seems to be a loftier expression than becomes a comic character." Nevertheless, Terence was not accused of breaking decorum here; for the character using the term is Chremes, who is somewhat indignantly repudiating the match between his daughter and Pamphilus. Chremes therefore has license to use more elevated expressions than ordinarily become comic fathers.

Tragic expressions, especially tragic exclamations, were permissible in comedy when the character expressed fear of going insane. Thus the irascible Demea, in the *Brothers* 111, very properly says to his easy-going brother Micio, "By Jupiter, you are a man to drive me insane." A similar expression is used in the *Brothers* 197, where Sannio, the pander, driven to distraction by Aeschinus, cries, "All-high Jupiter, I don't wonder that wrong drives men insane." Donatus remarked of the passage:

Moreover, notice how the careful poet, wheresoever he has raised a tragic voice in comedy, forewith calls the character insane. And so above [*ibid.*] 111: "By Jupiter, you are a man to drive me insane."

Upon occasion, the comic poet will employ rather complex expressions with subtle overtones suggesting meanings beyond the literal. In other words, the *colors* of rhetoric, the nuances of style, while more appropriate, perhaps, to serious oratory and poetry, are not denied the comic poet. For example, the comic poet, like the orator, may wish to use harsh language with an ultimate purpose of conciliation. Terence does so in the *Brothers* 685 ff. Here Micio, in order to arouse his nephew to a just sense of his heedless conduct, accuses him of wrong doing in rather harsh words. But Micio's ultimate purpose is to soften his accusation and so gain the confidence of Aeschinus, whom he loves, and perhaps even to soften the dour Demea.

Micio What country do you think you are living in? You have unlawfully wronged a girl. In the first place, that is a great fault, great, yes, but nevertheless a human fault; other honest men have often done the same.

Donatus, who may very well have had the advice of Quintilian and Cicero in mind,[23] namely, that the accomplished speaker should be able to blend all styles when necessary, admired this passage: "These are very difficult colors of eloquence, but Terence has taken pains to make Micio accuse gently and to induce the very harsh Demea to speak fair."

Serious, even tragic, terms, then, may appear in comedy. On the other hand, the comic poet could also depart from the mean of a simple, familiar, everyday style and occasionally make use of rather low, vulgar diction. (The disciples of the New Comedy, the Terentian commentators, never went so far as to approve obscene language.) In the *Eunuch* 96, Thais uses both *amare* and *diligere* (to esteem) in the same sentence. Doletus, the Ciceronian, remarked that Terence did not exercise the same care in using these words that Cicero did. "But," Doletus concluded, "what is not permitted to poets?" Nevertheless, he went on to praise the purity and propriety of Terence's diction in general. The comic poet had license to use vulgar speech if he assigned it to a vulgar person—if he avoided any breach of decorum. Thus Donatus and Barlandus excused the vulgar reply of Thais to Chremes, the brother of Pamphila, in the *Eunuch* 751. "But take care," says Thais, "that you don't lose her before you get her from me, Chremes." A better illustration of vulgar speech for the modern reader is another expression of Thais, in the *Eunuch* 90. Here she says to Phaedria, "*Missa*"—roughly the equivalent of the American slang expression "cut it out." Phaedria, apparently somewhat nettled by his mistress' rudeness, says, "Why 'cut it out'?" Donatus commented as follows:

The great virtue of the poet is not only to heighten sentiments drawn from middle-class customs and put them in comedy, but also to use certain words from common speech, and of such sort is what he now says, "Why *missa?*"

Donatus and his sixteenth-century followers justly admired Terence's decorum in diction, the Roman poet's happy faculty of fitting just the right word to the right character. There are innumerable instances of this propriety in Terence. In fact, it would be difficult to find illustrations of impropriety of diction in his plays. While the range of expression in Terence, compared with that in Shakespeare or Jonson, is narrow, and while the speech of his characters is seldom broad and lusty, he provided admirable models for the aspiring young poet or orator. Certainly no student would have picked up bad habits of diction in following Terence. One or two illustrations of this

---

[23]See Quintilian 6.5.5; 11.1.85. Cf. Cicero *De Oratore* 3.25.96; 3.52.199.

decorum in diction must suffice, for very few of them will flourish after being transplanted from Latin into English.

Donatus commended the propriety of a speech by Davus in the *Andrian* 606. The plans of Davus for helping his young master have gone awry and he now faces the wrath of Pamphilus, who approaches: "But yonder he comes himself. I'm a dead man. I would to God I might give myself the final shove over the edge!" Donatus remarked, "He did not say 'sword' or 'halter' lest it be tragic." An expression singled out for praise by several commentators comes from Demea in the *Brothers* 715. "I've crept (*perreptavi*)," says Demea, "over the whole town." Latomus remarked, "Crept is apt and proper for the slowness of the old man." Another expression of Demea, in the *Brothers* 877, illustrates good comic diction. Demea, who has found that severity towards his sons is unsuccessful, decides to try complaisance. "Now," he says, "let us try the opposite." The use of *we* here, observed Donatus, is more comic than if he had said "*I'll* try." The use of *we* in the mouth of a king, like King Lear, for example, lends majesty to tragic diction. In the mouth of a middle-class, fussy old man like Demea, however, the use of *we* suggests comic pomposity.

The high reputation of Terentian diction rested in large part upon its purity and neatness. Terence himself observed, in the Prologue (46), that his *Self-Tormentor* is "pure speech" (*pura oratio*), and this quiet play was much esteemed by Renaissance commentators. The *Self-Tormentor*, remarked Petrus Marsus, is "not glowing with passion, but quiet as befits graybeards." Its highest praise, said Barlandus, is "speech neat and comely." And said Melanchthon, "What, indeed, is more admirable than neat and comely speech?" One is reminded of Ben Jonson's well-known statement, "Pure and neat language I love, yet plain and customary."[24] While Jonson preferred Aristophanes and Plautus to Terence, whom he found inferior in "economy and disposition," he must have admired the kind of diction to be found in Terence. Indeed, it is difficult to conceive of any literate person who would not commend the language of Terence, though he might, as did Jonson and Scaliger, find Terence rather tame by comparison with some other comic writers.

If comedy is the mirror of daily life, and the Renaissance certainly thought it should be such a mirror, then the speech of the Terentian characters must be accepted as a standard of familiar discourse. Of course Terentian diction was accepted by most sixteenth-century arbiters of literature, and by eminent literary men long after the

---

[24]*Discoveries*, p. 72.

sixteenth century, as the highest standard of the familiar style. Rapin, one of the leading neoclassical critics of France in the seventeenth century, said in substance what Donatus, Erasmus, Melanchthon, Robortellus, and others had said before him. The art of comedy, according to Rapin, is "to keep close to nature, and never leave it; to have common thoughts and expressions fitted to the capacity of all the world."[25] Rapin also had Terence principally in mind:

Comedy is as it should be when the spectator believes himself really in the company of such persons as he has represented, and takes himself to be in a family whilst he is at the theater; and that he there sees nothing but what he sees in the world. For comedy is worth nothing at all unless he know and can compare the manners that are exhibited on the stage with those of such persons as he has conversation withal. 'Twas by this that Menander had so great success amongst the Grecians, and the Romans thought themselves in conversation whilst they sat beholding the comedies of Terence; for they perceived nothing but what they had been accustomed to find in ordinary companies.[26]

An English disciple of Rapin, John Dennis, who remains as good a critic of comedy as England has yet produced, upheld Terentian dialogue as the standard of comic diction. Dennis actually preferred Molière, Jonson, and Wycherley to Terence, but his preference was based upon the greater force of ridicule and the greater variety of characters to be found in the modern comedies. He acknowledged that Terence's diction was unrivaled. In 1717, Dennis wrote:

If the god of laughter does not always attend upon Terence, Venus and the Graces never leave him. 'Tis my humble opinion that there is no dialogue extant in any language which has half the charms of the Terentian dialogue; what comes nearest to it is that of Etherege in *Sir Fopling Flutter*. I, who have been acquainted with Terence above forty years, am now more delighted with him than ever. And sure that beauty must be no common charmer, in whom time shall discover new graces, whom long possession renders more desirable.[27]

Students of English drama will doubtless wonder why Dennis singled out Etherege here rather than his friend Congreve, whose dialogue throughout *Love for Love* and the *Way of the World* is purer, neater, and certainly more brilliant than the dialogue in the *Man of Mode*. Congreve himself admired Terence, and learned much from him. In the dedication of his masterpiece, *Way of the World*, he paid high tribute to the Roman poet, "the most correct writer in

[25]*Reflections on Aristotle's Treatise of Poesie*, p. 126.
[26]*Ibid.*
[27]*Critical Works* 2.161.

the world," and commended the "purity of his style." Surely Congreve has come close to Terence. Where else in all English comic literature is there such a consistent mastery of pure comic diction? Congreve is superior to Terence in range and variety of diction; for the Roman comic stage never produced a Millamant or an Angelica or a Lady Wishfort. Terence has no young men as genuinely comic as Ben the young sailor in *Love for Love;* he has no old men as genuinely humorous as Foresight the astrologer in the same play. It is true, nevertheless, that Congreve's diction is not uniformly as pure, neat, and customary as that of Terence; nor as that of Molière, whom George Meredith ranked with the Greek Menander as supreme among all comic writers of the world.

Meredith preferred Molière to Congreve, but acknowledged the vigor, precision, and naturalness of the English writer's diction. In fact, Meredith's tribute to Congreve's dialogue is one of the best in dramatic criticism:

> Where Congreve excels all his English rivals is in his literary force, and a succinctness of style peculiar to him. He had correct judgment, a correct ear, readiness of illustration within a narrow range—in snap-shots of the obvious at the obvious—and copious language. He hits the mean of a fine style and a natural in dialogue. He is at once precise and voluble. If you have ever thought upon style, you will acknowledge it to be a signal accomplishment. In this he is a classic, and is worthy of treading a measure with Molière. The *Way of the World* may be read out currently at a first glance, so sure are the accents of the emphatic meaning to strike the eye, perforce of the crispness and cunning polish of the sentences. You have not to look over them before you confide yourself to him; he will carry you safe.[28]

In Meredith's estimation, however, Congreve falls short of Molière. Terence he placed just below Menander and Molière, for he found in Terence that same "beautiful translucency of language" that distinguishes the best high comedy. "For us," he wrote, "Terence shares with his master [Menander] the praise of an amenity that is like Elysian speech, equable and ever gracious; like the face of the Andrian's young sister: *Adeo modesto, adeo venusto, ut nil supra.*"[29]

The sixteenth-century commentators and critics were familiar with Quintilian's praise of Menander:

> The careful study of Menander alone would, in my opinion, be sufficient to develop all those qualities of which my present work is concerned; so perfect is his representation of actual life, so rich is his

---

[28]*An Essay on Comedy*, edited by Lane Cooper (New York, 1918), p. 100.
[29]*Ibid.*, p. 109. See the *Andrian* 120.

power of invention and his gift of style, so perfectly does he adapt himself to every kind of circumstance, character, and emotion.[30]

Lacking any substantial remains of Menander, and much more conversant with Latin than with Greek, anyway, the sixteenth century made Terence just such a model as Quintilian suggested. Generations of schoolboys, and generations of playwrights, learned how to speak and how to write from Terence, whose sentiments and diction have shaped and colored most of western Europe's finest comic writing.

---

[30]Quintilian 10.1.69.

Chapter VII: Conclusion

THE FIRST published answer to the puritan attack on poetry and poets in Stephen Gosson's *Schoole of Abuse* (1579) came in the same year from Thomas Lodge. The *Defence of Poetry* by Lodge, a learned but somewhat chaotic essay, devoted some space to the drama. The author apparently felt that the best defense of the drama was a learned account of its origin, development, and function. He obviously was more familiar with the theory and practice of comedy than with that of tragedy. Why? The answer, I think, is clear: he knew more about comedy because his authorities on the history of the drama were the same authorities I have been pursuing in the preceding pages. Lodge's defense of playmaking, in modernized transcription, begins as follows:

First therefore, if it be not tedious to Gosson to hearken to the learned, the reader shall perceive the antiquity of playmaking, the inventors of comedies, and therewithal the use and commodity of them. So that in the end I hope my labor shall be liked, and the learned will sooner conceive his folly. For tragedies and comedies, Donate the grammarian sayth, they were invented by learned fathers of the old time to no other purpose but to yield praise unto God for a happy harvest or plentiful year. And that this is true the name of Tragedy doth import, for, if you consider whence it came, you shall perceive (as Iodocus Badius reporteth) that it drew his original of *Tragos, Hircus, et Ode, Cantus* (so called), for that the actors thereof had in reward for their labor a goat's skin filled with wine.[1]

Lodge's authorities here were Donatus (Evanthius) and Iodocus Badius Ascensius, author of the *Prenotamenta* on Terence. Then, after quoting the familiar definition of comedy ascribed to Cicero by Donatus—"the imitation of life, the mirror of custom, the image of truth"—he proceeded to discuss the development of comedy. Here he followed Horace, Donatus, and Servius, and illustrated from the plays of Terence. Lodge mentioned Aristophanes and Plautus in his essay, but it was Terence who provided the specific examples. Somewhere Lodge had picked up a notion of the Aristotelian concept of imitation. "I must confess with Aristotle," he wrote, "that men are greatly delighted with imitation, and that it were good to bring those things on stage that were altogether tending to virtue."[2] It is extremely doubtful that he took his notion directly from the *Poetics*.

---

[1] *Elizabethan Critical Essays* 1.80.   [2] *Ibid.* 1.83.

In other words, the Elizabethan Lodge took the normal sixteenth-century approach to the criticism of comedy; he relied upon the rhetoricians and the Terentian commentators for his theory and he turned to Terence for the standard practice. By 1579, to be sure, Englishmen were becoming acquainted with the *Poetics* of Aristotle and possibly with Aristotelian critics like Minturno, Scaliger, and Castelvetro. Even after they came to know something about Aristotelian dramatic criticism, however, they did not abandon Horace, Cicero, Quintilian, Donatus, and the Terentian commentators; they merely added the Aristotelian doctrines to the theory of comedy already well established.

Donatus and the Terentian commentators of the fifteenth and sixteenth centuries, with aid from Horace, Cicero, Quintilian, and other rhetoricians, provided a satisfactory theory of comedy. In fact, as I hope I have shown, Donatus and the rhetoricians took account of virtually every element that makes up comic plot, characterization, sentiment, and diction. Donatus' *protasis, epitasis,* and *catastrophe* formed the backbone of dramatic structure, not only for comedy, but for tragedy and tragicomedy as well. *Protasis, epitasis,* and *catastrophe* were the "beginning, middle, and end" of dramatic form. Aristotle's *Discovery* and *Peripety* are as useful analytical terms as any in dramatic criticism. Donatus' *cognitio* and *conversio,* however, described the same phenomena, and the plays of Terence offered admirable illustrations long before western Europe became familiar with Sophocles' *Oedipus Rex.*

As Robortellus and others demonstrated, Aristotle's brief but profound remarks on character in tragedy may be readily adapted to comic character. The details of comic characterization, however, the establishment of universal comic types such as the heavy father, the prodigal youth, the cunning servant, were worked out by the rhetoricians and Terentian commentators. It is true that the *Rhetoric* and *Ethics* of Aristotle provided, and very early in the sixteenth century, an important philosophical background for the analysis of dramatic character, though similar *dicta* on character in Horace's *Art of Poetry* were familiar to schoolboys before the *Ethics* and *Rhetoric* became widely known. For the intellectual content of the drama, for the power of rational thought displayed by the characters in a play, Aristotle's *Poetics* recommended a study of the art of rhetoric. But the early sixteenth-century students of comedy needed no prompting from Aristotle to turn to rhetoric; the theory of comedy has always been rhetorical. Again, the details of comic sentiment were worked out by rhetoricians, the figurists, the Terentian commentators, who found in Terence a congenial hunting ground for nearly every *sententiae*, nearly every figure of thought and figure of speech. The study of comic style has never owed much to Aristotle's *Poetics*. Robortellus, for example, when he came to discuss comic diction had to go outside the *Poetics*.[3] Donatus and the rhetoricians dictated the theory of comic style. Terence furnished the models *par excellence*.

Terentian comedy does not comprise the whole art of comedy, though the practice of Terence and the theory of comedy established by the Terentian commentators are by all odds the most influential elements in the literary comedy of western Europe. There are many kinds of comedy, some of which are not much like that of Terence. There is virtually no lyricism in Terence, for example, and no pastoral or rustic comedy. Terence scarcely touched burlesque, which in the hands of masters like Aristophanes, Shakespeare, and Fielding offers some of the richest rewards of laughter. The New Comedy never indulged in political satire, or in any kind of strong satire, for that matter. Consequently I have had to neglect many fine and important sources of comedy.

I believe I have never even mentioned medieval drama, for example, the morality plays, the interludes, the farces, the comic episodes in some of the mystery plays. Even here, however, it cannot be said that Terentian comedy is not to be reckoned with. We may all recall the pious imitations of Terence by Hrowswitha in the tenth century. I have neglected both Aristophanes and Plautus, who exerted a very considerable influence upon sixteenth-century comedy, and upon comedy of later centuries. With the celebrated examples of Udall's *Ralph Roister Doister*[4] and Shakespeare's *Comedy of Errors* in mind, plus Ben Jonson's avowed admiration for Plautus, it is unwise to argue that Terence influenced the actual comic practice more than did Plautus. I have wholly omitted any attempt to account for the enormous influence of native wit and humor, of the love for slapstick comedy, homely punning, and all the antics of the clowns of all ages, including our radio comedians of the twentieth century.

Comic practice has always been more important than theory, of course, and doubtless always will be more important. In this study, however, I have been concerned with the foundations of comic theory, and this theory, so far as I can judge, has been largely the work of the Terentian commentators. As Thomas Lodge indicated in his

---

[3] See p. 237.

[4] Nicholas Udall, author of *Floures for Latine Spekynge, selected and gathered out of Terence and the same translated into Englysshe*, would constitute a poor argument against the predominant influence of Terence, however.

Defence of Poetry, the sixteenth-century theory of comedy was the work of learned men addressed to learned men; it was an intellectual theory emphasizing a strict decorum of plot, character, sentiment, and diction, and emphasizing the philosophical lessons in human conduct to be gained from literary comedy. Consequently it is a relatively narrow theory, which fails to take account of the broader practices of comedians. But our modern theory of literary comedy is still intellectual. It is very like George Meredith's highly rationalized theory of comedy, and for a good reason; the foundations of Meredith's theory are the very foundations I have tried to describe. The great models of comedy in Meredith's eyes were Menander and Molière. Menander leads us forward to Terence. Molière leads us back to Terence.

Appendix

ON COMEDY

(Explicatio eorum omnium quae ad Comoediae artificium pertinent)

1548

By Franciscus Robortellus

COMEDY has the same purpose that all other kinds of poems have, to imitate the characters and actions of men. And since all poetic imitation is accomplished by three means, speech, rhythm, and harmony, these three have come to be used in Comedy, but separately, one after the other, not all together as in some other forms. This practice, however, it has in common with Tragedy, as Aristotle explains in the *Poetics*. Comedy differs, morevoer, from other forms in the subject matter which it treats; for it imitates the actions of the lower, meaner people, and therefore differs from Tragedy, which imitates the better sort of people, as Aristotle also shows. A third difference established among the kinds of poetry is attributed to the several ways of imitating. Comedy imitates men who are, as it were, carrying on business and acting, albeit this, too, it has in common with Tragedy; whence it has come about that Comedy as well as Tragedy were called by the ancients δράματα, i.e., acts, from δρᾶν which means to act or to carry on business.

Hence Aristotle explains, though obscurely, in the *Poetics* that at one time there was a quarrel between the Athenians and the Megarians (who were Dorians) over the claim to the honor of first inventing Comedy. The Megarians, those Dorians who lived in Greece as well as those in Sicily (for these Dorians had migrated from Sicily), alleged that they had invented Comedy at the time when democracy flourished in their cities. They relied upon this reasoning, that Epicharmus lived prior to Chionides and Magnes, who, the Athenians boasted, were their most ancient authors of Comedy. A second reason was drawn from the nature and usage of language; for the Athenians called their villages κώμους, the Megarians δήμους, which word gave the name to Comedy since it was first acted in villages and hamlets. Certain people, wandering through villages and hamlets at night, humorously directed their invectives against those from whom they

227

had received injury, with the resultant advantage that the insolence and wantonness of the wicked were considerably held in check. Therefore they were permitted to recite their railing verses in the theater, whence little by little Comedy arose. Varro,[1] indeed, relates the invention of Comedy in the same way as does Donatus,[2] but both as though it took place among the Athenians, which Aristotle seems not to approve. A third reason is that the Athenians say πράττειν for "to act," but the Megarians δρᾶν, and since from δρᾶν these poems are called δράματα it is indeed more likely that Comedy was first invented among the Megarians.

It seems that the invention and growth of Comedy are due to two causes: first because men have an aptitude for imitation which is implanted by nature as early as childhood, second because every one delights in imitation. Since, therefore, there were those who could fitly imitate and those who were glad to see imitations, it came about that this genus of poetry was held in high honor. At the beginning, Comedy was crude, trifling, and undeveloped, but little by little it was enriched when, as rills flow into a river, phallic poems, by reason of the affinity and likeness of subject matter, flowed into it, as Aristotle makes clear in the *Poetics*. What phallic poetry is like has been fully shown by me there.[3] Nevertheless, Aristotle seems to doubt whether or not Comedy in his day was yet fully formed; I think because he did not quite approve the form of Comedy then in use, what we call Old Comedy, because it was full of invectives and because its imitations went beyond the verisimilitude which the poet above all ought to seek. Aristotle avers in the *Poetics* that it was not sufficiently clear to him how Comedy developed. He offers this reason: poetry of this sort long lay neglected because very few took it seriously, owing to the harshness of its invective. It was forbidden by law to produce comic imitations in the theater; it was many years before the magistrate finally gave permission for some to perform Comedy. That much, he asserts, is known.

Phormis and Epicharmus first framed the comic plot in Sicily. Among the Athenians, it was Crates who abandoned the iambic invectives in which he had been engaged and turned his mind to writing Comedy. But who invented prologues, or the chorus, or the plurality of actors in Comedy are altogether unknown. It must be understood that Aristotle treats the prologue differently from the Latins; for in the prologue, which is the first part of the play, is put

---

[1] See *De Lingua Latina* 7.89.
[2] Evanthius, *De Fabula*.
[3] See Robortellus' commentary on the *Poetics*, p. 39.

a kind of episode for extending and embellishing the play; otherwise it would be something short and trifling.

If one inquires, however, whether Comedy or Tragedy was first invented, Donatus, the commentator on Terence, says that Tragedy sprang up first. He alleges this reason, that little by little society progressed from a rude culture and pastoral customs to a gentle, urbane way of living, and to mirth. But Aristotle, whose inquiry in the *Poetics* is more searching, seems to imply that both kinds of drama sprang up from nature at the same time. He says, indeed, that since some men were σεμνότεροι, that is graver and more serious, and others were εὐτελέστεροι, that is lively and merry, the former wrote grave works and the latter light and merry ones. Thus there grew up two kinds of poems, the one serious, the other merry. He proves his case by the example of Homer, in whom one may perceive both natures, the light and the serious; for insofar as Homer was of a grave and serious disposition he wrote the *Iliad* and *Odyssey*, and insofar as he was of a light and merry disposition he wrote the *Margites*. From the first kind sprang Tragedy, from the second Comedy, by means of narratives reduced to dramatic imitations. Homer himself first wrote in a dramatic style. Since Homer, therefore, wrote merry things in dramatic style, it seems that he first handed down the form of Comedy.

Little by little, "from improvisations," there arose what is called Old Comedy such as Aristophanes wrote, in which are mingled many fabulous things that are not put in the later New Comedy; for the personages of the gods often appear in Old Comedy, as in the *Amphitryon* of Plautus, but the New Comedy rather approached the imitation of manners which are perceived in the familiar, everyday intercourse of men.

Therefore, since New Comedy, I fancy, did not yet exist in his day, Aristotle intimates in his *Poetics* what we have pointed out in our explications, that Comedy did not seem to have reached the high level of decorum it later attained. Plutarch, also, in that little book in which he compares Menander with Aristophanes, produces evidence enough for one to perceive that Old Comedy is not much esteemed and that much more praiseworthy is the New Comedy whose author is Menander, whom our Terence above all has imitated. I here put down some words of Plutarch so that the matter may be more readily understood:

Now Aristophanes is neither pleasing to the many nor endurable to the thoughtful, but his poetry is like a harlot who has passed her prime and then takes up the rôle of a wife, whose presumption the many cannot endure and whose licentiousness and malice the dignified abominate. But Menander, along with his charm, shows himself above all satisfying. He has made his poetry, of all the beautiful works Greece has produced, the most generally accepted subject in theaters, in discussions, and at banquets, for readings, for instruction, and for dramatic competitions. For he shows, indeed, what the essence and nature of skill in the use of language really are, approaching all subjects with a persuasiveness from which there is no escape, and controlling every sound and meaning which the Greek language affords.[4]

There was much buffoonery and slander in Old Comedy, so much so that even the names of individuals were not spared. This can be observed everywhere in Aristophanes, especially in the *Clouds*, where that best of men, the most venerable Socrates, is ridiculed. Concerning this raillery, indeed, Horace speaks very well in the second book of *Epistles*, in the Epistle to Augustus. It became necessary to curb by law this whole breed of slanderous writings. Consequently it was carried over into satires such as Horace wrote, and before him Varro and Lucilius; after him Juvenal and Persius. For long ago satire was not of this sort, as we have shown at length in the discussion we have written on satire.[5] But if one wishes to know more about Comedy, both Old and New, he should read those writings that Platonius, the interpreter of Aristophanes, has left.

There was among the ancients a certain kind of Comedy called *mimus* because of the excessive mimicry; this contained obscenities which the actors tried to express even by gesture. Therefore Cicero, in the second book of his *De Oratore*,[6] advises the orator to eschew mimetic drolleries because of the obscenity. Those who wrote such Comedy were formerly called writers of mimes. Many kinds of mimes in Comedy may be recorded: some were *hilaroedi*, others *magoedi*, *Sicyonii, phallophori*.[7] The Latins called these *planipedes* because they acted without shoes. Lucian, in his book *On Dancing*, relates this kind to pantomime and the dancer who fitly expressed everything by ges-

---

[4]Plutarch's *Moralia*, translated by H. N. Fowler (Loeb Library), 10.469-71.

[5]Robortellus, *Explicatio eorum omnium quae ad Satyram pertinent*, Florence, 1548.

[6]2.59.242.

[7]Robortellus was evidently following Athenaeus, *Deipnosophistae* 14.621b-f. According to Athenaeus, *hilaroedi* were singers who parodied Tragedy, *magoedi* were lewd dancers dressed in feminine attire who parodied Comedy, *phallophori* were Bacchants. *Sicyonii* must have crept into Robortellus' list by mistake. Athenaeus has no such classification; he merely says of certain comic dancers, "The Sicyonians call them *phallophori*."

tures of his hands and feet. This means of dancing we know is called χειρονομία; see Quintilian in his second book.[8]

The kinds of Roman Comedy may be approximately reckoned as these many: *Stataria, Motoria, Mixta, Togata, Palliata, Tabernaria. Stataria* is such as the *Andrian,* for it is acted in the quieter manner; *motoria* is more boisterous, such as the *Eunuch; mixta* is in both manners, such as the *Brothers.* The word *praetextatae* comes from the general's *praetexta* (toga) in which the affairs, public or private, of generals were conducted; *praetextati,* in fact, were also generals and magistrates. Hence Cicero, in the first letter of the fifth book of the *Letters to Atticus:* "On that day I was a great *praetextatus* (magistrate)."[9] For a like reason the rest are named from the things they comprehend. The term *Atellanae* comes from the town Atella; these are drolls, concerning which see Donatus, the commentator on Terence.

The parts of Comedy are those which belong to the essence and can be called the essentials and those which belong to the quantity and can be called the parts that determine the magnitude. And first let us speak of the essentials.

These essentials are five or, as some reason, six in number: Plot, Character, Thought, Diction, Spectacle, Music. Aristotle allows just so many in the *Poetics.* As practice has demonstrated, no comedy can be recited if the Music and Spectacle are not employed so that the play on the stage appears to be enacted in city or town. Therefore these parts, Music and Spectacle, are necessary. The other parts are much more necessary, because without them Comedy cannot even be written. In composing a comedy it is first necessary to invent the matter which is to be written; this comprises the Plot *(fabula).* But, on the other hand, the Plot, because it imitates, must bring out Character *(mores)* and accurately express the manners of diverse people. Therefore another part, Character, is necessary. Not every speech expresses Character, as, for example, speeches in mathematics, medicine, physiology, dialectics.[10] Since it is necessary to express thoughts by means of speech *(oratio),* it is therefore necessary to add another part, Thought *(sententia).* But since Thought consists of words, it is necessary to add yet another part, Diction *(dictio).* One who is going to write Comedy properly should pay heed to all these parts; but let us speak of each one by one.

---

[8]See Quintilian 1.11.17.

[9]*Letters to Atticus* 6.1.22.9.

[10]Cf. Aristotle's *Rhetoric* 3.16.8. "The narration should depict character. . . . Mathematical discourses exhibit no moral character, for they reveal no moral purpose." (Lane Cooper's translation.)

The comic play ought to represent low, trifling matter; for this very reason it differs from Tragedy. Moreover, it should imitate not many but merely one simple action which can be completed within a single circuit of the sun, as Aristotle most learnedly advises in the *Poetics*, where he talks about the tragic play. I suppose I ought to repeat that a single circuit of the sun is not what the mathematicians generally call the natural day but rather the artificial day; I have fully said this in my commentary on the *Poetics*.[11]

The Plot ought to have magnitude and order. Magnitude distinguishes it from extemporaneous poems and from short ones. Order makes all the parts fit together; on the one hand, it should not be ended just anywhere, as though thoughtlessly, nor should it begin just anywhere. There is a very definite rule for fixing the limits of magnitude in any plot, namely, that in managing the single action it extend just so far as is meet, that is, so long as it seems to be more pleasing, and as I shall briefly describe. The right magnitude of a comic plot is whatever is necessary to make plain the change and interchange of disturbances and quarrels. All the parts of the plot, indeed, ought to be so joined together that no part can be taken away or transplanted without ruining or disjoining the whole plot.

Further, the names of all comic characters should be fictitious. This is not done in Tragedy because Tragedy uses stories of the more pitiful events that have befallen certain well-known people, whose names must be declared. Comedy, however, feigns in a verisimilar manner and therefore, as Aristotle very clearly informs us in the *Poetics*, invents its names.

The plot ought not to be episodic, for such a plot is faulty. I call that plot episodic in which many things are inserted over and above the one action that was set up in the beginning—what was done in the ancient contests by unskilled poets so that the play would appear longer and give more pleasure. Since the imitation in Comedy is not only of low and trifling affairs, such as take place in the private actions of people, but also of disturbances, there should also be present that which is taken from the nature and custom of human actions, which always have in them something troublesome or distressing. It is necessary to intermingle those things which are beyond our hope and expectation, such accidental events as bring unexpected joy, or grief, or wonder.

We say, therefore, that there are two kinds of comic plots: some are simple, others complex; and such, moreover, are the actions which they imitate. Simple actions are those which have nothing unex-

---

[11]Pp. 49-50. The natural day is 24 hours, the artificial 12.

pected[12] and contain no Discovery. Complex actions contain either one or both of these devices. Discovery occurs when we are led from ignorance to knowledge of some matter, out of which springs either grief or joy—nearly always joy, for Discoveries are, with good reason, placed in the last part of a comedy, where the disturbance in affairs begins to subside. An example of this sort can be drawn from the *Andrian* of Terence, and from many others in which there is Discovery.

There are five kinds of Discovery. The first is by means of signs, of which some are inborn and others accidental. These may be again divided into two classes, for they are either on the body, such as scars and birthmarks, or outside, such as necklaces. Some of the signs are of the better sort, some of the worse; some are artificial, others inartificial. Artificial signs are those which are invented by the poet himself. Inartificial signs are those in the material itself and already at hand in the plot. We call those signs inborn which have customarily been attributed to the habits of the characters—such as the club and lion's skin of Hercules. The second kind of Discovery occurs through memory: when, upon beholding something, the remembrance of something similar comes to mind and we acknowledge a likeness by means of a likeness. The third kind of Discovery is by means of inevitable reasoning: e.g., since we know that a certain man is like only one other person in the city, when we see one like this other person we therefore infer that he is this certain man.[13] Another rational Discovery, the fourth kind, is effected by a paralogism; this is a fallacy derived from a false foundation, as is a paralogism in dialectic. A fifth kind of Discovery is that which arises from conjectured likenesses more carefully considered and brought together.

Let these remarks, in short, suffice for Discovery; we have spoken more fully in our commentary on Aristotle's *Poetics*.

One ought not to proceed to write a comic play at random; rather, one ought to have a sure plan and method such as Aristotle describes. First, the poet should establish the plot, which should be set down in few words and put before his eyes so that he can readily see what is appropriate and what is not, just as the spectator does while the play is acted on stage. The language which he uses to unfold the plot should be clear and plain so that he may perceive contradictions if they have appeared; the greatest part of the mistakes committed by bad and unskilled poets proceeds from these contradictions. When

---

[12]Robortellus has in mind the Aristotelian Peripety or reversal of fortune.

[13]Aristotle's illustration in *Poetics* 16.55ª4-6 is clearer. Electra, upon seeing a peculiar lock of hair, reasons thus: "One like me is here; there is no one like me but Orestes; he, therefore, must be here."

the poet has set down the substance of the whole matter in this way, he should invent names for his matter which should be appropriate. Afterwards the poet should provide the episodes and set them in place. Episodes enrich the poem, embellish and enlarge the action. What these episodes are I might have explained with some examples from Terentian and Plautine plots, not more clearly but at greater length. Therefore it has seemed enough if I explained everything in few words, omitting examples.

In the art of writing Comedy it is important to recognize that its duration is limited by two goals, namely *dénouement* and complication.[14] All that extends from the beginning of the play to the point where the bustle of affairs turns and a change takes place is called the complication, as I have related above.[15] That part which extends from the beginning of the change to the end of the play is called the *dénouement*. He who will keep these things before his eyes will both readily judge the writings of the ancient poets and will himself write Comedy in an easier fashion. But let this be enough about Plot; now we shall discuss Character.

Four things should be considered in Character. First, one should see to it that goodness and badness are presented in the several kinds of people. If somebody is good, then the character assigned him should be good. Character is expressed by speech and by action, for we know from his speech and action whether some one is good or bad. This should be observed for all kinds of people, for it often happens that a trait which is praiseworthy in one person is not appropriate in another; persons may admit of great differences. Grant me that a certain slave is not a thief, and this is supreme merit and goodness in a slave; in a man of honor it is no commendation. To weave nicely, to embroider, to spin are commendable in a woman; these things ought not to be esteemed in a man. There is an old tale that Philip of Macedon rebuked Alexander when he once surprised his son singing in the midst of professional singers; such behavior, as it were, was not sufficiently becoming in a king. It was considered a blemish in Nero that he was a trained singer, in Commodus that he shot and wrestled well. Therefore praises becoming to men of low birth are not praises if ascribed to men of higher breeding. The character of a servant, if applied to a gallant gentleman, would not only lower the gentleman, but even make him bad. Whence it is evident that what was the highest goodness in a servant is a very great vice in the master.

---

[14]*Solutio* (*dénouement*) and *connexio* (complication) are Latin terms for Aristotle's λύσις and δέσις. See *Poetics* 17.55ᵇ24.

[15]See his Commentary on the *Poetics*, p. 209.

Second, what is requisite in Character is "appropriateness" (τὸ ἁρμόττον). As strength of body is certainly a very great virtue; if it be attributed to a woman, however, and if some poet or other portrays a woman in the same way Homer portrays Achilles,[16] he would be severely censured.

Third, Character ought to be what Aristotle, in the *Poetics*, calls "like the reality" (τὸ ὅμοιον); that is to say, the imitation of character in any role should be expressed according to his traditional reputation and the common opinion of mankind. For then this τὸ ὅμοιον is preserved when a poet introduces somebody acting and speaking as people know he is accustomed to act and speak. For example, we know that Achilles was fierce and ruthless,[17] and everybody thinks of him as so. Therefore he ought to be portrayed as such. The ancients report that Ulysses was shrewd and crafty. Therefore he is to be portrayed in this way. For a full treatment of this matter see Horace's *Epistle to Augustus*.[18]

Fourth, it is necessary to make Character "consistent" (τὸ ὁμαλόν); characters should be consistent throughout the poem. If you once show somebody as cowardly, greedy, proud, you should show him the same at all times; not cowardly sometimes and then brave, not greedy sometimes and then generous; for such practice is the greatest blemish in a poem. But we shall discuss this matter fully in our commentary on Aristotle's *Poetics*.[19] Horace also described it carefully in his *Poetica*.

It should be understood that characters are portrayed in two ways, either "according to the probable" (κατὰ τὸ εἰκός), or "according to the necessary" (κατὰ τὸ ἀναγκαῖον), as Aristotle says in the *Poetics*. If, therefore, known persons are introduced and we know that they actually existed, their characters should be represented according to necessity. If, however, the persons are new and have been created for the first time by the poet himself, their characters should be represented according to probability. As the poet understands and can execute this, he must note the characters of all ages and classes, just as Horace learnedly teaches in his *Poetica*,[20] and Aristotle in the second book of his *Rhetoric*.[21] Nor yet should the poet be ignorant, as

---

[16]For Robortellus' interpretation of Ἀχιλλέα ἀγαθόν (*Poetics* 15.1454^b14), see my article on the passage in *Classical Philology* 40 (1945), 248-49.

[17]Cf. Horace *Ars Poetica* 121.

[18]The *Ars Poetica* seems a better reference here than does the *Epistle to Augustus*.

[19]See pp. 164 ff.   [20]*Ars Poetica* 156-78.   [21]*Rhetoric* 2.12-14.

indeed we have said above, that he creates all the personages in his comedies, gives them whatever names he pleases, and that poems of this kind admit only the "probable." Albeit Old Comedy once took real persons, I speak of New Comedy, which is much more praiseworthy. It is different in Tragedy; for when real matters of real people are imitated the real names should be kept and the characters represented "according to the necessary," although all personages are not real and new ones were introduced even into Tragedy.[22] It suffices if some real names of people to whom the misfortunes befall are kept; the rest can be arbitrarily created by the poet in accord with probability, just as we say is done in Comedy.

Let this be enough about Character, upon which almost the whole art of the comic poet depends. Now, in what follows, we shall discuss Thought.

The power of Thought lies in fitly expressing the disposition of the soul; it encourages, stirs up, restrains, comforts, ridicules, disparages, and produces innumerable results of this sort, just as Aristotle learnedly describes in the *Poetics*. Since comic discourse is simple or, as the Greek rhetoricians say, ἀφελῆς, its thoughts ought to be humble and not at all lofty; otherwise it would not differ from political discourse, that is, the speech which orators use in public. For this reason Aristides the rhetorician has very rightly determined the whole matter in his book, "On Simple Discourse."[23] Aristides says, indeed: "Political thoughts are harsher, more illustrious, taken from more honorable matters, more striking since they are made up of striking turns of phrase, and therefore at the same time both less common and more illustrious. But thoughts in simple address are plain, common, insignificant, and taken from insignificant things."[24] There is a further difference between the thoughts of political and comic discourse and this rises "from the treatment"; for in political or oratorical discourse there are declarations of issues and careful proof in order that the hearer may attentively perceive and believe what is being discussed. In comic discourse, however, there are no issues, but everything is revealed as if it were already decided and proved. There is also another difference in the "figures of speech"; for the figures in a political discourse seem to be "harsh, critical, and forcible" (as, indeed, Aristides the rhetorician writes); in a comic or "simple" discourse, however, they are "loose, plain, by no means critical nor exemplifying

---

[22]Reading *novae* for *notae;* the context surely demands such a reading.
[23]The second book, Περὶ ἀφελοῦς Λόγου, of his *Rhetoric.*
[24]*Rhetoric* 2.3.513.

searching inquiry, but more common and obvious."[25] Just as the former figures produce a lofty discourse and one distinctly "political," just so the latter make the discourse simple and distinctly comic since they are "conversable" and "commonplace."

And this will be enough to say about Thought. Now we shall speak about Diction.

Diction in comic discourse ought to be simple, easy, open, clear, familiar, and finally, taken from common usage: for, as Aristides the rhetorician says, simple discourse, such as comic discourse is, does not admit lofty diction since, as has been said, it has thoughts that are simple and humble. Forensic and political oratory, however, since it is lofty, ought to be adapted to this lofty diction. Such, therefore, is the difference established so far as dictions go between comic and political discourse. In the one, that is, the "simple"—these are the words of Aristides—"the diction is delivered as if by chance, appearing careless and by no means studied."[26] In the political, however, the diction ought to be splendid, ornate, and symmetrical. I add also another difference which I have noted in the same passage in Aristides. Whatever one wishes to express in a political discourse must be separately uttered in distinct terms; the Greek words are: "In a political discourse only one meaning ought to appear."[27] In simple or comic discourse, however, one expression often indicates two or three things; the Greek words are as follows: "In the simple discourse one expression means one or two or three things . . . [for example] ἱπποφορβός (horse-keeper)."[28] Much that is splendid and ornamental is added by means of the composition. Now let us leave off our pursuit of Diction so that we may take up Spectacle.

Spectacle consists of the scene and the dress or costume of the personages. Therefore we shall discuss these one by one.

Vitruvius enumerates three kinds of scene: tragic, satyric, comic. He says that the comic scene was so fashioned that it represented, even as now, private buildings with doors and windows.[29] Valerius Maximus writes that Appius Claudius represented the scene in a vari-

---

[25]*Ibid*. 2.5.513.   [26]*Ibid*. 2.6.513.   [27]*Ibid*.   [28]*Ibid*.

[29]"There are three styles of scenery: one which is called tragic; a second, comic; the third, satyric. . . . The tragic are designed with columns, pediments and statues and other royal surroundings; the comic have the appearance of private buildings and balconies and projections with windows made to imitate reality, after the fashion of ordinary buildings; the satyric settings are painted with trees, caves, mountains and other country features, designed to imitate landscape." (Vitruvius 5.6.9. Translated by Frank Granger in the Loeb Library.)

ety of colors; formerly it was represented by unpainted panels.[30] The ornaments of the stage are main curtains, hangings, awnings, smaller curtains for comedy, and the rest of such things. The stage was strewn with flowers and saffron, as Crinitus, who first correctly expounded this passage in the poet, demonstrates from the verse in Horace's *Epistle*.[31] Donatus writes that ordinarily two altars were constructed on the stage, and Terence so intimates where he says, "Take some boughs from the altar here."[32] One altar was dedicated to Bacchus, the other to the god or goddess in whose honor the games were celebrated, for comedies were performed at the games of the Megalesia and of the circus. The aediles used to manage these comedies, as one may perceive from the inscriptions of the Terentian plays, which may still be read. The stage had an orchestra in which the dancers were stationed, and a platform where the speaking characters stood. Regarding this point, Horace says, "He trailed his robes as he rambled about the stage."[33] Under the stage machines were placed such as the *bronteum*, which imitated thunder. In tragedies there was the *eccyclema*, upon which, projecting from a part above the platform—since it was made in the shape of a wheel it could easily be turned—all those things were depicted which could not be viewed without horror, and as a result the audience could see what had happened. But enough about these matters.

Julius Pollux[34] relates that the comic dress or costumes were as follows. White robes were assigned to the old men because this attire was considered the most ancient. Purple and parti-colored dress was assigned to the younger men; to the slaves plain and ragged garments, signifying poverty. The slaves, in fact, wore short sleeveless tunics. The parasites appeared garbed in dark mantles. A white costume was assigned to a cheerful man, a dark one to the wretched or sorrowful man. To a slave dealer a varicolored mantle and a switch, which he carried in his hand. To priestesses long white garments reaching to the ankles. To old women or matrons pale yellow robes. The comic shoes were socks, the tragic cothurni. Beards, as Pollux writes, were fashioned either black or hoary, either long or short.

At some time or other the actors began to wear masks; formerly they smeared their faces with lees. Horace, in his *Poetica*,[35] reports

---

[30]Valerius Maximus 2.4.6: "C[laudius] Pulcher scenam varietate colorum adumbravit vacuis ante pictura tabulis extentam."

[31]*Epistles* 2.1.179. For the comment of Petrus Crinitus, see *Opera Horatii Flacci* (Basle, 1555), p. 1345.

[32]*Andrian* 726.   [33]*Ars Poetica* 215.   [34]*Onomasticon* 10.14 ff.

[35]*Ars Poetica* 275-77.

that Thespis was the inventor of speaking roles: Aristotle says that this is uncertain.

I would say something about Melody, which was mainly produced by flutes, if I did not see that it was sufficiently known to every one. I shall make an investigation in some other places as to the place and manner in which these things were used in the recitation of poems, and there is a fuller account of the whole matter in my commentary on Aristotle's *Poetics*.[36]

So much for my explanation of the parts of Comedy, that is, the essentials. The other parts, which appertain to quantity, are enumerated by Donatus as four, and what these are is explained: Prologue, Prothesis, Epitasis, Catastrophe. I think Aristotle wrote about these in the second book of the *Poetics*, which I suspect has been lost; for in the extant first book he carefully describes similar parts of Tragedy. Comedy ought to be divided into five acts, as Horace recommends in his *Poetica*. Donatus[37] observes that a character should not be permitted more than five entrances on the scene; in Tragedy the number should be even less. Finally, the Chorus would have been discussed, for the Old Comedy retained it; but since the New Comedy rejects the Chorus, it is not necessary to say more about these matters, especially since we have fully explained everything regarding the Chorus, the comic chorus moreover, in our commentary on Aristotle's *Poetics*;[38] we have given an account of its nature and of why it was removed from the New Comedy.

---

[36]Pp. 70-71, 266.
[37]See Donatus' Preface to *Andrian*.
[38]Pp. 41, 47, 118-24, 220-22.

Bibliography

The following is a selective bibliography of those books that have been most useful in the preceding study.

I. TERENCE

[*Comoediae.*] [With the comments of Donatus and Joannes Calphurnius.] Treviso, 1477.

[*Comoediae.*] [With the comments of Donatus and Calphurnius.] Venice, 1491.

[*Comoediae.*] [With the comments of Guido Juvenalis and Iodocus Badius Ascensius.] Lyon, 1498.

[*Comoediae.*] [With the comments of Donatus, Juvenalis, and Badius.] Strassburg, 1499.

Terentius in sua metra restitutus. [With *De comoedia* by Benedictus Philologus.] Venice, 1506.

Comoedie. [With the comments of Juvenalis and Badius.] Lyon, 1508.

Comicorum Latinorum principis comedie. [With the comments and annotations of Donatus, Juvenalis, Badius, and Paulus Malleolus.] Lyon, 1518.

Comoediae. [With *De comoedia* by Victor Faustus and *De comoedia et metris comicis* by Benedictus Philologus.] Mainz, 1522.

Fabulae. Edited with annotations by Iodocus Willichius. [With the *Libellus de fabularum origine et differentia, de ludorum ac tibiarum generibus* by Petrus Menenius, the annotations of Marcus Antonius Muretus, and a dedicatory epistle by Gregorius Wagnerus.] Zurich, 1550.

Comoediae. [A great variorum edition including the *argumenta* of Melanchthon; the *Liber de comicis dimensionibus* by J. C. Scaliger; the *Spicilegium* of Ioannes Theodoricus Bellovacus; the *De comoedia* of Victor Faustus; the arguments of Paulus Malleolus and Christophorus Hegendorphinus; the annotations of Donatus, Calphurnius, Erasmus, Antonius Goveanus, Petrus Bembus, Petrus Marsus, Adrianus Barlandus, Bartholomaeus Latomus, Ioannes Rivius, Stephanus Doletus, Henricus Loritus Glareanus, and Iodocus Willichius.] Paris, 1552.

Comoediae. [Edited by Vincentius Cordatus.] Venice, 1570.

In P. Terentii comoedias sex, novus commentarius. Edited by Stephanus Riccius. Vol. I, Weissenfels, 1566; Vol. II, Gorlitz, 1582. [This edition contains comments by Melanchthon, Rivius, Iacobus Milichius, Casparus Cruciger Senior, Ambrosius Bernt Iuterbocensis, Ioannes Stigelius, Andreas Misenus Senior.]

Comoediae. Edited by Matthias Bergius. Leipzig, 1574. [This edition contains annotations by Gabriel Faernus, Muretus, and Camerarius, the castigations of Rivius and Georgius Fabricius, annotations by Franciscus Fabricius.]

P. Terentii comoedia Adelphi. Edited by Nathan Chytraeus. Rostock, 1576. [Appended are Chytraeus' *Propositiones de comoedia.*]

Terence in English. By R[ichard] B[ernard]. Cambridge, 1598.

Comoediae. Edited by Nicolaus Camus. London, 1718. [This edition contains *prolegomena* by Donatus, Evanthius, Erasmus, J. C. Scaliger, Bembus, Rivius, Theodoricus, Daniel Heinsius, Melanchthon.]

The comedies of Terence. Edited with introduction and notes by Sidney G. Ashmore. New York, 1908.

Terence. With an English translation by John Sargeaunt. 2 vols. Loeb Classical Library, 1931.

II. MISCELLANEOUS

ABBOTT, KENNETH M. *Prolegomena to an edition of the pseudo-Servian commentary on Terence.* (Dissertation, University of Illinois), Urbana, 1934.

APHTHONIUS. *Progymnasmata rhetorica.* Salamanca, 1550.

AQUILA. [See Rutilius Lupus.]

ARISTOTLE. *Opera omnia quae extant, graece et latine.* 2 vols. Paris, 1619.

——. *Poetica per Alexandrum Paccium . . . in Latinum conversa.* Venice, 1536.

——. *Aristotle on the art of poetry. A revised text with critical introduction, translation, and commentary by Ingram Bywater.* Oxford, 1909.

——. *The art of rhetoric. With an English translation by John Henry Freese.* Loeb Classical Library, 1939.

——. *The Nicomachean ethics. Translated with an analysis and critical notes by J. E. C. Welldon.* London, 1920.

AVERROES. *Aristotelis Stagiritae omnia quae extant opera . . . Averrois Cordubensis in ea opera omnes ad nos pervenere commentarii.* 11 vols. Venice, 1550-52.

——. *Averrois paraphrasis in librum poeticae Aristotelis Iacob Mantino hispano hebraeo medico interprete; ex libro qui Venetiis apud Iunctas anno MDLXII prodiit. In Jahrbucher fur classiche philologie, Supplementband* 17 (1890), 351-82. Edited by Fridericus Heidenhain.

BALDWIN, T. W. *William Shakspere's small Latine and lesse Greeke.* 2 vols. Urbana, 1944.

CAMPBELL, GEORGE. *The philosophy of rhetoric.* 2 vols. London, 1776.

CASTELVETRO, LODOVICO. *Poetica d'Aristotele vulgarizzata, et sposta.* Basle, 1576.

CHARLTON, H. B. *Castelvetro's theory of poetry.* Manchester, 1913.

CICERO. M. T. *Ciceronis rhetoricorum ad C. Herennium libri, quos alii non esse Ciceronis asseuerant: eiusdem de inuentione libri duo. Interpretibus Francisco Maturantio, Antonio Mancinello, Iodoco Badio Ascensio, Mario Fabio Victorino Rhetore. . . .* Venice, 1542.

————. *De oratore. With an English translation by E. W. Sutton and H. Rackham.* Loeb Classical Library, 1942.

————. *Brutus, Orator. With English translations by G. L. Hendrickson and H. M. Hubbell.* Loeb Classical Library, 1939.

————. *The treatise on rhetorical invention.* In *Orations of Marcus Tullius Cicero, vol. 4. Translated by C. D. Yonge.* London, 1919.

————. *De partitione oratoria. With an English translation by H. Rackham.* Loeb Classical Library, 1942.

————. *Ad C. Herennium libri iv.* Edited by Fridericus Marx. Leipzig, 1894.

CINTHIO, GIRALDI. *Discorsi . . . intorno al comporre de i romanzi, delle comedie, e delle tragedie, e di altre maniere di poesie.* Venice, 1554.

COOPER, LANE. *An Aristotelian theory of comedy, with an adaptation of the poetics and a translation of the 'Tractatus Coislinianus.'* New York, 1922.

COOPER, THOMAS. *Thesaurus linguae Romanae et Britannicae.* London, 1565.

DANIELLO, BERNARDINO. *La poetica.* Venice, 1536.

DENNIS, JOHN. *Critical Works. Edited by Edward Niles Hooker.* 2 vols. Baltimore, 1939-43.

DONATUS. *Aeli Donati quod fertur commentum Terenti. Accedunt Eugraphi commentum et scholia bembina, recensuit Paulus Wessner.* 3 vols. Leipzig, 1902-08.

DRYDEN, JOHN. *Essays. Selected and edited by W. P. Ker.* 2 vols. Oxford, 1926.

ERASMUS. *Opera omnia.* 10 vols. Leyden, 1703-06.

FARNABY, THOMAS. *Index rhetoricus et oratorius . . . cui adjiciuntur, formulae oratoriae, index poeticus.* London, 1696.

FENELON, FRANCOIS DE SALIGNAC. *Dialogues concerning eloquence . . . with his letter to the French Academy concerning rhetoric, poetry, history. . . . Translated from the French . . . by William Stevenson.* London, 1723.

GILBERT, ALLAN H. *Literary criticism: Plato to Dryden*. New York, 1940.

GRANT, MARY A. *The ancient rhetorical theories of the laughable*. (University of Wisconsin Studies in Languages and Literature, No. 21), Madison, 1924.

HERMOGENES. *De ratione inueniendi oratoria*. Edited by Sturm. Strassburg, 1570.

―――. *De ratione tractandae grauitatis occultae*. Edited by Sturm. Strassburg, 1571.

―――. *De dicendi generibus siue formis orationum*. Edited by Sturm. Strassburg, 1571.

―――. *Opera*. Edited by Hugo Rabe. Leipzig, 1913.

HERRICK, MARVIN T. *The fusion of Horatian and Aristotelian literary criticism, 1531-1555*. Urbana, 1946.

HORACE. *Opera*. Basle, 1555.

―――. *Satires, epistles, ars poetica. With an English translation by H. Rushton Fairclough*. Loeb Classical Library, 1929.

JONSON, BEN. *Discoveries, 1641*. The Bodley Head Quartos. London and New York, 1923.

JOSEPH, SISTER MIRIAM. *Shakespeare's use of the arts of language*. New York, 1947.

LAWTON, HAROLD WALTER. *Terence en France au XVIᵉ Siècle*. Paris, 1926.

LITTLETON, ADAM. *Latine dictionary*. London, 1678.

MADIUS, V., and LOMBARDUS, BARTHOLOMAEUS. *In Aristotelis librum de poetica communes explanationes*. Venice. 1550. [The essay *De ridiculis* is on pp. 301-27.]

MELANCHTHON, PHILIPP. *De rhetorica libri tres*. Leipzig, 1521.

―――. *Latinae grammatices elementa. Item, syntaxis siue de constructione liber. Item, dialectices, libri quatuor*. Strassburg, 1533.

―――. *Elementorum rhetorices libri duo*. Strassburg, 1533.

MINTURNUS, ANTONIUS. *De poeta*. Venice, 1559.

MIRANDULA, OCTAVIANUS. *Illustrium poetarum flores*. Antwerp, 1549.

NANI MIRABELLI, DOMENICO. *Polyanthea*. Venice, 1507.

PLATO. *The dialogues of Plato translated into English, with analyses and introductions by B. Jowett*. 5 vols. Oxford, 1892.

QUINTILIAN. *Institutio oratoria. With an English translation by H. E. Butler*. 4 vols. Loeb Classical Library, 1933-36.

RAINOLDE, RICHARD. *A booke called the foundacion of rhetorike*. Cambridge, 1563.

RAMUS. *Scholae in liberales artes*. Basle. 1569.

―――. *Dialecticae libri duo*. Cambridge, 1640.

RAPIN, RENE. *Reflections on Aristotle's treatise of poesie*. London, 1674.

RICHARDSON, ALEXANDER. *The logicians school-master: or, a comment upon Ramus logick. . . . Whereunto are added, his prelections on Ramus his grammer; Taleus his rhetorik. . . .* London, 1657.

RICCOBONUS, ANTONIUS. *Poetica Aristotelis ab Antonio Riccobono Latine conversa: eiusdem Riccoboni paraphrasis in poeticam Aristotelis: eiusdem ars comica ex Aristotele.* Padua, 1587.

ROBORTELLUS, FRANCISCUS. *In librum Aristotelis de arte poetica explicationes.* Florence, 1548.

――――. *Explicatio eorum omnium, quae ad comoediae artificium pertinent.* Florence, 1548. [Bound with the commentary.]

RUFINIANUS. [See Rutilius Lupus.]

RUTILIUS, LUPUS. *De figuris sententiarum ac verborum.* Paris, 1541. [With *De nominibus figuraram* by Romanus Aquila and *De schematis lexeos et dianoeas* by Iulius Rufinianus.]

SCALIGER, J. C. *Poetices libri septem.* Editio secunda. Heidelberg, 1581.

SMITH, G. GREGORY. *Elizabethan critical essays.* 2 vols. Oxford, 1904.

SPINGARN, JOEL ELIAS. *Critical essays of the seventeenth century.* 3 vols. Oxford, 1908-09.

STURM, JOHANN. *In partitiones oratorias Ciceronis, dialogi duo.* Strassburg, 1539.

TALAEUS, AUDOMARUS. *Rhetorica, et P. Rami . . . praelectionibus observata.* Paris, 1572.

TAYLOR, WARREN. *Tudor figures of rhetoric.* Chicago, 1937.

TRAPEZUNTIUS, GEORGIUS. *Rhetoricorum libri.* Basle, 1522.

――――. *Aristotelis rhetoricorum ad Theodecten, Georgio Trapezuntio interprete, libri III.* Basle, 1534.

TRISSINO, GIOVANNI GIORGIO. *La poetica.* 2 vols. Venice, 1529-63.

VALLA, GIORGIO. *Logica.* Venice, 1498. [This book contains among other translations the *Aristotelis ars poetica.*]

VICTORIUS, PETRUS. *Commentarii in primum librum Aristotelis de arte poetarum.* Secunda editio. Florence, 1573.

――――. *Commentarii in tres libros Aristotelis de arte dicendi.* Florence, 1579.

WILSON, THOMAS. *The arte of rhetorique.* London, 1562.

Index

Abbott, K. M., 60
Aeschylus, 106, 184
Aesop, 90
Agricola, R., 15, 101
Alexander of Aphrodisias, 51
Aphthonius, 5, 9, 15, 16, 21, 117, 118, 132, 135, 189
Apollodorus, 86
Appius, Claudius, 237, 238
argumentum, 61, 91-94, 102, 112, 122, 176
Aristides, 134, 135, 235-37
Aristophanes, 5, 57, 58, 65, 85, 122, 179, 219, 223, 225, 229, 230
Aristotle, *Ethics*, 42, 49, 53, 54, 57, 131, 144, 150-52, 156, 171, 224; *Metaphysics*, 50, 90; *Movement of Animals*, 50; *On the Parts of Animals*, 50; *Physics*, 22; *Poetics*, 1-4, 8, 10, 11, 17, 20, 23-27, 30, 31, 34-38, 40-42, 44, 45, 48, 52, 55, 57, 61-64, 69, 72, 73, 76, 78-80, 82-84, 90, 92-94, 97, 105, 106, 110, 112, 115, 122-24, 144, 145, 149, 174, 176-79, 184, 190, 223-25, 227-39; *Posterior Analytics*, 49, 124; *Problems*, 50, 51, 62; *Rhetoric*, 3, 8, 14, 17, 19, 26, 27, 29, 43, 45, 57, 77, 80, 97, 106, 144, 147, 150-52, 154-58, 161, 173, 175, 176, 178-80, 184, 189, 190, 224, 231, 235
Athenaeus, 230
Atkins, J. W. H., 1, 96
Augustine, 90
Averroes, 17, 24-26, 30, 39, 49, 62
Badius, Iodocus, 4, 71, 112, 137, 138, 223
Baldwin, C. S., 135
Baldwin, T. W., 7, 8, 12, 21, 32, 60, 71, 107, 118, 131, 215
Barlandus, A., 4, 13, 21, 67, 68, 101, 123, 162-64, 166, 168-70, 187, 190, 193, 201, 205, 212, 216, 218, 219
Barrie, Sir James, 167
Barzizza, G., 9
Beaumont and Fletcher, 152
Bellovacus, I. T., 63
Benedictus Philologus, 72, 92
Bergius, M., 7
Bernard, R., 88, 91, 206

Berndt, A., 4, 75, 76, 169, 171, 172
Boccaccio, 34, 53, 63
Bryan, W. J., 8
Buchanan, G., 55
Calphurnius, 3, 13, 148, 151, 157, 162, 166
Campbell, G., 25
Castelvetro, 23, 24, 33, 37, 53, 61, 63, 79, 86, 128, 178, 224
catastasis, 109, 119-22
catastrophe, 6, 26, 32, 59, 73, 81, 106-10, 120, 122-29, 224, 239
Chapman, G., 143
Chaucer, 34-36, 96, 208
Chekhov, 89
Chionides, 227
Chytraeus, 4, 80, 81, 94, 144, 147
Cicero, 1, 2, 5, 7-9, 11-13, 18, 20, 22, 24, 25, 28-30, 37, 38, 40, 42-49, 52, 53, 56, 57, 60, 62, 64, 65, 67, 71, 75-78, 83, 95, 98-100, 117, 118, 122, 130-32, 136, 137, 141, 150, 154, 159, 173, 179, 189, 190, 215-18, 223, 224, 230, 231
Cinthio, Giraldi, 37, 82, 83, 85, 87, 112, 113
Coleridge, 25
Collier, Jeremy, 153, 154
conclusion, 17, 26, 30, 31, 33, 34, 99, 106, 125
confirmatio, See proof
Congreve, 114, 115, 153, 159, 167, 179, 187, 195, 196, 216, 220, 221
consilium, 14
Cooper, Lane, 44, 57
Cordatus, V., 109, 179
Corneille, 102
Cox, Leonard, 19
Crates, 228
Cratinus, 58
Crinitus, P., 238
Daniello, 10
Dante, 36, 84
Davenant, 121
decorum, 131, 132, 136-44, 147, 152, 154, 160, 163, 164, 167, 168, 173, 218, 226
Dekker, Thomas, 158, 159, 164
deliberative oratory, 14, 17
delivery, 18, 31-33

245